STORY TRUMPS STRUCTURE

How to Write Unforgettable Fiction by
BREAKING THE RULES

— STEVEN JAMES —

Foreword by Donald Maass

WRITER'S DIGEST
BOOKS

WritersDigest.*com*
Cincinnati, Ohio

For more resources for writers, visit www.writersdigest.com.

18 17 16 15 14   5 4 3 2 1

Distributed in Canada by Fraser Direct
100 Armstrong Avenue
Georgetown, Ontario, Canada L7G 5S4
Tel: (905) 877-4411

Distributed in the U.K. and Europe by F+W Media International
Brunel House, Newton Abbot, Devon, TQ12 4PU, England
Tel: (+44) 1626-323200, Fax: (+44) 1626-323319
E-mail: postmaster@davidandcharles.co.uk

Distributed in Australia by Capricorn Link
P.O. Box 704, Windsor, NSW 2756 Australia
Tel: (02) 4577-3555

ISBN-13: 978-1-59963-651-1

Edited by Rachel Randall
Designed by Laura Spencer
Cover Designed by Brianna Scharstein
Production coordinated by Debbie Thomas

DEDICATION

To my readers, who have allowed me to keep writing and learning as I live out my dream of being a storyteller.

ACKNOWLEDGMENTS

Thanks to my family for letting me disappear into the basement during the summer, and to Pam, Heather, and Trinity for their helpful editorial suggestions. Thanks to Jessica and Phil for believing in this book, to my agent, Meg, for encouraging me to write it, and to Rachel for taking it to the next level.

ABOUT THE AUTHOR

 Steven James is the best-selling author of nine novels that have received wide critical acclaim from *Publishers Weekly, New York Journal of Books, RT Book Reviews, Booklist, Library Journal*, and many others.

He has won three Christy Awards for best suspense and was a finalist for an International Thriller Award for best original paperback. His psychological thriller *The Bishop* was named *Suspense Magazine*'s Book of the Year.

Steven has a Master's Degree in Storytelling, serves as a contributing editor for *Writer's Digest*, and has taught writing and storytelling principles around the world. *Publishers Weekly* calls James "[A] master storyteller at the peak of his game."

CONTENTS

Monday Feb 6 - arleg
o'leary sentirt
call seklet
derma - Wrl n.ioo
Fri - Vince 1.00 1m

FOREWORD

Writing advice from writers is stuff I approach with caution. Does that sound odd? For me it's not. As an agent I've worked with writers for thirty-four years. I've talked with them about craft. I've read their articles, studied their books, listened to their audiotapes, and attended their workshops.

Most have a pretty good grasp of their methods, but oftentimes there's a problem: Their methods are incomplete. Don't get me wrong. Many writers can beautifully explain how they do what they do—*insofar as they understand it*—and tell you how to do it, too. They have principles that they follow, tricks that work, schematic breakdowns that explain story, and sparkling metaphors to describe the desired outcome and illuminate the process of creating it. That's all good, but it's only part of what's needed.

You see, there are big chunks of the craft that most writers do without thinking. They're good at explaining what they're conscious of but unaware of what they do intuitively. They avoid mistakes and add flourishes as they write because it just *feels* wrong—or right. A draft passage on the page smells bad or looks good in the way food does as soon as you open the refrigerator door. Before you've picked it up, taken a look, peeled off the plastic cover, and sniffed … well, you just *know*. Either it's good to eat, or it will make you sick.

There's a lot that most writers don't explain.

And then there's Steven James, whose book you are either holding in your hands or seeing on your screen.

Story Trumps Structure is something else again. If you have never before written a novel, this amazing guide will explain the basics like no other. Master the *Ceiling Fan Principle* and you will have a foundation for novel writing that will save you years of trial and error. But Steven digs deeper. Everyone knows that tension is the engine of story, but from where does it spring? Different teachers will give you different answers, but Steven smashes through the fog and reduces all disagreements to rubble. His analysis of openings, acts, interweaving, story development, genres, and more are also devastatingly simple and yet not simplistic. Rather than give you a roadmap, he sets you free to create your own.

"There are no rules" is a scary thing for new novelists to hear, but Steven makes it empowering. Yes, there are no rules, but you are not without strong principles to keep you out of trouble. Furthermore, if you are the kind of writer who feels secure with structure and frameworks, Steven offers those, too. This book contains charts, graphs, and diagrams that organize everything from character status to story fixes. There's even a formula or two, such as Context + Causality = Unity. Read on to see what that means.

From what I'm saying you might think that Steven is a formula guy, a my-way-or-no-way teacher of craft. Nope. Steven is both a deep thinker about story and someone who can make amorphous concepts as easy to understand as an Aesop fable. He is pithy and wise. I suspect he lives on a mountaintop. What for many novelists is intuitive, he makes concrete. *Pebble people vs. putty people. Keep your promises. Write from the center of the paradox.* Is that kindergarten reductive or Zen mystical? It's both. Keep a box of Post-It notes handy as you read *Story Trumps Structure*— you are going to need them. This book is a treasure chest of writing gems.

Most amazing of all to me is that Steven, a best-selling author of thrillers, is not an outline writer. He's a more organic and intuitive sort, a "pantser" supreme. Part II of this book is not only a manifesto of intuitive writing, it is the only practical guide I have ever read on *how to actually do it.* Believe it or not, literary writers will find his approach as useful as anyone. Steven can break down story like a professor of mechanical engineering, but he can also draw a memorable writing lesson from watching his daughter brush her hair. Never before have I read a book that's as useful to both sides of the outline/intuitive divide.

You'll see what I mean. When Steven relates a simple principle for conceptualizing how protagonists solve problems—*wit or grit, skill or will*—he quips, "I like that. It's easy for me to remember." Later on he tosses off sentences like, "We humans have agathokakological hearts." *Agathokakological?* Well, yes. Steven's discussion of this word that my spell-checker doesn't recognize is instantly memorable. And if you're looking simply for inspiration to write, just wait until Part IV of this book. His thoughts on theme have revolutionary force. The last line of that section is the best, truest, and most profound statement of the purpose of fiction that I have ever read, period. (Don't peek!)

Several years ago, Steven was looking for an agent. I had the pleasure of several long and enjoyable phone conversations with him. I didn't win the contest, but Steven won a fan. With this book he's won more than that: He's won a student and has made an admirer of a guy who's himself studied, written, and taught quite a bit about fiction craft. Whether you are new or a longtime pro, you'll learn much from *Story Trumps Structure.*

I don't think any fiction writer can fully explain the process or give you every tool, and maybe no one should. But Steven James comes close. Enjoy the journey to the mountaintop that you are about to take. The view from where Steven James sits is breathtaking.

Donald Maass
New York City, February 2014

INTRODUCTION

Step back for a minute.

Step back from your preconceptions about stories, from what you've been told about plot and three-act structure and archetypes and motifs and rising action, and how stories need to have a beginning, a middle, and an end, and how important it is to outline or "plot out" your novel, and how stories are either plot-driven or character-driven, and on and on and on.

Step back, take a breath, and give yourself permission to look at stories and storytelling from a new perspective, one you may have hoped existed but haven't yet found in the glut of plot and structure books that have flooded the fiction-writing and screenwriting markets in recent years.

Somewhere along the line, things have gotten flipped around backwards.

Here's the truth that gets lost in all the theorizing: Anything that gets in the way of readers' engagement and emotional investment in the story is not serving readers. The number of acts, the type of characters, the symbolism, the mythic elements—all those things that are trumpeted about in so many writing books and taught as gospel truth at so many writing conferences—they all need to be determined by the narrative movement of the story, not the other way around.

The greatest storytellers aren't afraid to break the "rules" of plot, characterization, or even grammar in order to enrich their stories and raise them above the status quo.

This book will teach you how to do just that.

Simply put, if you're courageous enough to ditch the formulas and templates and instead step into the heart of narrative, you can become a better storyteller. And if you're open to letting the stories you tell trump the structure you've been taught, it will transform the way you craft your stories forever.

PART I

THE ESSENCE OF
STORY

CHAPTER 1

DESIRE

The Ceiling Fan Principle and What It Means for Storytellers

When I was growing up, whenever we returned to school in the fall, my teachers would give us the assignment to "write about what you did over the summer."

The entries always ended up being lists of events: "*I played video games and then we visited my grandma and then I went to camp and went swimming and did archery and then ...*"

You remember that assignment.

Mind-numbing after a while.

Well, a few years ago I was visiting an elementary school while doing a residency on writing and storytelling. I arrived the day after spring break and told the students, "Please, please, please, do not tell me what you did over vacation. But can anyone tell me about something that went wrong?"

A fourth-grade boy raised his hand. "My cousin came over to my house, and we were having a contest to see who could jump the farthest off my bunk bed."

"What happened?" I asked.

"He went first and got pretty far, and I said, 'I can get farther than that!'" The boy was a natural storyteller, and by then everyone in the class was leaning forward, waiting to hear how things played out.

"Well, what went wrong?"

"I backed up to the wall to get a running start ... and I jumped off the bed ... and the ceiling fan was on. I got my head stuck in the ceiling fan, and it threw me against the wall—but I got farther!"

The class cracked up.

Now, if I'd said to those students, "Tell me about what you did over vacation," that boy would've replied, "I played with my cousin." But when I asked him to tell me what went wrong, he told me a story.

I call this the Ceiling Fan Principle. It's easy to remember, and it's the best place I know to start a discussion on storytelling.

Here it is: You do not have a story until something goes wrong.

Imagine that I'm telling you about my day and I say, "I woke up. I drank some coffee. I left for work."

Is that a story? After all, it has a protagonist who makes choices that lead to a natural progression of events, it contains three acts, and it has a beginning, a middle, and an end—and that's what makes something a story, right?

Well, actually, no.

It's not.

At its core, when you strip everything away, what is a story? Do all stories, regardless of genre, share some characteristics?

Yes: a character in tension, caught between his present condition and his unmet desire for things to be different.

Stories are transformations unveiled—either the transformation of a character or a situation, or, more commonly, both. If nothing is altered, you do not have a story, you simply have a series of images or a chronicle of events.

My description of what I did this morning contains no crisis, no struggle, no discovery, no transformation in the life of the main character or revelation of what he is really like. It's not a story. It's a report.

> To uncover the plot of your story, don't ask what should happen, but what should go wrong. To uncover the meaning of your story, don't ask what the theme is, but rather, what is discovered. Characters making choices to resolve tension—that's your plot. If your protagonist has no goal, makes no choices, has no struggle to overcome, you have no plot.

TENSION IS KEY

At the heart of story is tension, and at the heart of tension is unmet desire. So at its core every story is about a character who wants something but cannot get it. As soon as she gets it (or fails ultimately in her quest to do so), the story is over. If readers don't know what the character wants, they won't know what the story is about.

As storytellers we have to make all of that clear: desire, struggle, consequences, discovery.

In real life we avoid crisis events.

In fiction we seek them out.

In real life we want only the best for the people we care about. In fiction, we want things to get the *worst* for the characters we care about the *most*, at least on their pathway to the climax.

In fact, if all goes well, especially if things keep getting better and better for the main characters, we lose interest and put the book down.

With this in mind, it bewilders me that rather than dive into this essential aspect of story—tension—so many writers get stuck asking, "What should happen next?" or "What does this character do?" when the more vital questions are "What should *go wrong*?" and "What does this character *want*?"

The pursuit of fulfilling unmet desire is the key to unlocking your story. Where will that quest take your characters (emotionally, spiritually, physically, mentally, or relationally)? That's what readers want to know.

To write a story that draws readers in and keeps them turning pages late into the night, storytellers need to introduce more and more tension, not simply make more and more things happen.

Preventing your character from getting what he wants keeps things moving and propels the narrative forward.

In a romance story, as soon as the couple gets together, as soon as the relationship flourishes, the tension is gone: The characters have what they want, and the story is over. So when writing romance, we don't ask how we can make a scene more romantic but how we can ratchet up the *romantic tension*.

Unless we're writing erotica, we don't look for ways to get the couple into bed together but rather ways to *keep them* from climbing into bed together, thus drawing out that romantic and sensual tension for as long as possible.

Romance novels are not about romance but romantic tension.

One event happening after another isn't interesting for readers unless they can understand the unfulfilled desire of the main character (surviving, achieving justice, saving the world, etc.). Readers will get bored by relentless action.

Because of that, action/adventure stories are not so much about action and adventure as they are about the escalation of tension.

Fantasy isn't about making up worlds; it's about a clash between worlds. Tension.

Always tension.

Whatever genre you write in, when you discover your protagonist's unmet desire, you find the essence of your story.

WHY STORIES AREN'T DRIVEN FORWARD BY EITHER PLOT OR CHARACTER

There's a long-running debate among those who teach writing and storytelling about whether stories are "plot-driven" or "character-driven."

Some story theorists point to different genres of stories as plot-driven (for example spy and detective stories) and other stories as character-driven (literary fiction and coming-of-age stories).

Other people claim that all stories are both plot-driven and character-driven—at least to some degree.

However, in truth, there's no such thing as either a plot-driven or a character-driven story.

All stories are tension-driven.

Yes. All.

A story might be character-*centered* (revolving around personal growth), plot-*centered* (relating to tasks to be completed), or relationship-*centered* (focused on developing connections between people), but the story is never driven forward simply by character studies or the procession of events occurring.

This is an important distinction.

You can write a fascinating description of a character, but the longer you carry on about her, the less it drives the story forward—instead, it stalls it out. After a while, readers will grow tired of hearing about what the character is thinking or eating or wearing or doing if they don't know what her unfulfilled desire is.

In the same way, readers will eventually get bored by action (such as car chases, explosions, or giant robots fighting giant robots) unless they know what the characters involved in the action actually want but cannot get. Once again, a story isn't driven forward by events happening but by tension escalating.

Unmet desire equals tension.

And only tension moves a story forward.

Stop trying to decide if your story is "plot-driven" or "character-driven," and focus instead on your protagonist's unmet desires regarding his internal questions, external problems, and interpersonal relationships.

> Clarify what each character wants, not only in the sense of what he's hoping to accomplish, but also in the sense of what internal questions might be influencing his choices and relationships.

THE FICTION OF THREE ACTS

When I was a sophomore in high school, my English teacher told us that a story is something that has a beginning, a middle, and an end, and I remember thinking, "So does a description of a chair. How is that a story?"

Spend enough time with writing instructors and you'll hear again and again that oft-repeated dictum my English teacher gave me. Now, I know that the people who teach this definition mean well, but it's really not a very helpful one for writers.

Of course a story has a beginning, a middle, and an end—that's self-evident. Everything in the natural world, everything humans create or conceive of, has a beginning, a middle, and an end. But knowing that doesn't really help me finish writing my novel.

A shopping list has a beginning, a middle, and an end, but it's not a story. The sentence "Preheat the oven to 450 degrees" has a beginning, a middle, and an end, but it's not a story either.

When teachers refer to this "beginning, middle, and end" in reference to stories, they're usually viewing stories through the lens of three-act structure.

Act one: the beginning.

Act two: the middle.

Act three: the end.

But is that true?

Do stories need exactly three acts?

Centuries ago, Aristotle noted in his book *Poetics* that in a story, the beginning is not simply the first event but rather the emotionally engaging originating event. The middle of the story consists of the natural and causally related consequences, and the end is the unexpected and yet inevitable conclusive event.

In other words, stories have an origination, an escalation of conflict, and a resolution after which nothing would logically occur based on what precedes it in that story.

So, three acts?

Well, yes—sometimes—but Aristotle wasn't emphasizing that there are precisely three acts. He was emphasizing the contingent nature of stories—that the progression of the story, from start to finish, is not made up of random events, but of causally related ones, which give the story unity and closure.

As John Gardner pointed out in his book *The Art of Fiction*, Edgar Allan Poe's story *The Cask of Amontillado* has one act—the last one. It's a story with an ending but no beginning or middle, at least not in the typical sense that people refer to in terms of the structural acts of a story.

Regardless of how many acts or scenes your story has, for it to feel complete it'll need an orientation to the world of the characters, an origination of conflict, an escalation of tension, rising stakes, a moment at which everything seems lost, a climactic encounter, a satisfying conclusion, and a transformation of a character or a situation (usually both).

If you want to divide that into three acts, have at it.

Short stories may contain only one act. In theater you'll find one-act, two-act, three-act, four-act, and five-act plays. Epic novels may contain many more than three acts. A television series that runs for several seasons might contain, well, I don't even know how many acts. And most assuredly, all of those narrative forms with all of their different plot structures tell stories.

Readers couldn't care less how many acts are in your story. In fact, if you write it well, they probably won't even be able to keep track of them. Instead, they care about the forward momentum of the story as it escalates toward its inevitable and unexpected conclusion.

Let the shape of the story determine the number of acts, not the other way around.

Often the people who advocate funneling your story into three acts will note that stories have the potential to sag or stall out during the long second act. And whenever I hear that I think, "Then why not shorten it? Or chop it up and include more acts? Why let the story suffer just so you can follow a formula?"

I have a feeling that if you asked the folks who teach three-act structure if they'd rather have a story that closely follows their format or one that ends up with more acts (or fewer) but intimately connects with readers, they would go with the latter choice. Why? Because I'm guessing that deep down, even they know that in the end, story trumps structure.

Once, another writing instructor told me that the three acts form the skeleton of a story. I wasn't sure how to respond to that until I was at an aquarium with my daughter later that week and I saw an octopus. I realized that it got along pretty well without a skeleton. A storyteller's goal is to give life to a story, not to stick in bones that aren't necessary for that species of tale.

Give yourself the freedom to stop thinking of a story as something that happens in three acts or two acts or four or seven. Rather, think of your story as an organic whole that reveals a transformation in the life (internal, external, and interpersonal) of your character.

Note that words aren't necessary to tell a story. When a series of images shows disequilibrium, struggle, discovery, and change, the images themselves can tell the story without words. Comic books do this all the time.

Don't think of the material in this book as a structure to follow but as ingredients to include in your stories. This is not a system or a paint-by-numbers approach, but a framework for a better understanding of the narrative forces that shape the forward movement of a story. The ideas overlap with each other—believability relates to characterization and story flow and reader expectations and so on. You'll find that through the book, as we hold up the prism of story, you'll see the concepts being taught, sometimes from a number of different perspectives.

Gather the ingredients, then mix them together and let them merge and disappear into each other, forming something new and unique as you let the context determine the structure of the specific story you're telling.

Whether your story happens in one act or a dozen makes no difference to readers. They just want the tale to taste good.

Over the next five chapters we'll look at five essential story ingredients and how they combine to form a whole that is greater than the sum of its parts.

CHAPTER 2

ORIENTATION

The Eight Aspects Every Story Opening Will Include

While I was teaching at a writers conference in North Carolina, a woman gave me her story to critique. It started with an exciting car chase. I said, "Great, so this is an action story."

"No," she told me, "it's a romance. After the car crash, the woman goes to the hospital and falls in love with the doctor."

"But it starts with a car chase and explosion. Readers will expect it to escalate from there."

"I had a different opening," she admitted, "but my writing critique group told me I needed a better hook."

It may have been true that her story needed a better hook, but she landed on the wrong one. It promised something her story didn't deliver, and anytime you do that, you'll end up letting your readers down.

You have to keep the promises that the opening of your story makes.

And it needs to do more than simply grab your readers' attention. To be effective, story beginnings will do eight things.

1. Orient readers to the world of the story.
2. Lock in the genre.
3. Give readers a setting in time and place that they can picture.
4. Set the mood and tone.
5. Introduce the author's (or narrator's) voice.

6. Introduce a protagonist whom readers will care about or an antagonist they will fear. (Or, in some cases, both.)
7. End in a way that's both surprising and satisfying.
8. Snag readers' attention.

All eight facets intertwine. They can be accomplished quickly, sometimes in less than a paragraph, or they can happen over a chapter or two. It all depends on the story.

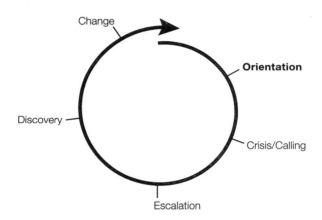

1. Orient readers to the world of the story.

This needs to be a consistent and coherent world. Once you lock readers into your story, don't insert anything that would cause them to start doubting the veracity of it.

Let's say you create a world in which gravity doesn't exist. Okay, readers will accept that, but now they want you to be consistent. As soon as someone's hair doesn't float above or around her head or someone is able to drink a cup of coffee without the liquid floating away, the consistency of that world is shattered. Readers will begin to lose interest or may mentally disengage from the story and begin to look for more inconsistencies—neither of which you want them to do.

Your historical romance takes place in 1850—people better not use modern slang. Your medical thriller explores cutting-edge technology—well, you'd better get your research right because as soon as you make a mistake, the believability of the story will be lost.

The narrative world you portray will create expectations that will need to be met as the story unfolds.

So what about snagging your readers' interest? How quickly does that have to happen?

If you're writing a full-length novel, you don't need to bend over backward trying to be clever in the first line or two. Readers will understand that there's a lot of story to tell, and they'll give you some space to do that. Don't rush the opening.

I've heard lots of advice about starting with action. People will tell you, "Hit the ground running!" While it's good to start "in the middle of things" (as Aristotle put it), hitting the ground running isn't good advice if, in the next chapter, you move back in time, diminish the tension, and show the character training, arriving at the track, warming up, stretching out, and then walking up to the starting line.

De-escalation like that can rip right through the fabric of the story and cause readers to lose interest before they've even gotten into the heart of your novel.

Really evaluate that hook. Too many times, openings grab readers' attention, but then the writer moves into backstory that destroys the forward momentum of the narrative. Trust your readers, orient them to the world of the story, and then move forward without having to explain why you started it the way you did.

In essence, the beginning of a story sets readers' expectations and reveals a portrait of the main character, typically by giving them a glimpse of her normal life. (Stories can also start with characters in abnormal situations trying to return to normal life. In that case, readers may not see "normal life" until the end of the book but they learn more about it as the story progresses because of the character's driving unmet desire.)

If your protagonist is a detective, readers want to see him at a crime scene. If you're writing a romance story, they want to see normal life for the young man or woman who's searching for love.

For instance, if you introduce readers to your protagonist, Frank, the happily married man next door who doesn't have a care in the world in his perfect, storybook marriage, readers instinctively know that Frank's idyllic life is about to unravel and be turned upside down—very likely by the death of either his spouse or his marriage. Something will soon rock the boat, and he will be forever altered.

Readers expect this.

Readers want this.

You've promised it to them because they intuitively know the Ceiling Fan Principle and they're waiting for something to go wrong to get the story rolling.

When they read about harmony at the start of a story, it's a promise that discord is soon to come.

Note that normal life doesn't mean pain-free life. The story might begin while your protagonist is depressed, hopeless, grieving, or trapped in a sinking submarine. When that happens, often another crisis (whether internal, external, or interpersonal) will serve to kickstart the story and take it forward on another, deeper level.

2. Lock in the genre.

Often this doesn't take much.

Back in the days before we streamed our movies, I rented a film called *Quarantine*. The DVD case showed a woman screaming, being dragged back into the darkness by some unseen force. The blurbs and reviews all raved about how scary the movie was.

The genre was perfectly clear before I even started watching the film.

Now, does anyone really think the director needed to hook my attention in the opening scene by "hitting the ground running"?

No. Of course not.

They'd already hooked me with the packaging. They could take their time setting up the story.

In a very real sense, the packaging served as a prologue to the story. As Robert McKee pointed out concerning films in his book *Story: Substance, Structure, Style and the Principles of Screenwriting*, "From the title to the poster through print and TV ads, promotion seeks to fix the type of story in the mind of the audience."

It's the same for books as it is for movies.

Even before readers begin the first page of your story they'll have certain expectations about it.

These expectations come from buzz, word of mouth, online recommendations, genre categorization, reviews, inclusion in a series, familiarity with your other books, your reputation, bio and photo, product packaging (back-cover copy, front-cover artwork), and so on.

Each of these factors makes promises to readers that will affect your story's flow. If you don't take your readers' expectations and familiarity with your story (even before they start it) into account, you may very well end up with a beginning that isn't as effective or impactful as it needs to be to draw them into this story.

Stephen King's name on a novel tells you it's probably not a safe little cozy mystery. Philip Roth's name on the cover is a good clue that it's not going to be an action-packed thriller.

Also, if you're trying to break into the publishing world, your query letter, pitch, plot summary—the entirety of your proposal—affects an editor's or agent's expectations. Think of it all as an orientation to the world of the story you're submitting.

Packaging is a promise. Titling is a promise. Length is a promise. If a reader purchases a six-hundred-page novel, he'll enter it with certain expectations about the pace of the story.

Remember the woman with the car chase/romance story? She locked in the wrong genre. Her opening undermined what she was trying to accomplish. The genre you set early on will affect readers' expectations right off the bat.

> Use the beginning to orient readers to (1) the main character, (2) the main struggle(s), and (3) the setting.

---

3. Give readers a setting in time and place that they can picture.

Until readers can picture a scene, they can't experience it.

Avoid disorienting openings:

> "Put down the gun."
> "Hand over the diamonds."
> "I said put down the gun!"
> "No. I want the diamonds and the antidote."
> "I'm telling you, I'll stab her if you don't put down your gun."

And on it goes.

Where are these people? Who are they? Who's talking? How many people are there? What do they look like? Readers have no idea.

Use the opening of your book to orient readers to a specific character in a specific time and place, and remember, you're making them a promise. You're saying, "Invest in this character. This is someone you should care about."

Fiction is composed of (1) narration (which might include what is happening, a summary of what has happened, or an orientation to what is about to happen), (2) description, (3) dialogue, and sometimes, (4) thoughts (which some people refer to as "inner monologue" or "inner dialogue"). (Since the character isn't talking to anyone, it's not technically dialogue—unless the character has two voices in his head, each vying for attention. This happens in real life, so it can be an effective technique to use judiciously in your story.)

Filmmakers draw attention to something through camera angles. We do so through description. Vivid descriptions early in the story will help readers picture the setting and acclimatize to the story you're telling.

Leave unsaid what your readers already know or will subconsciously fill in. So when writing about a familiar, everyday world—one that readers will immediately recognize and visualize—description is less important.

We can all picture a living room, a hospital, a city park. You don't need to spend much time describing them.

But what about a wizard's chamber? An intergalactic spaceship's control room? The inside of an Aztec temple?

Fantasy, science fiction, and historical fiction all rely more on description because the settings are so unusual. Their authors are, in a sense, dabbling in world creation, that is, striving to take the readers to an entirely different place and give them an immersive experience in a unique world.

So when writing your story, if it occurs in an unusual environment, you'll lean more on description. If you're writing about a place your readers are familiar with, you'll include less.

As you ground your story, include unique characteristics of that location or environment and let those help determine the direction of the narrative. Typically, the setting will be an integral part of the opening scene and the book as a whole. If your novel can be picked up from San Diego and dropped into Atlanta, you'll want to take a closer look at the importance of the city you've chosen and make it play a more prominent and indispensable role in the story.

However, if you want to create a closed-in, atmospheric novel that all takes place in one location (a hotel room, for example), you may want to make it purposely generic and universally transferable so it could be the hotel just down the street from your readers, wherever they are when they read your book. The story and its intended effect on readers determine the balance of the specificity or universality of the setting.

During your story's orientation ask yourself:
- Do I see this?
- Do I care?
- Do I worry about what's going to happen?

4. Set the mood and tone.

In her novel *Dark Places*, Gillian Flynn begins her story about Libby Day: "I have a meanness inside me, real as an organ. Slit me at my belly and it might slide out, meaty and dark, drop on the floor so you could stomp on it. It's the Day blood. Something's wrong with it. I was never a good little girl, and I got worse after the murders."

With an opening like that, there's no doubt about the mood of the story.

When someone says, "Watch your tone of voice," they don't mean volume, or even tone as they might in the music industry, but rather *attitude*—and that might be sarcasm or rancor or condescension. (Of course, tone can also be positive: humorous, optimistic, or lighthearted.)

Mood is different than tone.

When I think of mood I sometimes think of the varying moods at different times of the day—the hope of a new dawn, the oppression of a hot afternoon sun, the cool refreshment of an evening breeze, the breathtaking beauty (or foreboding nature) of a sunset, the shiver of a dark and lonely night.

Tone is the attitude of the story.

Mood is the atmosphere.

Create a mood, and use a tone consistent with the promises you want to make to readers regarding your narrative.

5. Introduce the author's (or narrator's) voice.

Voice is the distinctive writing style and unique perspective that saturates your story.

Think of a stage play. The mood is established by the lighting, sets, and music. The tone is conveyed through the dialogue and acting. The voice is the distinctive style of storytelling (terse, verbose, explanatory, etc.) that sets that play apart from others in the genre.

Just as story trumps structure, voice trumps grammar—not the other way around.

Mariette in Ecstasy by Ron Hansen begins like this:

> Upstate New York.
> August 1906.
> Half-moon and a wrack of gray clouds.
> Church windows and thirty nuns singing the Night Office in Gregorian chant. Matins. Lauds. And then silence.
> Wind, and a nighthawk teetering on it and yawing away into woods.
> Wallowing beetles in green pond water.
> Toads.
> Cattails sway and unsway.
> Grape leaves rattle and settle again.

Complete sentences?

Not on your life. Not until those last two lines.

Hansen's voice and storytelling style break grammar conventions and create a powerful opening to his novel.

Don't try to be different or memorable with your storytelling voice—be authentic. Complex sentences? Sure, if they're appropriate. Fragments? Why not? Elaborate descriptions, boiled-down language—okay, yes, they can all work.

Whatever voice you choose for your story, introduce it early and keep it consistent throughout your narrative or at least throughout a particular character's point-of-view portion of the story. In other words, you'll naturally have a different voice for each of the point-of-view characters. Let every one be distinctive and easily differentiated from the others.

6. Introduce a protagonist whom readers will care about or an antagonist they will fear. (Or, in some cases, both.)

Once, I started reading a novel with a protagonist who was immature and pouty, and after about fifty pages I just wanted her to get killed off so we could get on with the story.

That's definitely not what you want your readers thinking when they read your work.

If readers don't care about your protagonist, they won't care about your story. Your protagonist might be sarcastic, but she must not be smarmy. She might be unhappy, but she cannot be whiny. She might do undesirable things, but she cannot be unlikable.

If your protagonist appears childish, easily intimidated, or cowardly, readers will naturally look for someone else to cheer for. If the hero cowers in the face of evil, readers may end up liking the villain more. You'll need to fix this to keep readers on your protagonist's side.

Readers want to either empathize with or admire your protagonist. It all depends on the genre.

In an espionage novel, readers might not be able to identify with the glamorous, dangerous life of the secret agent, but they might look up to him.

It's the same for a superhero story: Until the masked crime fighter has a struggle that readers share, they won't necessarily identify with him, but they might aspire to be like him.

External struggles ignite reader interest and curiosity while internal and interpersonal struggles engender empathy. So in a mystery, readers will be intellectually curious about how the crime was done but not necessarily emotionally engaged in the story. However, if the protagonist's son gets kidnapped, making the crime more personal, readers will begin to feel more empathy and concern.

If your readers identify with someone other than your protagonist more than they do with him, they will likely end up being on that other character's side. In that case they'll care more for her than they do for your main character. To fix this, either reverse the characters' roles and give yourself a new protagonist or make your readers feel more empathy for your protagonist.

To touch readers on an emotional level, you'll need your main character to desire something your readers also desire.

For example, your protagonist might want to love or be loved, find freedom, pursue her dreams, overcome the wounds of the past, learn to forgive, or any number of things. But only when readers identify with that internal unmet desire of your protagonist will they be drawn into the story on a deep emotional level.

> When developing your story's struggles, don't assume your readers will care what happens. Make it impossible for them not to.

Regardless of how much or how little you describe a character, readers will form some mental picture of him. So when you first introduce a character, include any physical traits that are significant to the story.

If readers need to know that your protagonist has a scar on her left cheek, tell them when they first meet her or they'll get a different mental picture of her and become confused later when you refer back to the scar. Whatever is pertinent: Age, gender, hair color, build, tattoos, distinctive facial features, and so on should be conveyed early, when you're first bringing the character on stage in your story.

Trust your readers in all this. Tell them what's essential, and let them fill in the rest. In the seven novels I've written featuring FBI Special Agent Patrick Bowers, I've never described his hair or eye color, never told readers whether he has a thin chin or a lantern jaw, and so on. I want readers to envision their version of a hero, and I don't want to intrude on that with too many superfluous details. None of those other things mattered, so I never brought them up.

To give readers a memorable description of a character, you don't need much.

- "He was a tightly-muscled bulldog of a man."
- "A roll of stomach fat oozed out of the space between his shirt and his belt like the tip of a giant tongue."
- "One man's face looked like it was molded out of old clay. The other guy was an enormous, steel-fisted human wrecking ball."
- "She turned every step into a Spanish dance."
- "The woman had 'I have a two-year-old' written all over her face."
- "Her calves said stair stepper, her abs said yoga."

Sometimes a snippet of dialogue is all you need to show characterization.

"Sorry. I'm a married man."
"Hmm. That might be good news for me."
"Why do you say that?"
"You didn't say happily married."

To show beauty, emphasize a woman's elegance and grace. To draw attention to her sexuality, describe her body. The more you describe how physically alluring a woman is, the more readers will think she's promiscuous.

Besides physical descriptions, when you first introduce your protagonist, you'll want to show readers what he's capable of and what he wants.

If there are any significant attributes that the character will have or unusual skills he'll exhibit later in the book—for example, being a judo instructor, a psychic, a chess master, a shapeshifter, an expert marksman—whatever—reveal them early on.

When bringing characters into the story for the first time, show them in varying relationships with other characters, give them a universal desire readers will empathize with, make it clear what that desire is, and reveal what lies at the heart of your hero by allowing him to be heroic early in the story. (In other words, don't explain to readers how heroic your protagonist can be. Show them instead.)

This is also true of your antagonist. Show how evil and ruthless the villain is. What if he strangles a man with one hand while petting the man's dog with the other? What if he stands by the side of a swimming pool and calmly watches a child drown before jumping in to pull her out and then revive her?

Chilling.

Anything that interferes with the protagonist reaching her goal and fulfilling her unmet desire is the antagonist. That means it might not always be another person. It could be a storm or a demon or a dog. It might be the protagonist's past or her unfulfilled dreams or her grudge against her friend.

Since the antagonist isn't always a human being, some story theorists refer to the "forces of antagonism" in a broad sense, rather than "antagonist" in a narrow sense.

So my protagonist is a twenty-five-year-old single mom. What physical characteristics are vital for me to describe? What about her five-year-old autistic son? How can I show her commitment to him and her struggles by how she acts and what she does? What about her personality? What actions could she take to reveal it to readers? How can I pace the introduction of other essential characters so they don't appear so quickly that they confuse readers? And most importantly, what's her ultimate goal and what forces are keeping her from reaching it?

---

7. End in a way that's both surprising and satisfying.

Every story begins with a coincidence.

Of all the coffee shops in New York City, Joey just happens to bump into that specific woman in that specific shop on that specific day at 8:01 A.M. and accidentally spills that latte onto her blouse.

Of all the unsolved cases at the police department, the detective just happens to be assigned that particular case.

Of all the planets in the universe, and all the places on those planets, the aliens just happen to land in that field near the town where your protagonist is the sheriff.

Although coincidences *within* the story itself will jar readers, here in the orientation to the story we depend on a coincidence, or in other words, an uncaused or noncontingent event, to get things rolling.

So after fate or destiny or divine intervention or just blind chance brings together your protagonist, his desire, and the forces keeping it from him, your opening needs to end in a way that isn't contrived and predictable but has a twist that'll move the narrative forward.

We'll explore in depth how to do this in Chapter 10. For now, remember that readers want to be surprised, but they want that surprise to be logical and not come out of nowhere.

> Coincidences that start stories may be ones that (1) initiate the unavoidable conflict that follows, (2) ask the essential question the protagonist must answer, or (3) present the compelling desire that the character will passionately pursue.

8. Snag readers' attention.

Yes, your book's opening should be engaging enough to spark readers' interest, but the problem with these "gripping" hooks so many people advocate is the drop in escalation and tension that often follows them.

Typically it goes like this: The author starts in the middle of the action, or maybe in the middle of some dialogue, and then he has to go back and fill readers in on what led up to it.

That kills the pace and bores readers.

So hook readers, but do so while keeping the broader context of your story in mind. If the hook doesn't provide the platform for escalation, it becomes a gimmick and undermines your readers' engagement with the story.

So how long should your hook be?

Depending on who you talk to, they'll tell you the hook needs to happen in the first chapter, the first paragraph, or even the first sentence.

In his book *Winter Birds*, Jim Grimsley uses a gripping opening to not only snag readers' attention but to introduce the mood, voice, and setting. Breaking another convention, he also tells the story in second-person present tense.

> Out past the clapboard house in the weeds by the riverbank your brothers are killing birds. By the river flocks of wrens, starlings and a few faded female cardinals have gathered to feed on the leavings in the cornfield, and your brothers lie hidden in the weeds with their shared gun, waiting to burst open bird skulls with their copper BBs. At every shot you can hear your brothers laughing.

His opening merges naturally with the following chapters, and he never has to drop back and cause his narrative to languish with unnecessary backstory.

The length of the book determines the length of the hook. The importance of the first line or the first paragraph decreases with the length of your story. It's much more important to create an opening that readers can see, one that allows them to develop empathy or admiration for the character, than it is to come up with a clever first line.

Taking a closer look at the opening to my story, have I accomplished what I want or am I short-circuiting things by trying too hard to have a clever hook? What will my readers know about my story from packaging and promotion before they even read the first word? How will that affect how I begin the narrative, when I need to introduce the main character, and how much time I can take laying out the setting of the story?

WHAT ABOUT PROLOGUES?

Are they the first act? Part of the first act? Actually, they don't really fit well in the three-act paradigm. Since they seem to speak against that structure, some writing instructors tell authors flat-out not to include a prologue.

I've even heard people claim that prologues are always superfluous, that a story always stands on its own without them.

That's just ridiculous.

If the story demands a prologue, include one.

And yes, prologues are acts, and as such, they need to orient readers in the same way any story opening does.

There are six times when prologues might be used.

1. **When giving background information on the main character that, because of the pace, flow, or timing of the rest of the story, cannot naturally be woven into the narrative later on.** I needed to start my novel *Placebo* with a prologue since there's a span of thirteen months between the first scene and the rest of the novel, which takes place over just a couple of days.

   The only other way I could have included this vital scene later in the book would have been through a long, intrusive flashback, which would've killed the narrative momentum of the story. The

novel flows better by separating this scene and making it the prologue, and the pace of the story required readers to empathize
with my protagonist before the first chapter began. The story's
pace and *flow* required a prologue.

2. **To bookend the story.** When doing this, there will also be an
epilogue that ties the story together in a circular fashion. (This
is sometimes done in film through a voiceover.)

3. **To provide a flash-forward to a scene that's coming later in the
book.** In order to help the flow of the first chapter and introduce
characters who appear there, sometimes we include an excerpt
from later in the story to serve as the prologue.

4. **To avoid repetition within the broader context of a series of
books.** If your story is part of a series and you don't want them
all to start the same way—for example, a series of crime novels
that all begin with the detective arriving at a crime scene—you
may wish to include prologues in one or more of the books to
avoid falling into a predictable pattern.

5. **To orient readers from a different point of view than the rest
of the book uses.** For example, in R.J. Ellory's *A Quiet Belief in
Angels*, he includes a prologue in a unique third person-esque
point of view to ground the reader in the setting, and then moves
to first person for the first chapter.

6. **When introducing a subplot.** If your prologue introduces the
main plot and leads directly into the next scene, just change the
title from "Prologue" to "Chapter One."

If you choose to use a prologue that doesn't include your protagonist
(say, your prologue introduces a subplot), you'll want to introduce your
protagonist in the first chapter and keep readers with him long enough
for them to connect with him. (If you're wondering who your story is
really about and you find that a character appears in the first scene and
the last scene, it's a good clue that you've found your protagonist.)

But do you have to do that? Do you have to introduce your protagonist first?

No. But remember that readers need to be oriented to the world of the story. They anticipate meeting the character they're expected to care about the most early on. They want to know who to cheer for, whose side to be on, who to worry about.

If you can better serve your readers by juggling things around, do it. But realize that it will, at least initially, throw them for a loop or postpone their emotional engagement as they try to figure out what's going on and who the story is primarily about.

The character you introduce first is a promise to readers. If you introduce a point-of-view character and then kill her off in the prologue, readers won't be as emotionally invested in the story. They'll naturally be wary that you might take advantage of their time and emotional investment again.

Do whatever you need to do in your quest to help readers enter the world of your story. But don't resort to gimmicks just for the sake of being unique or artistic, or to impress critics.

If you don't know where to begin your story, try introducing readers to the protagonist's unmet desire, vividly show them the location, and give them something to worry about.

BRINGING YOUR CHARACTERS ON STAGE

Pacing the introduction of story characters can be tricky.

I've read novels in which eight characters were introduced in a single paragraph. I had to go back and reread it several times to make sure I could keep them straight. Some readers wouldn't even bother to double back like that but would just skim over the names, hoping it would all be clarified later.

Every time your readers have to look back through what they've already read, you've caused something to come between them and the story. Don't allow that to happen.

In the same way, every time you give them a reason to skim your work, you've allowed your laziness as an author to come between them and the story.

Every word matters.

Every word deserves to be read—once.

But only once.

It's our job to care for our readers. If they have to study our stories or if they feel sections aren't important enough to read and they choose to just skip or skim them instead, we've failed to serve the very people we depend on to make a living.

So as you work on bringing characters on stage, keep asking yourself if you've introduced them in an appropriate order, with adequate timing, and with enough detail to help readers picture them.

Readers know you need to introduce them to your characters, so at the beginning of the book they'll give you some grace as you do so.

> Look at a story as either (1) a final fulfillment of desire after a long series of setbacks or (2) a final plummet into despair after trouble overwhelms you.

THE END IS A GOOD PLACE TO START

Although the orientation appears first, it's not necessarily the first thing you'll write or the first part of the story that you'll finalize in the editing process.

Three centuries ago Blaise Pascal noted that "the last thing one settles in writing a book is what one should put in first."

What was true then is true today.

The opening scene to your novel will likely be the last one you hone. Why?

Because, unless genre has dictated the closure of your story (for example, an inspirational prairie romance will end in an uplifting way—with the protagonist either finding her true love or something better, such as God's forgiveness), if you know the ending of a story, you'll know the beginning, but if you know the beginning, you won't necessarily know the ending.

For example, if your protagonist is trying to find hope to start over again after her drug problems, she might do so at the story's end, or she might not and consequently give up on life. Just knowing her struggle doesn't tell you the culmination of the story. However, if you know that the story ends with her finding a new drug-free life, you know that the story begins with her searching for it.

If the story ends with your protagonist deciding to move from Cincinnati to London, you know that, at the beginning, this decision has to be his struggle. So when you get done, you'd go back and recast the beginning so it's inextricably tied to the end of the story. But if you only know the beginning—that he is trying to decide whether or not to leave the States—you won't know if he ever moves or not.

This is one of the reasons those "first-page critiques" performed at writing groups and writers conferences are so detrimental to writers—because they focus on a tiny glimpse of someone's writing taken out of context and dabble with it, over-sharpening it, when it might not even appear in the story at all.

These critiques are also damaging since they're often being done by people who aren't aware of all the narrative forces that press in upon a story to reveal its true shape, let alone the eight things the openings to novels need to accomplish. Just like in the case of the woman with the chase scene at the beginning of her romance novel, a well-meaning critique group can easily send a story spinning off in the wrong direction.

And perhaps most importantly, these critiques don't take the broader context of the story into account.

Sometimes, rather than focusing on the first page, the critique covers a section in the middle of the book. But even if the author gives a "plot summary" of her book, it'll always fail to provide adequate context since the people in the group haven't experienced what readers experience and won't have in mind the same things readers would, based on all that precedes that part of the novel.

The critiquers won't have any sense of pace or flow or characterization. Any writing taken out of context will end up being critiqued poorly.

A critiquer might say, "The pace is too slow," but he won't know that the scene occurs immediately following a mid-book climax in the course of your six-hundred-page novel and that the character needs some time to regroup, process what just occurred, and reorient herself before making the decision that will push the narrative forward again. The critiquer won't know that you're setting readers up for the final drive toward the story's climax.

Or, he might say, "This has good pace, but I don't really know what this character looks like. I can't picture her." But, of course, you've dealt with this two hundred pages earlier, and he doesn't know that either.

This is what goes on at these groups all the time.

I can't think of any other field in which people who aren't experts critique other people who aren't experts in the hope of everyone becoming an expert.

Instead of tinkering endlessly with your opening, it's vital that you work through your story, flesh it out, see where it leads, and then, once you know where it's going, head back to the beginning and start it off aimed in the right direction.

So, to review, grab the attention of readers, help them see what's happening, introduce a character they can identify with or aspire to be like, give them a feel for the mood, set their expectations in the right place for the story arc you're working with, and then get on with it. Don't stall out by giving too much background information. Press forward, make promises you can fulfill, and leave your readers hungry for more.

Which brings us to the second ingredient: Now that you've oriented your readers to the world of the story, it's time for something to go wrong.

CHAPTER 3

CRISIS/CALLING

Story Origins, Resolutions, and the Three Levels of Struggles

One night I was reading a bedtime story to my youngest daughter, who was five years old at the time. In the story, five sisters had a picnic, then danced around the meadow, then sang their favorite song, then played dress-up in the attic, then played outside again. Finally, my daughter sighed and told me she was bored.

"You don't like the story?" I said.

"Course not!" she exclaimed. "Nothing's going wrong!"

Ah. Yes.

Even at five years old, my daughter understood that a story is not simply a list of events. It's the account of a character facing a struggle.

The Ceiling Fan Principle all over again.

The crisis that tips the world of your character upside down must be one that cannot be immediately solved. It's an unavoidable challenge that sets the rest of the story in motion.

If your protagonist can solve a problem right away, it's only an event that might lead to a story, not the story itself. His life needs to be disrupted in a way that he can't immediately overcome or step away from.

After all, if he can just walk away from the problem, readers will wonder why he doesn't. Something will happen that makes it impossible for him to turn back. His engagement needs to be a requirement, not a choice. He must progress through the story.

Remember, stories aren't essentially about what happens or what a character is like but about what goes wrong and how the character pursues what she desires most.

Without injecting tension into your book early on or delivering on your promise to make something bad happen, readers will quickly lose interest.

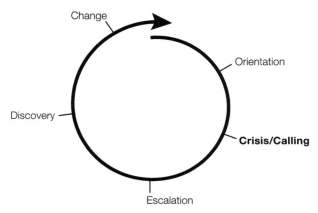

Stories revolve around dilemmas, not action. To build a story, you don't try to make the right things *happen* but rather make the right things go *wrong*.

Using the example from Chapter 1 of me waking up, drinking a cup of coffee, and leaving for work, if I simply brew a cup of coffee and then drink it, that's not a story, it's just a series of events that might happen within a story. If we want a story, we need to create a complication that disrupts normal life and sends a promise rippling forward through time to inextricably touch the eventual climax.

If I were to find that the coffee jar is empty and consequently have to go to the store to get some, or if the coffee is poisoned, or if there are bugs crawling in the beans, or if peering into the coffee pot tugs me into an alternate universe, well, then we might have the genesis of a story. But until something goes wrong, we don't have a story; we simply have an episodic record of events.

The crisis or calling disrupts the equilibrium of the protagonist's world and carries with it the promise of what the story will be about. The door to normal is closed forever. The protagonist will search for it but will only find doors that lead to other rooms where things get progressively worse for her until all appears lost in the dark moment right before the climax.

Depending on the genre, the crisis that alters your protagonist's world might be a call to adventure (perhaps a quest that leads to a new land or a prophecy or revelation that he's destined for great things). Mythic, fantasy, and science fiction novels often follow this pattern. Frodo Baggins, Harry Potter, and Luke Skywalker all experience a dramatic calling and end up embarking on the epic journey that destiny has waiting for them.

When the calling comes, your protagonist might initially welcome it or he might resist it, but he'll eventually embrace it. Otherwise, you don't have a story; you just have an account of someone whining about how he doesn't want to do something great or heroic.

In crime fiction, this calling might be a new assignment to a seemingly unsolvable case. In a young adult novel, the crisis might be moving across the country to a city where the protagonist doesn't know anyone and has to start trying to fit in at a new school. In a romance, it might be the crisis of a troubled marriage, a bitter divorce, or the sudden breaking-off of an engagement.

In each instance, however, life is changed, and it will never be the same again.

George gets fired. Amber's son is kidnapped. Larry finds out his cancer is terminal. Whatever it is, the normal life of the character is forever altered and he or she is forced to deal with the difficulties this crisis brings.

Note that sometimes an event that appears good can serve as the precursor to the crisis or calling event.

- The cute football player whom Angie has had a crush on all semester finally asks her out.
- Monique finds a suitcase full of cash under the floorboards while remodeling the living room.
- Sebastian finally lands the big account that's going to make him a partner in the firm.
- In the wardrobe, the children find a doorway that leads to a magical land.

Giving the character what he longs for (or believes that he longs for) early in the story is a way to promise readers that things are going to go very wrong very soon. If nothing goes wrong, this good event offers only the potential of a story but never matures into one. You don't have the beginning of a story, you just have the *ending*: your main characters living happily ever after.

So after those good things come the bad ones.

Struggles and setbacks might appear in the form of facing threats, overcoming an obstacle, confronting a problem (personal, interpersonal, spiritual, emotional, physical, political), competing for prestige or acceptance, sacrificing for something you passionately believe in, dealing with loss or tragedy, recovering something that had been lost, or a myriad of other types of conflicts.

In a romance, what's the crisis that initiates the story? Well, it might be the end of one relationship (perhaps before your novel actually begins) or the encounter between the two soon-to-be lovers in which the equilibrium of their lives is shifted and the promises that will drive the story forward are made. In that case, rather than a crisis, we really have more of a calling toward a new and different life.

There are three ways to introduce the crisis or calling into your story.

1. **Give your protagonist what he desires most, and then snatch it away.** Let readers see his idyllic life, and then turn everything on its head. In this type of story, he has something, loses it, and tries to get it back.
   - A happily married woman finds out that her husband is having an affair, and she tries to restore sanity, intimacy, and a sense of belonging in her life.
   - The jewels your protagonist values so highly are stolen and must be recovered.
   - Under the wise king, peace has finally settled over the land, but a cold-hearted invading force lurks on the horizon.

2. **Show him what he desires most, and then dangle it in front of him.** This is common in heists, sports (underdog-team-makes-it-big) stories, and romances.
   - Six students from an inner-city high school form a math club and shoot for the state championship.
   - An underappreciated accountant sees her best friend get a promotion at a neighboring firm and maps out a way to imitate her friend's success.
   - The lonely bachelor meets the woman of his dreams and sets about courting her.

3. **Force what he dreads upon him, and make him escape from it.** Your protagonist is presented with a problem that must be solved or there will be dire consequences.
   - The man who values his freedom more than anything else is wrongly imprisoned and must find a way to escape.
   - The sailor is trapped in a sinking ship and must escape before he runs out of air.
   - Your detective must catch the killer before he can strike again.

To initiate your story, your protagonist will either (1) lose some-thing vital and try to regain it, (2) see something desirable and try to obtain it, or (3) experience something traumatic and try to overcome it.

DIFFERENTIATING THE CHARACTER'S STRUGGLES

Three types of struggles all interweave in stories and create different types of reader engagement and reaction: internal struggles (a question that needs to be answered), external struggles (a problem that needs to be solved), and interpersonal struggles (relationships that need to be started or restored).

All three struggles do not necessarily have to be present in every story. For example, a solo pilot crashes a plane in the middle of the Alaskan wilderness. He must survive (external struggle) and keep up his optimism/hope (internal struggle), but there's no one else there for him to have interpersonal struggles with.

Internal and interpersonal struggles create reader *empathy* and an emotional connection with the story, while external struggles create *curiosity*. Depending on your writing goal, your genre, your readers' expectations, and your story's content, you may focus on one type of struggle, making it the primary one in your story—although most contemporary, marketable fiction includes all three to some degree or another.

Today's readers are discerning and demanding. You're fighting against thousands of television shows and video games, millions of books and movies, and billions of websites and tweets for people's attention. Writing multilayered tales that emotionally engage readers is the best way to keep them enthralled by your story.

Each of the three struggles will interweave with the others. If they're simply parallel to each other, readers won't feel that the story has unity.

If one or more of the storylines can be dropped and the ultimate story resolution doesn't consequently change, recast the story so every storyline is essential or delete the unnecessary ones from the narrative. (More on subplots in Chapter 16.)

Let's examine the three interwoven struggles more carefully.

1. Internal struggles

The more profound the internal struggle, the more profound the change. The question is not just "Does the character get what he wants?" but "How does that closure and that new normal affect the character?" Inner journeys always change us. There must be a satisfying payoff.

To move readers emotionally, you'll need to create a sense of empathy and concern for characters. How? Through choosing struggles readers can identify with.

- We all want to love and be loved. Let your protagonist yearn for that and seek it through the story's struggles.
- We want a sense of meaning, purpose, and belonging.
- We want to find pleasure, truth, and happiness.
- We want adventure, freedom, and peace.
- We want to be forgiven for the times we've done something wrong and a second chance to make things right.

Let your character yearn for the same things.

Or, choose one of these universal desires.

identity	acceptance	justice
respect	success	fulfillment
authenticity	joy	survival
significance	value	security

To find the heart of your story, ask yourself what your character desires more than anything else. Once you've landed on that, decide if you're going to give it to him at the start of the story and then snatch it away, let him seek what seems just out of reach, or force him to deal with the opposite of it.

2. External struggles

These involve overcoming other people or dangerous situations or phenomena. They center around tasks. External struggles often have to do with the quest for survival or justice (and its close relative, revenge). Readers are curious about how the protagonist will solve the problem.

The suitcase with the launch codes is stolen. The congressman's son goes missing. Somali pirates take over a yacht, and the elite Special Ops team is called in to save the crew. None of those situations are primarily about internal questions or personal growth but rather about solving daunting problems in the external world.

When your story is centered on external struggles, readers won't typically be as emotionally engaged or as invested in the story as they would be if they also closely identify with the internal struggle of the protagonist.

We're thrilled by chase scenes, but we're rarely moved to tears by them.

However, we might be moved to tears if the protagonist's wife is killed in that chase. Loss, grief, pain, love—those are all internal issues we can identify with.

Emotion comes from identification with the protagonist's unmet internal or interpersonal desires.

We identify with Batman's struggle to overcome the loss of his parents when he was a boy and his pursuit of justice, but we have a harder time with seemingly impervious Superman until he gets into relational problems with Lois Lane. You threaten Superman when you threaten Lois. You hurt him when you hurt her. He becomes interesting when he becomes vulnerable.

If you want your readers to simply admire your protagonist, don't give him a strong internal or interpersonal struggle; just keep the story focused on a protagonist overcoming great odds to accomplish a vital task. If you want readers to be emotionally gripped by the story, weave in internal and interpersonal struggles.

3. Interpersonal struggles

Every relationship holds the potential for conflict, intimacy, and misunderstanding.

Your main character will inevitably have numerous interpersonal struggles—getting along with an ex-spouse, connecting with a teenage son or daughter, relating to an overbearing boss, and so on. However, in most cases, one of these will move to the forefront and constitute the protagonist's central interpersonal struggle.

In a sense, interpersonal struggles are both internal (since they deal with our feelings) and external (since they deal with our relationships with others).

Okay, internally, Jane is dealing with guilt that she could have been there more for her husband before he passed away. Externally, she has no source of income and needs to find a way to pay the bills. Interpersonally, her sister blames her for ruining her relationship with her boyfriend because of the one-night stand she had with him last year. Now, let's see where all of this leads ...

ORIGINS AND RESOLUTIONS

Some writing instructors talk about an "inciting incident" and teach that it must happen on the pages of your novel or screenplay.

Yes, every struggle (internal, external, and interpersonal) has an inciting incident. Depending on the story, that might be the same event or different ones for each struggle. And contrary to what you may have heard, those incidents might be either known or unknown to the protagonist, they might appear during the story or before it begins, and they might end up being essential for readers to know or, perhaps, best kept secret.

A complex story has many interwoven struggles and might have many "inciting incidents."

And not all of them have to appear on the pages of your novel.

Think of the Harry Potter novels. What's the inciting incident that gets the entire seven-book series started? It's the confrontation between Harry Potter's parents and Lord Voldemort, the fight that left Harry scarred and his parents dead.

Yet, throughout the entire series, readers never see that inciting incident on the page, they just read references to it and see short flashbacks to it.

In the first book of the series, readers are oriented to Harry's normal life, and then he receives his calling to attend the school of wizardry and the story is off and running. So is *that* the story's inciting incident, or is it the confrontation between his parents and Lord Voldemort?

Both are. Both are necessary.

But only one is rendered on the pages of the book.

Don't get sidetracked by this game of identifying every specific "inciting incident" or "plot point." Instead, focus on how you can tell this story best. You're not here to dissect it, you're here to breathe life into it.

Tell your story by introducing the disequilibrium in your character's internal, external, and interpersonal world in the right order and with the right timing for this specific story.

Note, however, that if all your protagonist's struggles begin before the first page of your book, you'll have to dump an awful lot of backstory onto your readers after the narrative begins to catch them up on what's happening. Also, and more importantly, readers will feel like they missed something vital to the story, and the last thing you want is for your reader to start out the story disappointed.

So, typically, you'll render the origin of at least one of the central struggles. If you notice that all three struggles begin before your novel's opening, you can probably improve your story by moving back the story's beginning so readers take in one of those crisis/calling events for themselves.

So how do these interwoven struggles play off each other in a novel? How and when do we introduce and resolve them?

Imagine you're writing a 250-page novel.

The following chart represents a story in which the character's internal struggle begins on the first page, while the external and interpersonal struggles are introduced at around page 50. To close the story, the external struggle is wrapped up first, at around page 200, the interpersonal struggle (or struggles) resolve after that, and finally, the character's primary internal struggle is resolved at around page 250.

(Remember, this is just an example and not a formula that you or anyone else should follow for any particular story. It's simply a way to visualize what's happening as one particular story's multivariate struggles originate and resolve.)

	ORIGINATION	RESOLUTION
PAGE	1 ...50...100...150...200...250	
INTERNAL STRUGGLE	⊢————————————⊣	
EXTERNAL STRUGGLE	⊢————————⊣	
INTERPERSONAL STRUGGLES	⊢—————————⊣	

The three struggles might be caused by the same event or by different events. It all depends on the story.

In the same way, the three struggles might be resolved simultaneously, but most often one resolution gives the character the impetus, insight, or wherewithal to solve the remaining struggles.

Most often, a choice related to the external struggle (to overcome the climactic confrontation with the antagonist) helps the main character overcome her internal struggle and mend or move on from her interpersonal struggles.

Why? Well, because internal and interpersonal struggles are more closely tied to our personality, our nature, our dreams, and our most intimate aspirations, desires, and loves. If the internal and interpersonal struggles are solved before the external problem, well ... you guessed it. The story would de-escalate, and the end would seem anticlimactic. Most resolution will come near the *very* end of the book for the same reason—we don't want the tension of the story to de-escalate.

Here's a representation of another story. This time, the internal struggle and the interpersonal struggles originate before the first page of the novel. Then, as the story opens, the external struggle is introduced, launching the narrative. You can see in this example that the three struggles all resolve at the same time, on the last page of the book.

	ORIGINATION	RESOLUTION
PAGE	... 1...50...100...150...200...250	
INTERNAL STRUGGLE	├─────────────────────────────┤	
EXTERNAL STRUGGLE	├──────────────────────┤	
INTERPERSONAL STRUGGLES	├──────────────────────────┤	

In my first novel, *The Pawn*, after a prologue, the protagonist is called to a crime scene to investigate a homicide in the mountains of western North Carolina.

As he's flying in a helicopter on the way to the scene, readers learn that he's been working a desk job and not in the field for the last six months. He's depressed because of the premature death of his wife to breast cancer, and this has deeply affected his relationships with his stepdaughter and his co-workers.

So his internal struggle (depression) and the resulting interpersonal struggles he's experiencing originate before the novel even begins, similarly to the story represented on the chart above.

In the next example, you can see that the struggles all begin on the same page and are all resolved at different times, beginning with the interpersonal struggles and ending with the internal struggle.

	ORIGINATION	RESOLUTION
PAGE	1...50...100...150...200...250	
INTERNAL STRUGGLE	├──────────────────┤	
EXTERNAL STRUGGLE	├────────────────┤	
INTERPERSONAL STRUGGLES	├────────────┤	

It might be helpful to think through the timing of the origins and resolutions of your story's central struggles. Always be aware of the dynamics and interplay the struggles have with each other.

If some of them can be initiated before the novel's first page, can some be resolved after the last one? Do we have to resolve everything on the pages of the book?

No, we don't have to resolve everything, but we have to resolve enough to satisfy our readers. And they want some sort of resolution, or it'll feel like the story isn't done. They'll feel cheated, like they've invested their emotional energy and time in a story that ends prematurely.

When I was growing up, I had to read Frank R. Stockton's short story "The Lady, or the Tiger?", first published in 1882, for one of my English classes.

In it, a king has devised a way of judging those accused of high crimes. He has constructed an arena containing two doors at one end of it. Behind one of them waits a tiger, behind the other a lovely, suitable bride. The accused man must choose one door—either life and happiness, or a bloody death. There is no way to tell which door holds which fate.

But when a young man of a low social class falls in love with the king's daughter, he ends up becoming one of the accused. The princess he loves has seen him talking with another girl, the one who now stands on the other side of one of the doors, and the princess knows that if he chooses that door, he would be with her rival—but he would be alive.

She discovers which door has the tiger.

Now, when the young man appears, she indicates by a slight gesture that he should open the door on the right. No one else sees this gesture except the young man, who immediately goes and opens that door.

Was she sending him to his death so he wouldn't be with that other girl?

Or was she saving his life because she loved him more than she resented his attention toward her rival?

The story ends like this: "The question of her decision is one not to be lightly considered, and it is not for me to presume to set myself up as the one person able to answer it. And so I leave it with all of you: Which came out of the opened door—the lady, or the tiger?"

What? Seriously? No closure?

Man, that ending annoyed me.

After investing my emotion and attention in the story, the author just ended it without finishing it.

Often when this story is taught, it's used as the impetus to a writing assignment—*Alright students, what was behind the door? Why did the princess send him there? Go ahead and finish the story.*

That kind of ending would never fly today.

Write a story so it stands on its own and doesn't require an explanation or a scene to be written by readers in order to have closure. Satisfy your readers. Don't betray the trust they put in you.

So one last question: Can the crisis/calling be part of the story's orientation?

Sure.

It's just that both of these factors—a glimpse at normal life (even if that's in the rear-view mirror) and the disruption of that equilibrium (which is what initiates the story)—need to be made evident to readers and happen in ways that serve the readers' engagement with the narrative.

The crisis or calling might come first, followed by a more in-depth orientation to the world of the story. You can play with all the aspects of the story as long as you escalate the tension and surprises so that the best ones come at the end. You cannot make progressively smaller promises and revelations, or readers will lose interest.

So now that you've introduced the struggle, it's time to make things worse.

CHAPTER 4

ESCALATION

Adding Complications and
Weeding Out Repetition

A story is not about something *else* going wrong; it's about something *worse* going wrong.

Escalating conflict doesn't mean just piling on tragedies—Maria's son dies while she is going through a divorce, then she's on the phone rushing out of her burning home and into the heart of an oncoming hurricane when she finds out from the doctor that she has a brain tumor while she's watching her dog get run over by a car.

When we talk about escalation, that's not what we mean.

We intensify the struggles rather than just compounding them.

Those three struggles—internal, external, and interpersonal—will all continue to deepen as the story progresses. Typically, they'll reach their darkest moment right before the climactic encounter with the antagonist or the forces that are hindering the protagonist from getting what he desires most.

Scene by scene, the tension will continue to escalate until your story reaches the climax.

Since things must continually get worse for the protagonist, characters actually descend through difficulties and pain into transformation. They do not slowly ascend into change.

It's a little counterintuitive. Things steadily get worse and worse, rather than better and better, as the story progresses. The protagonist's journey only reaches the highest peak at the moment when it appears to be plummeting into the deepest crevasse.

As the story moves forward, the consequences of not solving the struggles become more and more personal (or universal) and devastating. As the stakes are raised, the three levels of struggles serve to add increasing tension and deepen your readers' engagement and interest.

During this stage of the story, the character takes steps to try to resolve the struggles he's having in order to get back to the way things were earlier, before his world was tipped upside down.

But he does not succeed.

The plot must always thicken. It must never thin.

There's a common misconception that stories need rising action. Often, this is taught using a chart with a jagged line that looks like it might be the outline of a mountain range. There's usually a sharp rise near the right-hand side of the chart to signify the rising action as the story reaches its climax.

But be very careful with this.

Action does not equal tension. In fact, it might be counterproductive to developing it. Simply making more things happen doesn't ensure that readers will be interested, but tightening the tension from unmet desire does. You don't need rising action; you need escalating tension, and that can often come from making *fewer* things happen rather than *more*.

Think of the climax of a suspense novel. Flashlight in hand, the detective slowly descends the stairs into the serial killer's basement lair. Readers know what the detective does not—the killer is lying in wait for him deep in the recessed shadows of the next room.

The author milks the scene: Step by step the detective slowly and cautiously makes his way down the stairs as readers' hearts pound in anticipation of the climactic encounter that's about to ensue.

He angles the narrow flashlight beam into the darkness.

Reaches the last step.

And begins to search for the killer.

Is this rising action?

Hardly.

In fact a man walking slowly down a set of stairs might be the least amount of action for the last fifty pages—but it can be part of the climactic scene of a book because of *escalating tension*.

Keeping this distinction between rising action and escalating tension in mind, as the story progresses, struggles do need to escalate rather than diminish.

Repetition undermines escalation.

Every murder you include decreases the impact that each subsequent murder will have on readers. Every explosion, shootout, argument, and sex scene means less and less to readers because repetition short-circuits that crucial escalation that moves stories forward.

The value something has is directly proportional to the amount of pain it causes when it's lost. So having one person after another after another get killed diminishes the value of human life—if no one grieves after a murder, it basically tells readers that the life wasn't worth grieving over. And by implication, that *their* life isn't worth grieving over either.

Personally, this is one reason why I've never tackled writing a cozy mystery.

They're essentially narrative puzzles. They appeal more to intellect, are more lighthearted, and aren't as emotionally charged as other genres (such as thrillers or psychological suspense). If a cozy mystery showed how much death really does sting, it would run the risk of turning off those readers who are hoping for a "safe" story.

Because of that, authors of cozies don't want their readers to weep or grieve, so it's very difficult for them to be honest about death in the homicides their detectives solve. Often murder will be dealt with in a trite, light, almost off-handed way.

This genre presents a difficult balance of trying to care for your readers' expectations while not diminishing the value of human life—a challenge for even the most gifted authors.

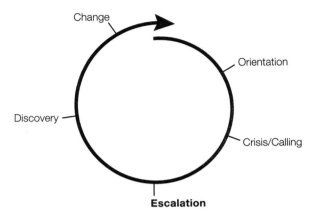

Change

Orientation

Discovery

Crisis/Calling

Escalation

WRITE YOUR WAY TOWARD THE IMPOSSIBLE

Just when readers think things can't get any worse, they need to.

The number and depth of the setbacks will be in the context of the escalating tension of the story. This may include numerous scenes or acts.

To intensify the strength of your story, make the struggles more emotionally charged and difficult to overcome. Escalate the problems, increase the setbacks (or difficulties), and make the danger (or consequences) more serious and imminent.

So if you blow up the moon in the prologue, you might need to put the entire galaxy at risk by the end of the book. If, instead, you settle into a slow-paced coming-of-age story on a new planet, you ended up making a promise that you didn't fulfill, and you let readers down since you de-escalated the tension of the story.

Four things keep readers flipping pages—concern, curiosity, escalation, and enjoyment. If readers don't care what happens, or they stop wondering what will happen, or they sense that the most important things have already happened, or they're not entertained by what is happening, they'll lose interest in the story.

Actually, that last reason—enjoyment—can hardly be overrated. As ludicrous as a story may be, as long as readers are having fun with it, they'll be forgiving and keep turning pages.

Depending on the type of promises you make within your story, you can appeal to four different emotions in your reader:
1. **Anticipation:** I can't wait to see what will happen next.
2. **Inquisitiveness:** I wonder what will happen next?
3. **Anxiety:** I'm scared to see what will happen next.
4. **Pleasure:** I'm having so much fun I know I'll love whatever happens next.

Context and escalation dictate the pace of the forward movement of your narrative. In one novel, a shootout in the streets of L.A. might be the climax, while in another it might be only a small moment in the escalation toward the potential destruction of the entire city by a rogue country's nuclear bomb.

When escalating the tension, ask yourself, "Is there a time limit? Is the danger real and immediate? Is there a seemingly impossible predicament to escape from? Does the resolution feel natural?"

Here are nine specific ways to escalate the tension of your story.

1. **Escalate in proximity.** The danger that was distant gets closer and closer.
2. **Escalate in magnitude.** The danger that was small, manageable, or localized (one person abducted) is increased (a bus is taken over by terrorists).
3. **Give a countdown to the impending tragedy.** Hour by hour, minute by minute, second by second, tick toward a deadline. However, be aware that countdowns can work against you if they become repetitive or don't fuel the story's escalation.

For example, if every chapter is one hour closer to the climax, after a while readers will get bored with the countdown and it'll lose its impact. Instead, begin the countdown in the middle or toward the end of the book and use it to accelerate the story toward the climax.

4. **Decrease the amount of time available to solve the problem.** This is related to the previous point. At our climax, a SWAT team has three minutes to disarm the bomb, but then something goes wrong and the timer speeds up, giving them only thirty seconds.

Good. That'll work.

But you wouldn't render the scene the other way, where they would start with thirty seconds, but then something happens and gives them an additional three minutes. That would de-escalate the tension. That's what you want to avoid.

5. **Let readers see impending threats or menace.** You can create a sense of escalation when you allow readers to see danger that the protagonist or the other characters in that scene are not aware of.

For instance, write a scene about how the rapist goes to the parking garage, picks the lock, and then hides in the backseat of a woman's car.

Then flip to the woman's point of view and show her leaving the office, taking the elevator down to the parking garage, exiting the elevator. Pulling out her keys.

Back to the rapist. He's watching through the window, and when he sees her, he drops out of sight, flicking out his switchblade and removing a roll of duct tape from a sack at his feet.

She approaches the car.

Unlocks the door ...

And then—

What are readers thinking right now, at this moment? Are they worried? Concerned?

If they care at all about what happens to this woman, yes. They're apprehensive. Absolutely they are.

By letting readers see the peril that the story characters don't see, you'll increase the suspense and escalate the tension.

6. **Include progressively more difficult moral dilemmas.** Rather than just having to choose between a professional obligation (a work deadline) and a personal one (attending his son's baseball game), force your protagonist to choose between two intimately personal ones. Or have him make a life-and-death decision such as choosing between (1) going against his anti-euthanasia beliefs by aiding a quadriplegic who's begging him to help her commit suicide or (2) letting her continue to suffer in mental anguish. (More on moral dilemmas in Chapter 19.)

7. **Make it personal.** Don't just let New York City be in danger, let Gramma live there. Don't have a random person get abducted, let it be the main character's son.

8. **Raise the stakes.** Deepen the danger, make the consequences of failure more severe, challenge the characters to perform under greater and greater threats of harm. Include tension on every page, eliminate potential solutions to the problem, and drive a deeper wedge between what the character has and what she wants.

9. **Isolate your protagonist.** Alfred Hitchcock believed that doing this helped create more suspense. In many of his movies the tension deepens and progresses as the protagonist becomes more and more isolated.

How can we make this happen in our stories?

Look for realistic and believable ways to remove the protagonist's tools, escape routes, and support system (buddies, mentors, helpers, or defenders). This forces him to become self-reliant and makes it easier for you to put him at a disadvantage in his final confrontation with evil.

The flow of a story relies on:

1. **Promises**—about where the character's storyline is heading
2. **Tension**—by having progressively worse things go wrong
3. **Surprises**—as the story goes in a direction readers don't expect
4. **Resolution**—that might be positive or negative for the protagonist

How does all this work together? How can these nine ideas relate to different genres? Well, think of a romance story.

Introduce more cultural or societal pressure to keep the couple apart, add misunderstanding between them, create meaningful deadlines, or make one of the lovers choose between rescuing the other or saving him- (or her-) self.

Or, let's say you're writing a medical thriller. Show readers that the drug conspiracy isn't just limited to one city but is a national problem, that a shipment of counterfeit drugs is about to be sent out. But guess what? The deadline is moved up. Rather than having five days to stop the distribution to pharmacies, the protagonist now only has three hours. In the end, make your hero choose between saving a hospital wing full of patients or his own family, whom the conspirators have abducted.

ESCALATING THE SETBACKS

When you're deciding about your character's action or response to a situation, ask yourself, "Where will things escalate from here?" If your story begins with a woman horrified, overwhelmed with terror, screaming, and tearing out her hair, where will you take things from there? How will you escalate from a scream? Where will you escalate from someone being "horrified" or "overwhelmed with terror"?

You may decide you need to start in a different place, or you may find you're rushing too fast to the climax and need to slow things down so you can escalate them more as the story progresses.

Even though I'm not a big fan of writing exercises, they can at times be helpful, and this narrative force of escalation is so important that it's a good place to pause and think through how to escalate stories in various genres.

Take a few minutes, and write out the progression of four events that would escalate each of the following situations. Ask yourself what would naturally happen next to deepen the tension. What would happen after that? What would make things worse from there?

1. There's an outbreak of hemorrhagic fever in an African village.
   - Event #1:
   - Event #2:
   - Event #3:
   - Event #4:
2. A demon is released from hell.
   - Event #1:
   - Event #2:
   - Event #3:
   - Event #4:
3. Terrorists blow up the White House.
   - Event #1:
   - Event #2:
   - Event #3:
   - Event #4:
4. The emotionally disturbed teenager breaks up with the love of her life.
   - Event #1:
   - Event #2:
   - Event #3:
   - Event #4:

Without escalation, you'll bore readers, even if your story has danger, intrigue, and intensity.

A few years ago I saw a movie based on a best-selling novel. In the first scene, we meet a father and his son in danger from a cannibalistic gang in a dreary, post-apocalyptic world. They narrowly escape.

Next scene: They're in danger from a cannibalistic gang in a dreary, post-apocalyptic world. They narrowly escape. Enter some flashbacks: They travel down the road, talk to some other endangered people, and then ... you'll never guess ... yes! Surprise, surprise. They meet a cannibalistic gang in a dreary, post-apocalyptic world and narrowly escape.

But by then, I didn't care. I was bored by the gang-of-cannibal-attack sequences.

I don't know if the book was any good, but the movie was episodic, not escalatory, and because of that, even a life-and-death struggle against a gang of cannibals became tedious and caused me to lose interest.

Repetition will eventually make anything boring.

So the protagonist's struggles should escalate scene by scene until the story's climax.

Be on the lookout for repetition in its various forms.

1. **Role repetition:** If you have two characters playing the same role, you can usually help the story out by conflating them into one character.

   Evaluate your story to see if you have several characters who are all serving the same narrative purpose. Are there too many gatekeepers? Too many helpers? Too many people acting as roadblocks to your protagonist's success at the ad agency? If so, search for ways to combine them or eliminate all but one of them.

2. **Action repetition:** You include one motorcycle chase scene, then another, then another. You have a sex scene, then another, then another. You have a character pray for divine help again and again. Instead, eliminate some of the instances of the event and then intensify and escalate the remaining sequences.

3. **Struggle repetition:** Some authors believe that a story's inner unity dictates that all the point-of-view characters share the same internal struggle. For example, all of these people are conflicted about forgiveness—either giving it or receiving it or figuring out what it means to forgive yourself (if that means anything more than just moving on)—and so on. This will only work if each of the characters finds a different resolution (one finds forgiveness, one doesn't, one extends it to someone who doesn't deserve it, etc.). Otherwise, you have repetition of the lessons the characters all take from the story.
4. **Voice repetition:** Characters sound the same, use the same idioms, or share the same idiosyncrasies.

DON'T STALL OUT YOUR WRITING

The strength of your protagonist is measured against the difficulty of the struggle (or the strength of the antagonist) he has to overcome.

So give your character a worthy opponent. If your detective simply has to face a run-of-the-mill cat burglar, he won't have to be very clever or heroic. Let it be the most cunning criminal the city has ever seen.

If your sailor only has to navigate through mildly choppy waves, he doesn't have to be very skilled to survive. Instead, make him face the perfect storm, the one that no one could be expected to live through.

Depression can be a form of antagonism. However, if it's just a regular, easily manageable case of depression, the kind your character can solve with a pill, it's not worth writing about. It needs to be the razor-blade-against-the-wrist kind of depression. Take her all the way to the edge. Don't back away.

Readers only worry about the main character when three things are true.

1. They can picture what's happening.
2. They care about the character.
3. They see increasing danger or an impending threat.

Compassion for the character and concern for her safety create the worry that draws readers emotionally into a story.

Remember that tension drives a story forward, and when tension is resolved, the momentum of the story is lost. As soon as you bring resolution, add more tension. As soon as you resolve one problem, add another one, a deeper one. If you resolve physical danger, immediately escalate the emotional or relational danger.

De-escalation is the death of the forward movement of a story.

Here are a few subtle examples.

1. **Verb strings:** Even the verbs you choose in chase sequences need to escalate in intensity. You wouldn't write, "She dashed across the lawn and then ran toward the pier," because running would be de-escalating from dashing. Instead you would write, "She ran across the lawn and then dashed toward the pier." The intensity of the chase needs to increase, not decrease.

2. **Punctuation:** Once an editor told me it seemed like there were a lot of exclamation points in the book I sent in. Of course, I didn't believe her until I searched the document and found over four hundred of them. Oops. I had a little editing to do on that one.

   Use exclamation points judiciously, and make sure they serve to escalate the tension. Look at the effect of the punctuation marks in the following three examples.

   "Get away from the lava! Now! Do it! Hurry! Go!" (You wouldn't write this. There are too many exclamation points—by the end that repetition has diminished their effect.)

   "Get away from the lava! Now! Do it. Hurry. Go." (You wouldn't write it like this either since the urgency is de-escalated by using the exclamation points in the first two sentences and periods in the last three.)

"Get away from the lava. Now. Do it. Hurry! Go!"
(This could work. The use of the exclamation points
escalates the tension of the string of sentences.)

3. **Paragraph length:** Shorten scenes, paragraphs, and sentences as you build toward the climax to move things along faster and to let readers' eyes fly down the page.

4. **Word choice:** Use fewer adjectives and adverbs as the story progresses. Avoid flowery descriptions or unusual words in tense situations. If readers have to intellectually unpack the text they're reading rather than be emotionally present in the blunt, vivid language of the climactic scenes, it'll distance them from the story.

5. **Release of tension:** Emotional or physical release de-escalates the tension and can allow readers to relax, something you don't want as you're escalating your story. Crying and screaming, just like sex scenes, offer a release from narrative tension. You'll typically want to hold out as long as possible before allowing your characters to cry, scream, or sleep together.

   Think of a television series with a romance subplot between the protagonist and his love interest. It's fascinating until the two characters get together, but then it loses something significant. Some series go on for years with this dynamic in play. It's easy to make it believable that a couple would get together. Your goal is to make it believable that they *don't*—at least not yet.

6. **Pace considerations:** Don't introduce unique settings, special skills, or important characters at the climax.

   Once I read a book in which the climax happened in an old, abandoned southern mansion. The flow of the story was disrupted and the escalation came to a grinding halt while the author spent two pages describing the mansion when he should have been rocketing toward the climax.

This could have easily been solved if he had included a scene earlier that took place at the mansion. He could have described it then, when the escalation wasn't so vital to the story's progression.

So, ideally, find a way to describe the setting of the climax before it occurs—especially if it requires you to slow the story down to describe it. Then, when the climax comes, readers will be able to immediately picture the scene. (This is different in film, of course, where readers instantaneously see and orient themselves to the setting of the climax by what's onscreen. This is one area where screenwriters have an advantage over novelists.)

CURIOSITY VS. CONCERN

Clarity about the protagonist's goal will draw readers deeper into the story.

In a scene, readers will either know what the character wants or they will not. If they don't know what the character wants, they'll wonder what it is, what's going on, what the point of this scene is—they'll be confused about what is going on and why.

If they do know what the character wants (and they're on his side), they'll worry about whether or not he'll get it. In other words, they'll be concerned about him accomplishing his goal or overcoming the obstacle before him.

Since curiosity and concern are in opposition to each other, readers cannot be wondering about what is going on in the story and worried about the outcome at the same time. That is, the more they're confused, thinking, "Why is he doing that? I don't get it," the less worried they'll be.

Yes, they might wonder *how* he will achieve his objective, but the more empathy they have, the more they'll worry—rather than detachedly sitting back trying to figure out what the goal is.

So decide what you want your readers to be feeling at that moment in the story—curiosity or apprehension—and write toward that response.

For example, imagine your protagonist enters his attic and discovers a large, sturdy wooden box. If you have him glance at the box, walk over to the window and look outside, go and stand on the box, and then pull out his cell phone and call his sister-in-law to chat about chicken alfredo recipes, readers will be wondering, "What's going on? Why is he doing that? I don't get it." If they trust you at this point in the story (that is, you've kept your promises up until now), they'll *probably* keep reading. If not, they'll put the book aside and say, "It just didn't make sense."

Readers weren't worried, they were confused. The protagonist's objective remains a mystery, and how can you cheer for someone when you don't know what he's trying to accomplish?

On the other hand, if you want your readers to be concerned, you could have your protagonist open the box, find a ticking bomb with two minutes left, and then hear the attic door close. Someone has locked him up there. After rushing over and finding it impossible to open the door, he tries the window and finds it too small to escape through, then looks at the timer on the bomb and thinks, *You need to disarm this thing, and you have less than ninety seconds to do it or you're going to die.*

Both his desire and the consequences that would result if he doesn't get what he wants are crystal clear. If readers care about your protagonist, they'll be concerned.

Remember, the tension needs to become more and more intense until you reach the climax. Keep it building by deleting superfluous scenes, removing dead-end dialogue, and scrapping all extraneous material.

As far as "getting worse," the whole story needs to keep moving in that direction, with the flow determined by (1) the importance of that scene, (2) the pace of the story at that point, and (3) the placement of that scene in the overall sweep of the story.

As tension escalates, the protagonist will come to a dark moment in which all seems lost, in which it appears impossible for him to get what he desires most.

And that brings us to the fourth story ingredient: discovery.

CHAPTER 5

DISCOVERY

Crafting a Satisfying Climax

Because of the narrative force of escalation, things will always be the worst just before the climax. That's where the clouds are the darkest, the despair the most heartrending, the villain the most ruthless, the situation the most dire.

And that leads to the protagonist's discovery about either (1) how to resolve his struggles or (2) how to move on from them. Conflict is the proving ground for your protagonist.

He'll make a significant choice that leads to a changed situation or a discovery that leads to a changed self.

Or both.

Depending on the genre, it might be a moment of insight, triumph, or despair.

This discovery and resolution help reshape the person's life and circumstances from that point forward.

It might be helpful to think of a story as a journey. During the journey, the protagonist travels from one specific place in time, space, or relationship to another.

Along the way he'll encounter various struggles, overcome or succumb to temptations, confront enemies, and face obstacles until he eventually accomplishes (or in a tragedy, fails to achieve) some goal.

He'll eventually arrive at a state of affairs different from those he was experiencing before the journey occurred, before the story began. He may have learned a lesson, matured in some way, gained a new perspective, discovered new meaning, grown up, or possibly given up.

The discovery relates to the struggle and helps the protagonist learn what he's capable of doing (external struggle), who he's capable of becoming (internal struggle), or how he's capable of relating to others (interpersonal struggle).

Often, all three struggles will be resolved, making him a fuller, more connected human being.

If they're not all resolved, we need to make sure that readers will be pleased by the fact that they're not. As I'll mention repeatedly throughout this book, we strive to give them what they want or something better.

So how do we gauge that? How can we tell if we've fulfilled the appropriate amount of promises? First, we need to develop the ability to look at our stories from a reader's perspective, asking the questions they might ask, entering their mindset.

Second, we carefully evaluate the promises we've made and make sure that the biggest ones are fulfilled in ways that are satisfying and surprising for readers. Usually, reading the book with this in mind and keeping track of the story's major promises will help verify that they are fulfilled in the right way and at the right time.

Often, when one or more storylines remain unresolved, it's left as a promise or cliffhanger to another installment in a series of books.

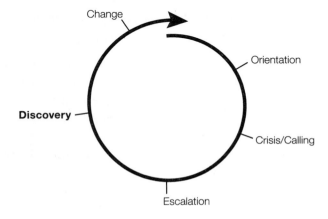

KEEP YOUR READERS GUESSING

In one of the paradoxes of storytelling, readers want to predict how the story will end (or how it will get to the end), but they want to be wrong. They'll be frustrated if they solve the crime before the fictional detective does. No matter what genre you write in, readers will be let down if there are no twists, if all goes just as they guessed it would. Readers want an ending that they could not have guessed but in retrospect seems like the only acceptable one.

Depending on the story and the emphasis on the various interwoven struggles, the discovery can be part of the climax or lead directly to it.

In either case, the climactic resolution of the story will occur in a way that makes sense to readers when they get there but is also completely unpredictable.

So the climax needs to (1) be believable within the narrative world of that story, (2) be logical and the only inevitable conclusion to all that precedes it, (3) end in a way that's unexpected and yet satisfying, and (4) contain the culminating moment of tension and excitement after which nothing can sensibly and naturally escalate within the context of that particular story.

WAYS AUTHORS CHEAT

The final resolution should come from something other than chance, coincidence, or the advice or intervention of an answer-giver or problem-solver.

1. The storm can't clear just as the ship is about to be smashed to pieces on the rocks (chance, in this case, an act of God).
2. The main character can't suddenly know karate at the climax and fight off all the bad guys (coincidence).
3. The protagonist can't just go to a wise answer-giver and have that person tell him the lesson he needs to know to overcome the climax (sermonizing).

4. The main character's friend can't just show up and shoot the villain to save the day (*deus ex machina*).

While mentors might guide a character toward self-discovery, ideally the decision and courage that determine the outcome of the story will come from the protagonist. It's weak storytelling to have the mentor step in, take over, and face the antagonist on behalf of the protagonist. (Unless, perhaps, the mentor is defeated, consequently giving the protagonist the motivation and opportunity to face the villain himself in the final climactic encounter.)

Characters who give advice need to do so from a place of weakness or vulnerability (low status) rather than strength (high status). (We'll cover status more in depth in Chapter 21.)

So a child can tell an adult the meaning of life and readers will accept it because of the contrast between the character's youthfulness and the wisdom he's exhibiting. However, if the local megachurch pastor tells a character the meaning of life (and he nails it!), readers might (and probably will) feel that the author is trying to preach at them.

Who can be the voice of truth, then? Minorities, the underprivileged, the physically or mentally impaired. I've even flashed back to a character who was dead and let her give advice posthumously. There's not much lower status than being dead.

Regardless, avoid sermonizing—unless the rug gets pulled out from under the person who has all the answers. I like to think that if someone is an answer-giver, he or she needs to also be a problem-haver: the alcoholic priest can give advice, as can the elderly woman who's afraid to leave home and needs to remember what it's like to venture out into the world—but don't make the advice-giver too perfect or saintly.

Is there a cause for everything that happens? Don't rely on bad luck or inexplicable coincidences. Choice, not convenient circumstances, should dictate story direction.

Coincidences drive a stake through believability. Foreshadowing removes them. Foreshadow any skills or tools needed at the climax and introduce readers to any vital characters before you reach that point in the story, or the climax will seem too contrived or coincidental.

So if the diver suddenly needs a harpoon gun to fight off the killer barracuda and he reaches down and—how convenient!—has one, readers won't buy it. Show them the harpoon gun earlier so it makes sense that he has it in the climactic fish battle. Make sure every special skill or gadget needed in the climax is foreshadowed earlier in the story.

Readers naturally cheer for the underdog, so we want the protagonist to be in that role in the story's climax. Let him enter the final showdown with evil while he's at a disadvantage—weaponless, injured, poisoned, or exhausted from fighting his way past all the antagonist's henchmen. He might be outnumbered, outmanned, and outgunned, but he will somehow believably prevail.

Evil is never constrained by compassion, but your hero must be. The villain might indiscriminately kill, or attempt to kill, bystanders or captives, while your hero not only has to save them by stopping the antagonist but must also do so in a way that readers will feel is morally justifiable.

Often it's satisfying if the protagonist can use his expertise or emblem to solve the major external struggle—the archer shoots an arrow to slice through the rope that's about to hang someone; the acrobat drops to the ground and does the splits to avoid getting run over by the oncoming semi; the compass that the boy always carries with him serves to direct him to the utopian village hidden deep in the Himalayas.

I've heard it said that the resolution should come from the wit (that is, cleverness) or grit (perseverance and tenacity) of the main character. I've also heard it referred to in terms of skill (gifts and special abilities) or will (courage and resolve).

I like that. It's easy for me to remember.

Wit or grit.

Skill or will.

ENGAGING YOUR READERS

Stories pivot on struggles and discoveries, so when you're coming up with ideas, explore your own life and your own:

- **Struggles:** mistakes, temptations, questions, regrets, and secrets
- **Discoveries:** decisions, lessons, consequences, life transitions, and insights

Generally speaking, women prefer to see fictional characters in relational conflict, and men like to see them in situational conflict. To draw in a broader audience, weave both kinds of struggles into your stories.

In my writing seminars, I sometimes assign the students to write a knife fight scene and also the scene of a woman on the ocean shore, looking out across the water, hoping to see her lover's ship returning.

Now, while there are always exceptions, men seem to connect better with the knife fight scene and the women do a better job with rendering the shore scene.

But it makes no difference if you're writing action, romance, or suspense—unmet desire gives the story the energy and momentum it needs to move forward.

As soon as readers stop understanding what the character wants, they start disengaging from the story. They begin *wondering about it* rather than *walking with the characters through it*.

The secret to keeping your readers engrossed in the story is no secret at all—keep the foremost unmet desires in their minds, draw them close to the protagonist, and make them care so much about him that they cannot look away. Then, bring the story to a satisfying close as the transformation of the situation or the protagonist's life becomes clear.

And that brings us to the fifth storytelling ingredient: change in the character's internal or external world.

CHAPTER 6

CHANGE

How Situations and Characters Are Transformed by Conflict

Imagine throwing a ball of putty at a wall. As a result of its impact, the putty will change shape. However, if you throw a pebble at the wall, it'll bounce off and won't change shape at all.

Every character in your book will be either a pebble person (static) or a putty person (dynamic). When you throw them into the struggle of your story, some come out unchanged, others are transformed.

Putty people are altered.

Pebble people remain the same. They're like set pieces. They appear onstage in the story but don't change in essential ways as the story progresses. They're the same at the ending as they were at the beginning.

Usually, protagonists are putty people. They are the most interesting, the most malleable characters.

In his book *Writing for Story*, two-time Pulitzer Prize winner Jon Franklin writes, "In the best stories, the odyssey from complication to resolution changes the character profoundly. ... If all is done properly, the most dramatic aspect of any story is growth and change in the main character."

But can your protagonist be a pebble person? For example, what about Sherlock Holmes or James Bond? They're not transformed in every progressive story, are they?

External struggles exist more to reveal the characteristics of the protagonist, while internal and interpersonal ones serve to transform him. Since Bond is tackling cases that mainly involve external problems rather than inner questions or intimate relationships, the stories will serve more to reveal what he is like than to alter who he is. It's the same with Holmes and with many series characters.

We'll explore this relationship of revelation and transformation in Chapter 23, but for now don't necessarily think of change as a complete conversion from one type of person to another but rather something that results in a new kind of normal. Most of the time, a series character will have both a broad consistency and a certain degree of development in each story installment.

In stories that primarily focus on external struggles, the change might be characterized by a transformed situation or a subtle lesson.

1. **A new set of circumstances:** The city is safe from the terrorists.
2. **A new outlook or attitude:** The spy realizes the importance of working with his team rather than going it alone.
3. **A new set of skills or abilities:** The heroine now knows how to disarm bombs. If she encounters them in her next adventure, she'll be prepared.
4. **A new insight or revelation:** The detective discovers that he can face his fear of tight spaces when the safety of others is at stake.
5. **A new (or renewed) relationship:** The guy gets the girl.

Even if your protagonist is a putty person, it doesn't mean that he must be altered in a wide, sweeping way. Instead, it means that when his life is disrupted by the crisis or calling event, he'll try to get back to normal but he won't be able to do it and will end in a place of a new normal, a new set of circumstances and challenges.

Remember, any point-of-view character who's dealing with those internal struggles that relate to the universal desires your readers can identify with (love, acceptance, freedom, adventure, etc.) will be a putty person.

In that case, the struggle of the story changes them, reshapes them. They have something they want but can't get. They take steps to try to get it. Typically, after they're tossed into the crisis of the story, they try to reshape themselves so they look like they did before they were thrown against the wall. But of course they can't do it, and at the end they look different than they did at the beginning.

Here are a few rules of thumb for deciding whether your characters are pebble people or putty people.

1. Does this character have a clearly expressed internal or interpersonal desire or goal? The more time you spend defining or elaborating on what your character wants from himself or his relationships, the more you're promising readers that this person is a putty person who'll be transformed by being thrown into the struggles of the story.

2. Most of the time, point-of-view characters are putty people. By making someone a point-of-view character, you're promising readers that his struggles will be resolved, that his situation in life will be different, or that he'll be transformed by weathering the struggles of the story's escalating tension.

3. With stories that involve internal and interpersonal struggles, you can discern who the protagonist is by asking, "Who struggles? What does she discover? How does she change?" Her world is disrupted. She tries to get back to normal but finds that it is irrevocably altered.

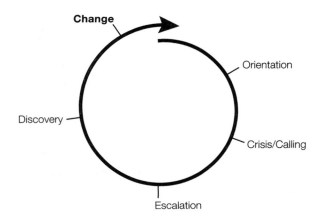

LET A CHOICE REVEAL THE CHANGE

Your character has learned to forgive again, has found hope in the future, has rediscovered that life can be an adventure, or whatever. The whole story has been building to this point, so don't let readers down by just summarizing what happened—render the scene.

This gets back to the old axiom "show, don't tell." While there are times to tell, at the moment your character reaches his emotional or spiritual climactic moment, it's time to show. Do that through action rather than reflection. Readers want to see the character make a decision at the end of the story that shows how the struggle has affected him.

- He chooses to sprint through the airport to catch up with his love interest before she gets on that plane back to Thailand.
- She lays a flower at the grave of the father she has always resented.
- He pulls out his old baseball glove and invites the son he's been neglecting to go outside and play catch with him.
- She finally tells her husband about the affair. He might leave her or he might forgive her, but at least the truth is out in the open at last.

Another way to look at it: Think of a caterpillar entering a cocoon. Once he does so, one of two things will happen: He'll either be transformed into a butterfly, or he'll die. But no matter what else happens, he will never climb out of the cocoon as a caterpillar.

So it is with your protagonist when he faces internal and interpersonal struggles.

As you frame your story and develop your characters, ask yourself, "What is this caterpillar doing?" He'll be changed into someone more mature, more insightful, or more at peace. Or in dark stories or terrifying tales with a dramatic plunge at the end, your character may realize that the last glimpse of hope has just disappeared or readers may see the last chord of sanity finally snap.

A butterfly.

Or a cold, dead cocoon.

Genre dictates the direction of this transformation—horror stories will often end with some kind of death (physical, psychological, emotional, spiritual, or relational). However, since readers generally prefer a happy ending, most genres are butterfly genres and end with the protagonist experiencing new life—whether that's physical renewal, psychological understanding, emotional healing, intellectual satisfaction (for example, solving the case), a spiritual awakening, or a transformed relationship.

This change marks the resolution of the crisis and the culmination of the story.

MOVE TOWARD A NEW NORMAL

So how does all of this work in practice, in the actual crafting of your story?

The Old Testament contains some of the world's best-known and most enduring stories. In it, the book of Ruth begins by showing us a portrait of a woman named Naomi. She's living in Bethlehem with her husband and two sons when a famine hits the land and they're forced to move to another country called Moab to find food.

Now, hunger is certainly an external struggle, but since they solve it right away without any real trials or trouble mentioned in the text and without any escalation, that's not the central story.

Think of it as the prologue that sets up the context for the rest of the narrative.

When they arrive in Moab, the young men get married, and life goes on until a crisis event disrupts normal life—Naomi's husband and sons all die.

As a result, she decides to return to her hometown—an attempt to get back to normal.

One of her daughters-in-law, Ruth, ends up joining her, committing herself to both Naomi's people and her God.

When they arrive in Bethlehem, the women who live there run up to Naomi (whose name means "beautiful") and exclaim, "Is it really you, Naomi?"

"No," she replies. "Don't call me Naomi. Call me Mara because I went away full and I came back empty and it is God Almighty who has brought this bitterness into my life."

In Hebrew the word *Mara* means "bitter."

So we have an escalation of her struggle—dead husband, dead sons, bitter against God. She has no food, no immediate family, and, being unmarried, no hope of having more sons. Her beautiful life has turned bitter in just about every way.

Well, she and Ruth arrive at just the right season, and she sends Ruth to just the right field at just the right time of day to glean leftover wheat for them. In that field, Ruth meets a man named Boaz who shows kindness to her.

Fate? Destiny? Divine intervention? Contextually, it's clear that there are greater forces at work. And since it's a biblical narrative, it's clear that God is working in the background, bringing a new beauty to Naomi's life.

After Ruth returns home and Naomi sees how much food Boaz has generously given her, she's encouraged and she offers Ruth a lesson in seduction—or how to woo a drunk Jewish man into proposing to you in five easy steps. (It's a little comical. You'll have to read it.)

In the end, Ruth and Boaz get married and have a son. When they do, the women of Bethlehem return to Naomi and encourage her, telling her that God has given her a new family. And when they do, they don't call her "Mara" but "Naomi."

Her life has moved from beauty through bitterness into a new kind of beauty.

Her normal life was disrupted, but she has reached a new normal. She moved from full to empty to a different type of fullness that can only come from the perspective of standing on the far side of a tragedy.

In the story, Ruth is a pebble person. While she surely mourned the death of her husband in Moab, we don't hear about her grief. Instead, she's portrayed as faithful and obedient all the way through the narrative. No flaws. A perfect little pebble.

Naomi, on the other hand, is a putty person. She's the one readers hear about at the beginning and the end of the story, she has the most relatable struggles, she's the one who journeys through agonizing bitterness to arrive at an emotionally scarred but renewed place in life.

What about the three levels of struggles?

Well, internally, Naomi struggles with bitterness against God for the emptiness she's feeling. This is something readers can identify with—we all want happiness and peace, and we all tend to question God (either his existence or his goodness) when tragedy strikes. Naomi's interpersonal struggles aren't as present in this story but subtly appear as she faces the cultural forces of being a widow in a patriarchal society.

Her external struggles (no food, no sustenance) serve as ways to move the story forward.

To develop your protagonist's journey through the story, think about four things:

- Desire: What does he want?
- Setbacks: What keeps him from getting it?
- Stakes: What will happen if he doesn't get it?
- Outcome: What will change in his life when he does fulfill his desire?

What about nonlinear storytelling?

Can these ingredients—orientation, crisis/calling, escalation, discovery, change—appear in another order? For example, could you start the story right before the discovery, drop back with a series of flashbacks to orient readers, and then weave in the crisis as you build to the climax?

Sure—if doing so better serves your readers and their engagement with the story. If you end up disorienting or confusing them or causing them to be lost trying to figure out where exactly you are in telling the story, then you need to go back to the drawing board.

Each of the chapters we've covered so far has dealt with vital story ingredients. There's no set formula for precisely how to mix them together. Remember: story trumps structure.

Go ahead and break the rules, flip expectations, twist the story world around backwards—as long as it's in the service of your readers. If it's a way of showing off, it doesn't belong. If it's a way of drawing readers in, go for it.

So stories include an orientation to the world of a character we care about, an introduction of a dilemma, escalating tension, a moment in which all seems lost, a discovery, and a resolution that leaves the character in a different situation or mindset than he had at the beginning.

Develop those meaningful struggles for the protagonist to overcome, make things get worse, climactically resolve the conflict, and then show how his life is altered, and you'll snag readers' attention early and keep them engaged until the very last page.

Orientation

We meet the protagonist. What's his normal life like? If he has what he wants, he's about to lose it. If he doesn't have it yet, he's about to pursue it.

Crisis/Calling

Crisis: Something bad or unexpected turns the protagonist's world upside down. What is it? What is he trying to overcome, avoid, or obtain?

Calling: Something good beckons the protagonist on a great adventure toward his destiny. How will he respond?

Escalation

Your protagonist tries to solve his problem, answer his life-defining question, repair or begin a relationship, or get back to normal. What does he do as he seeks to accomplish this? How does he progressively fail or face bigger and bigger challenges until his final climactic encounter with the forces of antagonism?

Discovery

The protagonist reaches a moment of realization. What does he learn about the world or about himself?

Change

Your protagonist's situation in life or understanding of life has been transformed. Clearly reveal his lesson, change, or new direction.

Mixing up a story is an organic process and is affected by the narrative forces that press in upon the tale—a concept that might be completely new to you, but that we'll examine in depth throughout the rest of this book.

In the next section, we'll start by exploring how to write organically rather than mechanically.

Read on.

You may be surprised by how quickly your stories will take shape when you start pressing the right questions against them.

PART II

SECRETS TO ORGANIC WRITING

CHAPTER 7

RESPONSIVENESS

Eight Secrets to Discarding Your Outline to Write Better Stories

Thirteen years ago I had an idea for a series of mysteries featuring a one-armed detective. I attended a seminar by a well-known novelist who taught us to carefully and meticulously outline our fiction and then stick to the outline as we crafted our stories. In some cases he would write a forty-page, single-spaced outline and then spend his actual novel-writing time pretty much filling in the blanks.

Well, I didn't get too far in that one-armed detective project. In fact, it went absolutely nowhere. The process of outlining seemed daunting, not a whole lot of fun, and a very artificial way to approach an art form—sort of like telling an artist to use a paint-by-numbers approach.

I realized that in my heart of hearts I'm a storyteller, not an outline-maker.

I began to wonder if there was another way to climb into the heart of the stories that I wanted to tell. Was it possible to create them without outlining them or plotting them out? Was it possible that stories really could unfold as you wrote them?

You'll hear the importance of outlining, or "plotting out your story," taught at writers conferences across North America, and when you don't follow their formulas you'll quickly be labeled an SOPer (that is, a "seat-of-the-pantser," or sometimes just a "pantser," and no, I'm not making this up).

While outliners have a very detailed, well-constructed approach to writing, I've come across very little advice on the actual process of writing organically. In fact, I have a master's degree in storytelling, and after seventeen years of studying story, I can't think of a single time in all my years of schooling (before, during, or after graduate school) when I received a grade for, or even advice on, writing a story *without* an outline.

And as far as instructional writing books that cover the subject, of the thousands of pages of craft books on my shelf, I found only five pages—yes, *pages*—that offered any specific advice on organic writing. (These were all in a single book. The author's take in a nutshell: *If you write this way, you're going to have to cut a lot of stuff out in the process.* That's not necessarily the case, but at least she took a shot at it.)

Consequently, working as a professional novelist over the last decade, I've had to uncover the principles of organic writing for myself.

I've found that when I tell people to stop outlining their stories, I get strange looks, as if writing organically is against some sort of rule of writing.

Well, in that case, I invite you to the rebellion.

Discarding your outline and uncovering your story word by word might be the best thing you can do for your fiction, just as it was for me.

Here's how to get started.

1. Ground yourself in story.

As we covered in the previous section, there are a lot of misconceptions out there about what makes a story work.

Rather than straightjacketing your story by forcing it into three acts or trying to make it "character-driven" or "plot-driven," ask if it has an orientation, a crisis or a calling that disrupts normal life, relentless escalation, and a satisfying climax. Make sure readers care about the main character, feel enough emotion to stay intrigued by the story, and gain enough insight to see the world with new eyes when they're done.

When you focus on what lies at the heart of story—tension, desire, crisis, escalation, struggle, discovery, transformation—you'll begin to intuitively understand what needs to happen in each scene to drive your story forward.

For example, let's say you're writing an epic fantasy novel about a young apprentice to a blacksmith who gets caught up in a grand adventure that leads him to face a dragon and—perhaps, but you're not sure yet—marry the princess of the land.

So of course you want to tell your story in a way that fans of the fantasy genre will love but also in a way that avoids clichés, is full of twists, and is unlike anything they've ever seen. After all, you're trying to take your tale through territory that's familiar to fantasy readers but is also so unique that they won't feel like they've heard this story before. Our stories are the best when they walk that fine line between novelty and familiarity.

But where do you start?

Well, based on what you know about story (broadly speaking), what do you already know about this story in particular?

Readers need to be oriented to the protagonist's normal life. You might use a prologue or jump right into the main storyline, but whichever direction you go, readers will need to meet the protagonist and get introduced to his world. Does magic exist? Is the land at peace? What does the village look like? If there are dragons, are there other mythical creatures? Explore the options. Brainstorm a little. Feel it out as you move forward. Write a rough draft of an early scene. Don't worry yet about "getting it right."

Step in. Look around. Picture it. Describe what lies around you. Dip your toes into the water of the story and see how it feels.

At some point, your protagonist's life will be tipped upside down in a way that drives him into the conflict that propels the story forward.

He might initially resist this call to adventure or he might embrace it, but either way he needs to act believably. He'll face escalating danger and setbacks until he finally faces the terrifying dragon.

At one point, all will appear lost, but then (unless this is a tragedy) he'll vanquish the dragon in a way that's both unexpected and inevitable.

His life situation will be forever transformed. Perhaps he'll marry that princess and get ready for his next epic adventure as the new prince of the land, or he might end up joining an army that's trying to save the land from a vast horde of cruel invaders. But whatever happens, he won't be simply a humble blacksmith's apprentice anymore.

So you begin to write, fleshing out any of the scenes above, showing readers the inside of the blacksmith's shop or the young man receiving his grand calling or entering the dragon's lair. Whichever one you begin with, feel out how that scene contingently relates to the other scenes that might precede or follow it.

To get started, you don't need an outline, you just need a premise. With that much in hand, you can embark on telling your story, writing the scenes you expect will be included, and then going back over what you've written to make sure that what *is* happening is informed by what *has* happened.

Of course, your story will veer into unmapped territory as you listen to it and follow where it leads.

Of course it will.

And it should.

That's what creativity is about.

The dragon encounter might end up being only a mid-book climax before the hero faces off with an army of trolls. The blacksmith might become a sailor. The princess might love him but be pledged to marry someone else—or she might turn out to be the blacksmith's apprentice herself with a little gender-bending in the genre. Who knows? That's part of the excitement, the adventure, the discovery process of writing.

The point is: You can relax.

You know what makes a story work, what the key ingredients are. You don't need to follow some plot "blueprint" or try to map out where everything will lead. You don't need to rein in your imagination, you need to give it some breathing room.

And since every story is different, you definitely don't want to follow some prepackaged novel-writing template—complete with instructions on when to introduce subplots or resolve each act—or you'll produce a cookie-cutter story that doesn't impact anyone.

As you work with your ideas, ask yourself if you've adequately oriented readers to the world of this story. Is there a disruption that initiates the main character's central struggle? Does the conflict continue to escalate, becoming more and more intimate and intense? Is there a moment of discovery about the world or about your protagonist that transforms his situation?

This doesn't mean you're plotting out a story, it just means you understand what happens in a story. When you root yourself in the ingredients that lie at the heart of a story, you'll find the pieces begin to naturally fall into place.

2. Let narrative forces, rather than formulas, drive your story forward.

Imagine a giant ball of clay being held by a group of people. As one person presses against the clay, it changes shape.

The clay is your story. The people surrounding it represent the narrative forces pressing in on it. These narrative forces include:

- **Believability:** The characters in your story need to act in contextually believable ways. All the time.
- **Causality:** Everything that happens in a story will be caused by the thing that precedes it.
- **Inevitability and Surprise:** The end of every scene must not only be logical but, in retrospect, the only possible conclusion to that scene. Scenes will end in a way that's unexpected and yet satisfying to readers.
- **Escalation:** The tension must continue to escalate, scene by scene, until it reaches a climax after which nothing is ever the same again.

- **Scenes and Setbacks:** If nothing is altered, you do not have a scene. If your characters solve something without a setback, you do not have a story—you have the setup for a story, an event, but that's all.
- **Continuity:** Think of pace as the speed at which things are happening, and think of narrative momentum as the energy that's carrying them along. Together they affect the story's continuity.
- **Story and Genre Conventions:** Readers enter a story with expectations based on their understanding of story and of the genre they're reading. You need to know the principles of storytelling and be familiar enough with genre conventions to meet or exceed your readers' expectations without resorting to clichés.

All of these, plus voice, mood, flow, context, and other narrative forces we'll be exploring in depth in the upcoming chapters, press against the story in a continual give-and-take relationship, affecting each other and forming the shape of your tale.

As you write, rather than starting with a preconception of what the clay should look like, constantly review and evaluate the pressure each of these concepts places on the story.

Okay, so I need to escalate this chase scene—I had a foot chase before so I can't do that again. Maybe a helicopter chase? But will that be believable? Well, I'll need to foreshadow that someone knows how to fly the helicopter and make it inevitable that he ends up at the helicopter landing pad at this moment of the story. But does that fit in with the pace right here? Can I pull all this off without relying on narrative gimmicks or coincidences?

When you know the right questions to ask, your story will open up before you in unique, unpredictable, and fulfilling ways.

Believability

What would this character naturally do in this situation?

Is he properly motivated to take this action?

Causality

Is this event caused by what precedes it?

How can what I want to happen bow to what needs to happen based on the context?

Inevitability and Surprise

Does this scene end in a way that's both unexpected and yet inevitable?

How can I ensure that readers don't see the twist coming?

Escalation

Does this scene ratchet up the tension of the one before it?

How can I make things worse?

Scenes and Setbacks

Have I inadvertently included scenes just for character development?

Is there an interlude or moment of reorientation between each scene?

Continuity

Do my revelations happen at the right moments within the story?

Have I used foreshadowing to eliminate coincidences, especially at the climax?

Story and Genre Expectations

What requisite scenes are inherent to this genre and to this story?

How can I render them in a way that's not clichéd?

3. Trust the fluidity of the process.

I love Stephen King's analogy in his book *On Writing* where he compares stories to fossils that we, as storytellers, are uncovering. To plot out a story is to decide beforehand what kind of dinosaur it is, how big it should be, and so on. As King writes, "Plot is, I think, the good writer's last resort, and the dullard's first choice."

His analogy helps me realize that a story is not something I create as much as it is something I uncover by asking the right questions.

When people outline their stories, they'll inevitably come up with ideas for scenes they think are important to the plot, but the transitions between these scenes (in terms of the character's motivation to move to another place or take a specific action) will often be weak.

Why?

The impetus to move the story to the next plot point is so strong that it can end up overriding the believability of the character's choice at that moment of the story.

Stated another way, the author imposes the plot onto the clay without allowing it to be shaped by the essential forces of believability, causality, and context.

You might have had this experience: You're reading a novel, and it feels like there's an agenda to the story that isn't dictated by the narrative events.

You can often tell that an author outlined or "plotted out" her story when you read a book and find yourself thinking things like:

- *"But I thought she was shy? Why would she act like that?"*
- *"I don't get it. That doesn't make sense. He would never say that."*
- *"What?! I thought she was ...?"*
- *"Whatever happened to the ...? Couldn't she use that right now?"*
- *"I don't understand why they're not ... "*

These types of snags come up when an author stops asking, "What would naturally happen next?" and starts focusing too much on what he has decided needs to happen to get to the climax he has in mind.

As soon as your character doesn't act in a believable way, it'll cause readers to ask, "Why doesn't she just ...?" And as soon as that happens, they're no longer emotionally present in the story.

As you learn to feel out the direction of your story by constantly asking yourself what would naturally happen next based on the narrative forces that shape all stories, you'll find your characters acting in more believable and honest ways and your story will flow more smoothly, contingently, and coherently.

Here's one of the biggest problems with starting by writing an outline: You'll be tempted to stick to it. You'll get to a certain place and stop digging, even though there might be an awful lot of interesting dinosaur left to uncover.

4. Follow rabbit trails.

Forget all that rubbish you've heard about staying on track and not following rabbit trails.

Yes, of course you should follow them. It's inherent to the creative process. What you at first thought was just a rabbit trail leading nowhere in particular might take you to a breathtaking overlook that far eclipses everything you previously had in mind for your story.

You'll always brainstorm more scenes and write more words than you can use. This isn't wasted effort; it's part of the process. Every idea is a doorway to the next.

So where to start? Put an intriguing character in a challenging situation, and see how he responds. Sometimes he'll surprise you in how he acts or when he demands a bigger part in the story.

And sometimes a random character will appear out of nowhere and vie for a part in the story.

As J.R.R. Tolkien noted one time, "A new character has come on the scene (I am sure I did not invent him, I did not even want him, but there he came walking through the woods of Ithilien): Faramir, the brother of Boromir."

For fans of *The Lord of the Rings*, it's a good thing Tolkien didn't stick to some predetermined outline.

Where do ideas and characters like this come from? Tolkien's contemporary and the author of *The Chronicles of Narnia* series, C.S. Lewis, wrote, "I don't believe anyone knows exactly how he 'makes things up.' Making up is a very mysterious thing. When you 'have an idea' could you tell anyone exactly *how* you thought of it?"

While the exact genesis of ideas will always be, as Lewis pointed out, somewhat mysterious and impossible to pin down, we can tip the scales in our favor when we remember that they often come from the questions, attentiveness, observance, and responsiveness of the artist, the author, the poet, or the musician.

Allow your characters the opportunity to flex and adapt and grow, revealing to you their quirks and inconsistencies, even as you push them to the limit to see how they respond. Then let the story shape them even while they shape the direction of the story.

The key is responding to the story as it reveals itself, being honest, keeping it believable, letting the characters act and develop naturally, and following where the trail of the story takes you. Give yourself the freedom to explore the terrain of your tale.

Without serendipitous discoveries, your story runs the risk of feeling artificial and prepackaged.

5. Write requisite scenes.

Because of the movement of a story and the expectations of readers, certain scenes end up becoming obligatory in different genres.

If you find yourself at a loss for what to write next, write a scene that fulfills a promise you made earlier in the book or work on a requisite scene that readers expect based on the genre and the story you've told so far, as we explored earlier in the apprentice blacksmith example.

In a lighthearted love story, readers need to be introduced to each of the prospective lovers at the beginning of the story and see their lives without each other. At some point there'll be a scene where the two meet. They'll develop an interest in each other, romantic tension will deepen, and they'll eventually have to face and overcome obstacles (societal, geographic, socioeconomic, etc.) as they strive to be together or begin a relationship.

Start there. With what you have. With any one of those scenes. Don't worry about where it'll all lead. The questions we'll explore in the following chapters will point you in the right direction.

So you might choose to write (1) the lonely girl scene (maybe she's at work, maybe at home), (2) the single guy scene (maybe he's a workaholic and not even aware that he wants to be in a relationship), (3) the scene where they meet, or (4) the scene where something goes wrong and it looks like they'll never get together.

Or, take a police procedural. You'll need to have a crime occur in the beginning of your story that's ruthless, grisly, or seemingly impossible to solve. The detective will visit the scene or at least review the evidence. He'll search for clues, find something no one else notices, and then follow up on it, but he'll run into dead ends as he evaluates evidence and pursues suspects. The villain will be bigger than life, and the case will become personal to the detective.

He'll often have a close encounter or chase scene with the villain, and there'll be a final climactic confrontation between good and evil in which justice is served (or perhaps delayed) and the antagonist either is killed, is caught, or, in rare cases, escapes.

And you'll want to render these scenes in ways readers haven't seen before.

Or, maybe you're writing a romantic suspense novel.

1. **A chase scene:** *What about parkour or free running? I've never used that before. That's very visual, easier to do in film. Can I pull it off in print? I don't know. Let's give it a shot. They're in New York City, chasing the villain through the back alleys. Let's see what happens ...*

2. **Romance:** *Hmm ... I like the idea of my protagonist defending his love interest in a bar to show his chivalry, courage, and fearlessness. Write up how some thugs disrespect his woman and how he responds ...*

3. **Arrest and apprehension:** *If I let my hero catch the killer in the middle of the book, it'll be a promise to readers that the guy is going to escape or get freed on some kind of technicality. They'll intuitively know this based on the book's length. So let's say he escapes. How could he do so in a way no readers will expect but will accept as logical later when they see the broader context of the story? And it all needs to be shown in a way that's never been done before but that readers will really be drawn into ... Jot down some ideas. See where it leads.*

4. **Clues:** *I need my detective to notice what no one else does. Go on, write what happens when he arrives at the crime scene: What is he looking for? Exit routes? Entrance routes? Trace evidence? Lighting and sight lines at this time of day? The position and condition of the body? Step in, look around, try to see what you notice that wasn't evident before ...*

5. **Climax:** *What's a moral dilemma my hero might face? Having to choose between saving his fiancée and saving his daughter? Okay, how would I need to set that up? Think location, dilemma, and decision. What setting that hasn't been overused in this type of novel would lend itself naturally to this kind of a climax?*

When we write, we're inevitably making promises to the reader about what will happen (the would-be lovers need to get together or be torn apart; the detective must face the killer; the hero must find the dragon, etc.). So as I'm working on a story, I might focus on writing a promise scene and a payoff scene the same day even though they might appear hundreds of pages apart in the manuscript. That way, I can make sure the scenes are tied together in intricate and subtle ways that I might not be able to render without the context of the promise kept so closely in mind.

Organic writers are never directionless because we can always work on scenes that fulfill the promises we've made earlier in the story or go back and foreshadow the fulfillment of promises we think of as the story takes shape.

6. Reevaluate where you're going.

So in practice, what does all this look like? When you get up in the morning and sit down at the keyboard, what do you do if you don't have an outline to work from?

1. Reorient yourself to the context. Print out the previous ten, fifty, or one hundred pages (sometimes I'll do the whole novel) and read it, looking at it through the eyes of a reader, not an editor. Remember, readers aren't looking for what's wrong with the story but what's right with it. Ask yourself what your readers are thinking or expecting in each scene as they move through the story.
2. While considering the context and maintaining the story's continuity, draft the scene that would naturally come next. The length and breadth of the scene need to be shaped by the narrative forces we're discussing in this book. Type up your ideas.
3. Because of the necessity of a story's unity, what you write will have implications on the story you've already written, so be ready to go back and rework earlier sections of the manuscript.
4. Print out what you've worked on, read it again in context, mark changes, and then type them in.
5. Keep track of unanswered questions and unresolved problems, and review them before you read through your manuscript again.

Often I imagine that the first time through a scene I'm tilling the soil. Sometimes the earth is fertile and easy to churn up, but more often than not, it's unyielding and I have to really work at it to break up the ground.

At this early point, I'm not trying to get things right or even get down a "rough draft." I'm just preparing the path for the story seeds to fall into place. I'm not trying to force things, just trying to get a sense of what the scenes might be about.

Start with what you have.

Some people write descriptions first, but most of the time for me it ends up being dialogue. I hear it, almost audibly, in my head. I write what I hear and explore where that leads. Often I have to rework the scene later to fill in the descriptions, speaker attributions, and the narration as I figure out who's talking, where they are, and what they want, and I bring myself to the point where I can see the scene as well as hear it.

I might have an idea for one of these scenes and work on that in the morning before printing it out and reading it in context with the adjoining parts of the story in the afternoon.

I tend to work on a scene until I can see it. Then I reread the story before that scene to get the context and pace as I move forward. (However, there are some transitional scenes that I don't shape too much until I know what happens next so I'll know what needs to have happened to cause them to happen.) As details emerge and the story grows, I'll frequently go back to refine the scenes that lead up to the one I'm working on.

Don't pressure yourself to do too much on the project at the start. Use your free writing to break up the soil.

Listen to the story, ask the right questions, and let them press in against the clay, and the narrative will begin to take shape.

Be aware of the questions and transformations of the characters. Let the people in your stories struggle desperately, choose valiantly, act believably, and chart their course to an ending that is both inevitable and unexpected, and you'll craft a story worth reading.

By understanding the essential characteristics of every story (tension, believability, escalation, reader empathy, character intention, causality, twists, and so on) and the expectations of readers, a story will unfold as you write it.

This isn't outlining, and it's not writing by the seat of your pants. It's intuitive, natural, and based on an informed understanding of reader expectations and a clear grasp of what makes a story work.

7. Let the scene evolve.

Since so few people teach how to shape stories organically by intentionally *not* outlining, it's hard for some folks to really picture how all this plays out in real life.

I thought about making up a generic example for you, but then I realized that giving you one from actual experience would be much more practical and beneficial.

So here's a glimpse into an organic writer's thought process. This is from when I was working on the climax to my thriller *The Bishop*.

I should start by admitting that when I was partway through the book, I decided to give outlining a shot to nail down the ending. I figured I could at least plan out *that much* of the story.

I had a scene in mind where my protagonist, FBI agent Patrick Bowers, is called in after his supervisor, Margaret Wellington, makes a terrible discovery. I wrote up the whole 3,000-word scene. It fit in with where I anticipated things were going. It was a good scene. I thought I was on target to making this outline thing work.

But when I went back and reread the previous scenes, I realized that at this point readers would be more concerned with what was happening in the other storyline involving Patrick's stepdaughter, Tessa. Also, because of his love for her, Patrick would have naturally been there to help her and not gone to be with Margaret.

However, the only way I knew all this was by the narrative weight of the scenes within the broader context of the story.

What do I mean by narrative weight? Well, as we'll discuss more in detail in Chapter 11, every word of your story is a promise, and every word carries a certain amount of weight with the reader.

The amount of time you spend on a scene will determine how significant readers expect that scene to be to the overall story. In other words, the number of words or the detail and length of a scene directly relates to the importance of that scene to the story.

You might have a one hundred-point outline, but you don't know that point fifty will be four pages and point fifty-one will be one page. There's no way to know that until you get into the story. It's simply not possible to plan out how many words you'll need for a scene until you write that scene.

Remember that dinosaur? You won't know what it'll look like until you've uncovered it. You can't just decide it's going to be eight feet tall or that you want it to have wings. And if you've decided beforehand what it should look like, when you get to a certain place you'll stop uncovering it.

> You won't know where the story should go, or should have gone, until you evaluate how each section, in context, is able to bear the overall weight of the narrative.

So in light of the context (Patrick would have other priorities), the narrative weight (the original scene was too long for the build to the climax), and my readers' priorities (they'll be more concerned about Tessa at this point in the story), I scrapped the scene with Patrick and Margaret and went back to the drawing board, back to asking the natural questions that shape the clay, to feel out where the story should go. I figured, why make it so hard on myself by trying to outline? Why not do it the easy way? Only then did the end of the story come together.

Here's the context:

In a previous book, a dismembered body was found in the trunk of Margaret's car. Now, it's beginning to appear that the same killer (or at least a copycat) is operating in the area.

At the build to the climax, she arrives home. Opens the door. Steps into the house.

But her golden retriever, Lewis, who is always there to greet her at the door, doesn't run up to meet her.

Understand that while I was writing this scene I didn't know what had happened to the dog. So I began by running through the questions that help organic writers shape their stories: *Believability: What would Margaret naturally do? Well, she would realize something's wrong, so she would look for her dog—but she would be careful about it. After all, either the dog is dead or unconscious somewhere in the house, or someone obviously got in there and took him.*

Margaret pulls out her gun and searches her home.

Meanwhile, in the other storyline, my protagonist's stepdaughter is being tracked by a serial killer, and Bowers is trying to stop him. While Margaret looked for Lewis, I switched the point of view to keep the reader up to speed on Tessa's storyline.

Flip point of view back to Margaret—she can't find the dog.

Where is Lewis? What happened? What would the killer have done with him? Probably something concerning the trunk of the car—he's done that before. It would make sense. But in the context of this book, she wouldn't think to look there yet. What will lead her to search in there? Well, she's meticulous, detailed. Maybe she notices a clue in the house ...

But what?

I didn't know.

I reread the previous pages, taking a look at the flow, keeping in mind the narrative weight of the scene.

Finally, I wrote the next sequence: While searching her home office, Margaret notices that the desk chair is turned slightly to the side from how she left it.

She sits down, and, using her fingernail so she won't disturb any fingerprints that might be there, she taps the spacebar of her computer and a note comes up ...

Okay, so what does it say? Whatever it says, it needs to drive the story forward but also escalate the tension. What kind of message would the man who took her dog leave her?

She read the note: Check your trunk, Margaret.

Okay, now we're getting somewhere. But don't forget about Patrick and Tessa. Readers are worried about Tessa, and they want to know what's going on. Get back to them now, or readers will get annoyed.

I flipped to their storyline, showed readers that the killer was getting closer to Tessa, then returned to Margaret's story.

Now, she's outside the house, staring at her car.

What next? Well, she'll make sure it's not some kind of a trap.

She scans the shadows nearby, the neighborhood, sees no one. She checks inside the car, under it, nothing.

She walks toward the trunk.

Unlocks it and reaches out to open it up.

So what does she find?

I had no idea.

But I knew one thing—it couldn't be the dismembered corpse of her dog.

That would be too predictable, and because of the importance of having scenes end in a way that readers can't anticipate, that option was off the table.

The sequence needed to be believable as well as ratchet up the tension—and I needed to give readers what they wanted or something better. Most of them wouldn't want Margaret to find Lewis's dismembered corpse in her trunk. No. That would not be a good call.

Back to context.

I reread the preceding scenes, then returned again to the narrative forces that inform storytellers, that press in upon the clay: *To build the escalation, since I have no idea what happened to Lewis, how about I put off the resolution to increase the suspense?*

Slowly, she opens the trunk.

And finds a DVD with a note beside it: "I hope you enjoy watching this as much as I did filming it."

Yes, good. That escalates things, drives everything forward. It's believable. Readers are still worried about Lewis but don't feel cheated or let down because things are too predictable.

Flip to the storyline of Patrick and Tessa.

A countdown to an explosion is going on while a shootout ensues.

Then to Margaret again—she pops the DVD into her computer.

Now, it was time for me to review. When I reread this section in context, I realized that, while readers are worried about the dog, at this point they're far more worried about Tessa. Her life is more important to them than that dog's, no matter how much they might be dog lovers.

Also, continuity. There was no logical place to break the action sequence with Patrick, Tessa, and the killer, so I needed to stay with them and write a scene so intense that, for the time being at least, readers would actually forget about Lewis. I couldn't leave my hero and his daughter while they were in the middle of the action or I would have frustrated readers and chopped up the scene.

Besides, readers might have just flipped past or skimmed over Margaret's section to get back to the life-threatening situation with Tessa. And as we noted earlier, we never want that as writers. If we're going to spend the time carefully crafting a sentence or even choosing a specific word, we want it to be important enough for readers to read. Otherwise, why on earth would we even write it down?

The best way to serve readers: stay with Patrick and Tessa until I could resolve their sequence with the serial killer before flipping back to Margaret.

Which was fine by me because I still didn't know what was on that DVD.

Because of the narrative forces of inevitability and surprise, it couldn't be a video of the killer slaughtering her dog—that's too predictable—just like dismembered dog in the trunk would have been. But whatever the footage contained, it needed to be believable and, once again, escalate the tension.

I needed something that would satisfy readers.

Something that wasn't clichéd.

And to increase that all-important tension, something *worse* than a video of the killer dismembering a golden retriever.

It took me a couple of days of reviewing the story to think of what that might be. Finally, I resolved the climax with Tessa and Patrick, and just at the point where readers would be relaxing a bit, I inserted the first draft of the closure with Margaret and Lewis.

(In the following excerpt, I've changed the names of the characters so it doesn't give everything away if you decide to read the novel. However, there are some plot spoilers included, so if you haven't read the book and plan to, you might want to skip these next few paragraphs.)

It wasn't footage of her dog Lewis being slaughtered as she'd feared, in fact, after Adrian's death, the task force found Lewis in the backseat of Adrian's car, drugged but okay.

Thankfully.

Thankfully.

Lewis was okay.

But still, the videotaped images were grisly and disturbing.

The DVD contained videos of seven of Adrian's victims: Linda Walker screaming as the two chimpanzees attacked her, Julianne Rodale lying unconscious in the back of the van, Monica Tomlinson struggling to escape a shallow grave in the body farm. And four other victims who still remained unidentified.

But to Margaret, some of the most unsettling footage was at the end of the DVD. It wasn't video of another victim but of her lying asleep in her own bed. The video had been recorded from inside her bedroom.

He'd been there, in her room, watching her. Standing over her as she slept.

> He'd even leaned close, filming only inches from her face, and she'd never known, never even suspected a thing. *How many nights was he there, standing by your bed, watching you sleep?*
>
> But now, she assured herself, it was over. He was dead. And he was not coming back.
>
> She tried not to think about the one remaining fact that no one was talking about—there was no actual proof Adrian was the one who'd taken the video of her lying asleep in her bed. It might have been someone else that they still hadn't identified.

Apparently, the killer had invaded her home and filmed her—something I found chilling. But actually, since he was dead, there was no way of *knowing* it was him—so as I resolved one struggle, I introduced a new one: Who really filmed Margaret sleeping? I wasn't sure. It was something I would need to address in a future book.

Another promise.

Another storyline.

Another question to discover the answer to as I proceeded into another story.

All part of the adventure.

This is how organic writing works in practice. It's an interplay of responsiveness to the movement and context of the unfolding story. It only comes from a constant awareness of where the story has been, where it might go, and what readers want and expect. You trust the narrative forces to reveal the story to you as you let them press against the clay of your tale.

Move into and out of the story, big picture, little picture, focusing one day on the forest and the next day on the trees.

Scary?

Maybe.

But the more you trust the questions and the narrative forces that shape all stories, the more you'll begin to see your tale emerge. As Ray

Bradbury noted, "Remember: *Plot* is no more than footprints left in the snow *after* your characters have run by on their way to incredible destinations. *Plot* is observed after the fact rather than before. It cannot precede action. It is the chart that remains when an action is through."

Rather than outlining, focus on (1) narrative progression, (2) genre conventions, and (3) reader expectations.

8. Nurture the story.

If I'm stuck coming up with what to write next, I might reread some scenes, research information for the book, flip through my idea files and review lines of dialogue I've thought of, character descriptions, clues, or unique phrases. I might free write or work on a requisite scene. By then, I have plenty of story fodder, and I'll need to center myself in the book again by looking carefully at the context.

Then I type in all the changes, and that ends up altering some of the content and the story direction. So I weave that in and begin moving through the narrative once again.

Come up with your own personalized system to organize your blossoming ideas. In addition to files of character descriptions, phrases, clues, and so on, I have four word-processing files that I use to organize my thoughts: (1) questions, (2) reminders, (3) discarded ideas, and (4) stuff from notebooks. The categories are pretty self-explanatory, the last one referring to notes I've typed up but haven't yet inserted into the story itself.

Most of us were taught to outline our stories at some point when we were growing up. Whenever my teacher assigned an outline, I would write the story first and then go back and write the outline so I'd have something to turn in for my grade. Over the years I've met a lot of other people who did the same thing. So why would this process be taught if it's not helpful for so many writers?

Honestly, I think it's because people haven't been exposed to organic writing so they simply don't know how to teach it.

Abandoning an outline isn't something to be ashamed of. You don't have to "confess" or "admit" that you write without one. It's a natural and bold approach to your art form.

I love how David Bayles and Ted Orland put it in *Art and Fear*: "Art is like beginning a sentence before you know its ending. ... Many fiction writers, for instance, discover early on that making detailed plot outlines is an exercise in futility; as actual writing progresses, characters increasingly take on a life of their own, sometimes to the point that the writer is as surprised as the eventual reader by what their creations say and do. ... Uncertainty is the essential, inevitable and all-pervasive companion to your desire to make art. And tolerance for uncertainty is the prerequisite to succeeding."

If you don't have an element of trust in the process, you will never become an artist.

Writing a story isn't a straightforward, step-by-step, mechanical process. In my view, it's more like growing a houseplant than drawing up the blueprints to the house.

When you nurture a plant, you provide the right environment by watering it, giving it the nutrients it needs, making sure it's in the sunlight, and then trusting that it'll grow.

Even though you know what species of plant it is, in the end, it'll never look exactly like you expected it to. Though you might have had a general idea, its leaves and branches will develop in ways you would never have been able to predict.

The more you try to force the plant into your preconception of what it should look like without giving it time to flourish, the more you'll interfere with its natural growth. You need to trust the process. And you need to give it time to grow.

These narrative forces we're exploring form the environment I use when growing my stories. They're a way to water and nourish my stories to enable them to thrive. In the research and literature on creativity, incubation is widely cited as a vital part of the creative process. So before you even begin, understand that it takes time for good ideas to grow. The span of time between the initiation of your creative endeavor and the completion of it is all part of the process.

When you're working your way between drafts without any specific plan of what will come next, it doesn't mean you've reached a dead end or have writer's block. It doesn't mean you've stalled out. It means your mind is working in ways you don't even notice to solve the problems you might not even be able to articulate.

Go back, get the context in mind, and, once again, let it press against the evolving shape of your tale.

And as you do that, there are three questions you can ask yourself that will solve every "plot problem" you'll ever have. In the next chapter we'll take a careful look at them and at the implications they have for developing your story—even if you're used to working from an outline.

CHAPTER 8

EMERGENCE

The Three Questions That Will Solve Every "Plot Problem" You'll Ever Have

Initially, most authors land somewhere on the continuum between outlining and organic writing. If you try to fit your story into a predetermined number of acts or a novel template, you're more of an outliner. If you don't care how many acts your story has as long as you let your characters struggle through the escalating tension of your story in a believable way, you're more organic.

Both organic writing and outlining have their inherent strengths and weaknesses. (Yes, even organic writing can, in some cases, lead you astray if you don't let all three questions listed on the next page guide your writing.)

Outliners often have great high-concept climax ideas. Their stories might escalate exponentially and build to unforgettable endings. However, characters will sometimes act in inexplicable ways on their journey toward the climax. You'll find gaps in logic. People will do things that don't really make sense but that are necessary to reach the climax the writer has decided to build toward.

Organic writers are usually pretty good at crafting stories that flow well. The events are believable and make sense. However, sometimes the narratives can wander, and although the stories are believable, they might also end up being anticlimactic as they just fizzle out and don't really go anywhere.

So outlining often results in problems with continuity and causality, while organic writers often stumble in the areas of focus and escalation.

Outliners tend to have cause-effect problems because they know where they need to go but don't know how to get there. Organic writers tend to have directionality problems because they don't necessarily know where they're going, but things follow logically even if they lead into a dead end.

Of course, as you know by now, I'm bullish on organic writing for reasons I've already expressed and for additional ones I'll be detailing throughout the rest of this book. However, I know it's a new concept to many people, so whichever approach you've been using, you can build on its strengths and solve its weaknesses by asking the following three questions and letting the answers influence the direction of your story.

1. **"What would this character naturally do in this situation?"** This focuses on the story's believability and causality—everything that happens in a novel needs to be believable even if it's impossible, and because of the contingent nature of fiction, everything needs to follow causally from what precedes it.

2. **"How can I make things worse?"** This dials us in to the story's escalation. Readers always want the tension to tighten. If the story doesn't build, it'll become boring and they'll put it aside.

3. **"How can I end this in a way that's unexpected and inevitable?"** Here we're shaping the scenes, and the story as a whole, around satisfaction and surprise. So the story has to move logically, one step at a time, in a direction readers can track—but then angle away from it as they realize that this new direction is the one the story was heading in all along. However, readers don't want that ending to come out of nowhere. It needs to be natural and inherent to the story.

The first question will improve your story's believability. The second will keep it escalating toward an unforgettable climax. The third will help you build your story, scene by twisting, turning scene.

Organic writers are good at asking that first question; outliners are good at asking the second one. As far as the third, organic writers will tend to have believable endings and outliners will tend to have unpredictable ones.

The way you approach writing will determine which of those questions you most naturally ask and which ones you need to learn to ask in order to shape effective stories.

I hope you'll give organic writing a shot, but whichever way you lean, by focusing on letting *all three* questions shape your stories, you'll add to the strengths of your approach and overcome its weaknesses.

- Outliners need to ask, "What is actually going on here? What are readers thinking at this point? What do they want?"
- Organic writers need to ask, "Is this scene essential to the story? Have I spent too many or too few words on it considering its overall importance to the narrative?"

The more time you spend asking questions of your narrative and listening to your story, the more it will tell itself to you.

DIVE INTO THE QUESTIONS

At one of my seminars, a student wrote a story about an FBI agent who found out that the killer she was tracking was in L.A. What would that agent naturally do? Well, obviously, she would go to L.A., or at least tell her supervisor what she found out, or call law enforcement in L.A. to bring them up to speed. Any of those responses would be reasonable and believable.

Instead, the author sent this character to a meeting with her supervisor where she never even brought up the fact that someone knew the location of the killer. It didn't make any contextual sense.

I don't think most organic writers would have made that mistake, because when we write we're continually asking, "What would naturally happen next?" And since it just wouldn't be believable that the agent would neglect to bring up the killer's location, we wouldn't write that.

Outliners need to remember that (1) everything that happens needs a reason to do so, (2) that reason grows from the story events that precede it, and (3) what you feel needs to happen is not always what would naturally happen.

	ORGANIC WRITING	OUTLINING
INSTINCTIVE QUESTIONS	1. What is happening? 2. What would naturally happen next?	1. What needs to happen? 2. How can I escalate to the climax I'm trying to build toward?
STRENGTHS	1. Logical, contingent, believable 2. Strong continuity	1. Conflict escalates exponentially. 2. Mind-blowing climaxes
WEAKNESSES	1. Stories can wander and not escalate. 2. Stories can end abruptly. 3. Climaxes can be anticlimactic.	1. Scenes aren't always believable. 2. Transitions between scenes are weak. 3. Climaxes can seem contrived.
TO SOLVE THE PROBLEMS, ASK:	"How can I make things worse?" "How can I make the end of this scene, and the story as a whole, surprising?"	"What would this character naturally do in this situation?" "How can I make the ending causally related to everything that precedes it?"

I should mention that, in regard to the first of the three key questions listed above, some writing instructors teach that we should ask ourselves "If I were this character in this situation, what would I do?" rather than "What would this character naturally do in this situation?"

There's a subtle but significant difference.

One of these questions puts you in the scene, and the other emphasizes the character's response.

It's important that you move yourself out of the story and let the characters you've created take over. I don't want to imagine myself as the character. I want to observe the character responding as *she* would, not as I would if I were her. Step further away from yourself, and remove your own views as much as possible from the situation.

Incidentally, the first two questions also help authors who strive to write books that are either character-centered or plot-centered (remember, however, that no story is character-driven or plot-driven because all stories are tension-driven).

The first question helps plot-centered authors develop deeper characterizations. The second question helps character-centered authors develop plots that are more gripping.

"You don't have to see where you're going, you don't have to see your destination or everything you will pass along the way. You just have to see two or three feet ahead of you. This is right up there with the best advice about writing, or life, I have ever heard."
—Anne Lamott in *Bird by Bird*

The central struggles of the main character (internal, external, and interpersonal) will only be ultimately satisfied at the story's climax. As we write the scene-by-scene lead-up, we are constantly deepening and tightening the tension in those three areas.

Some climaxes implode because they lack believability, others because they don't make sense or they're too predictable, others because they don't contain escalation of everything else in the story and end up being disappointing.

Let me reiterate: The solution to most of these problems is keeping the promises you've made to your readers by maintaining believability, creating endings that are inevitable and yet unexpected, tightening the tension, ratcheting up the action, relentlessly building up the suspense, heightening the stakes, and escalating to a finish that reaches its pinnacle at just the right moment for the protagonist and for your readers.

Let those three questions filter through every scene you write.

1. "What would this character naturally do in this situation?"
2. "How can I make things worse?"
3. "How can I end this in a way that's unexpected and inevitable?"

If you're attentive to them, they'll crack open the nut of the tale for you.

GETTING TO KNOW YOUR CHARACTERS TAKES TIME

The more time you spend with any particular character, the more you'll get to know him and how he would naturally respond in a given situation.

As you work on your novel, you'll be spending weeks, months, maybe years with the characters. And as you do, you'll begin to realize how they would react to things and why they have the attitudes they have toward religion, politics, art, hip-hop music, and Kit Kat bars.

Think about getting to know someone in real life. It takes time before you can accurately predict how she'll respond in a given situation.

Think of your relationship to the characters in your book as you would your relationships to people in life. Could I sit down and outline how I think someone I just met might act when getting a divorce or finding a rattlesnake in her yard or discovering a wormhole to another galaxy in her cubicle at work?

Obviously not. The better I know the person, the more accurately I'll be able to anticipate how she would act when faced with those situations.

The more time you spend with your fictional characters, the better you'll be able to write believable stories. This is why the process of writing, the time involved in it, is essential to and inextricably tied to character development, and why sitting down beforehand and writing an outline is counterintuitive to the process.

As you spend time getting to know your characters, you'll begin to understand more clearly what they want, what they fear, and what their attitudes and goals are toward other characters and toward their surroundings. That'll inevitably affect what you've already written and ineluctably alter the unfolding story.

This will, of course, mean that as you write, you'll be continually going back over the book to shade each scene, each interaction, toward the character's true nature, desires, and fears. Accept from the start that you won't know a character well enough when you begin the book to know what he or she is thinking, hoping for, or feeling in each and every scene, on each and every page as you shape your story—and accept that the characters' reactions will affect the story's trajectory, both where it comes from and where it's going.

This will only come with time.

Just as it is with real people.

SURPRISE IS PART OF THE CREATIVE PROCESS

Truthfully, I've been shocked by the endings of all the novels I've written. I've never completed a novel with the same ending I had in mind when I began it. Yes, I have ideas about where the story will go, but as it unfurls, it also surprises me. Since the beginning and ending are necessarily tied together by the promises that connect them, changing either the beginning or the ending will necessitate reworking the other end of the promise—either as it is being made or as it is being fulfilled.

As Robert Frost wrote, "I have never started a poem yet whose end I knew. Writing a poem is discovering."

It's the same for storytelling as it is for poetry.

So start with what you have, and follow it. See where it leads.

Writing effective fiction requires being aware of the interplay of the unfolding narrative and your evolving ideas as you watch and respond to how everything merges and reforms itself into the final product. It's a dance, and we're just here to help introduce the two partners—character and unmet desire—and then listen to the music and watch them take it from there within the constraints of our art form.

GIVE READERS WHAT THEY WANT OR SOMETHING BETTER

When I write my novels, I'm constantly asking myself what readers are thinking at this point in the story. Our job as writers: Give them what they want, when they want it—or add a twist so we give them more than they ever bargained for.

Continually ask yourself, "What are readers wondering about, worrying about, hoping for, or expecting at this moment in the story?" Then give it to them, or draw them deeper into the story by giving them something even better.

Try to watch your story unfold through the eyes of your readers. Think in real time: What's on stage in your readers' minds *right now* as they read these words, having just read the previous ones?

These four questions are so vital for understanding readers' expectations and their relationship to context that it's worth taking a look at each of them a little more closely.

1. **What are readers wondering about?** These are the questions that are rolling around in their minds, questions that you've brought up through the promises you've made in regard to the narrative weight of certain scenes, characters, and situations.

This has to do with what's currently happening in the story and how it relates to what you promised earlier.

2. **What are readers worried about?** Here's where empathy and concern come into the picture. You're trying to figure out what's at the forefront of your readers' minds in regard to anxiety and apprehension about what is going to happen.

3. **What are readers hoping for?** Based on the context, readers will hope for different things: that the bad guy suffers for what he's done, or the dog doesn't get killed, or the couple gets together by the end of the story, and so on.

   This will be affected by genre, the depth of the readers' emotional concern for the well-being of the story's characters, and virtues readers want to see, such as justice, forgiveness, and self-sacrifice.

4. **What are readers expecting?** This is based on context and what's foremost in readers' minds considering what they've just read. In order for you to twist the story forward, you'll need to have a clear idea of what readers will be expecting next. If you give them what they expect, and only what they expect, they'll be disappointed. So use expectations to your advantage, and play them against your readers as you're building in twists.

There are certain places in your story where readers might set the book down and other places—climactic scenes or action sequences, for instance—where they'll likely stay in the story. Keep this in mind as you edit.

To climb into the context, read the story as a reader would.

Since readers probably won't stop reading in the middle of a chase scene, when you're editing, don't start reading in the middle of the chase scene to get the context. You're trying to enter the mind of your readers, to see it from their perspective, through their eyes, looking for the things they'll be looking for.

Before I start working on a new scene, I reread the context of the story to get the pace and flow in my mind. Typically, I try to start at a different place than I did the last time so I can catch the rhythm of the story and keep from getting in a rut.

Developing the ability to see things from a reader's point of view is one of the most important things you can do as a storyteller.

If you're not aware of what your readers will likely be experiencing (both feeling and thinking) at each progressive moment of your story, you won't be able to craft a narrative that affects them and accomplishes your narrative goals—either an emotionally impactful climax (whatever emotion that might be) or a tantalizingly satisfying intellectual puzzle (for example, in a mystery).

Read what they would read, pause where they would pause. Keep in mind what they will be thinking when they're reading the scene you're working on.

So what do my readers want to know about Marianne's past? How long will they be happy not knowing it? What do they need to know in order to understand the progression of the story? Where's everything naturally heading based on what I've written so far and the promises I've made? How will the narrative weight of the previous scenes influence the content, pace, length, tone, and mood of this scene?

Okay.

Time for a short breather.

This would be the point in one of my seminars where we might naturally stop for a little Q & A. Here are some of the questions that often come up in my workshops when I start talking about organic writing, and my responses to them.

Q: "But how do we listen to a story? What does that even mean?"

A: When I refer to listening to the story, I mean constantly asking questions of it as you move forward into the narrative and then letting the answers inform the direction you take as you write it. Let the narrative forces we're talking about press in on the clay, and try to keep as many of them in mind as you can while moving forward with each scene.

Q: "Why do you need to write the whole story this way? Why can't you just use this process as you're outlining it?"

A: As we explored earlier, it takes time to get to know characters and allow them the freedom to respond to the situations you present them with in the story.

Also, you'll only know the narrative weight of scenes after you've written them and studied them in context. There's no practical way to do this when outlining.

Finally, if you're not surprised by the twists in the story and the direction that it takes *as you're writing it*, it's likely many of your readers won't be surprised *as they're reading it*. It might take me six months of thinking about how to resolve a certain plot question before I come up with a workable solution. I'm nowhere near smart enough to solve all those issues before I get started. And unless you're a prodigy or a creative genius, you probably aren't either.

Q: "How long should my book be?"

A: As short as possible for you to tell your story. Some novels require 200,000 words, some require 50,000 words. Don't add fluff or eliminate vital storylines just to hit a certain word count.

Q: "But if you don't outline, how do you know how long your book will be?"

A: I don't. I can't know how many words my book will have until I've uncovered the story.

I might know some general ideas based on the genre, number of point-of-view characters, the complexity of the plot, and so on, but novels are not sitcoms. The art form allows us freedom that those who are constricted by a twenty-two-minute time limit don't have. Don't let a predetermined word count handcuff you and interfere with telling the story that needs to be told.

Q: "Are you saying organic writing is best for everyone? Doesn't it depend on the person?"

A: I wouldn't feel right suggesting that anyone approach writing a story in a way that I believe is counterintuitive to the creative process. So yes to the first question, no to the second.

Q: "But won't I have to go through more edits if I write organically? Won't it take me fewer drafts if I outline?"

A: There seems to be an impression out there that writing a novel organically takes longer than writing one using an outline. Some people outline their books and go through dozens of drafts, while some people write organically and hardly have to edit the manuscript at all. Some of it is skill, some artistry, some intuition.

Writing great fiction takes a lot of time no matter how you approach it. I've had a number of professional novelists confess to me that the more they write, the less they outline simply because they don't have time to write detailed outlines and still meet their deadlines.

Writing organically doesn't mean approaching your book with a blank slate in your brain—you know about story, about genre conventions and reader expectations. If you're writing a series, you've made promises in previous books and readers will look forward to finding payoff for them in the book you're working on now.

If you ask the right questions and let the story continually unfold before you by letting the narrative forces press in upon it, you'll be able to write the book much more quickly than if you were to outline it and then have to make edits because of continuity or causality problems.

Q: "What do you do if you get writer's block?"

A: I reread the story in context, keep the promises I've made, or make more promises and ask the narrative questions we're examining in this book. Since you're always analyzing the direction and content of your story when you write organically, you'll find that you don't run out of ideas very often. It makes it a lot easier for those of us who make a living doing this.

Q: "How many chapters should you include in your book?"

A: The minimum necessary to tell your story. In his best-selling novel *The Ruins*, Scott Smith has no chapter breaks. On the other end of the spectrum, I've read (and written) novels with more than a hundred chapters.

Q: "But without an outline, how do you know when to end your story?"

A: Stories are over when the change in the life of the character has occurred, the questions readers have been asking are answered, and the promises you've made have been kept. At that point, readers expect no more from the story, and the next logical step would only be the introduction of a new internal, external, or interpersonal struggle for the protagonist—in other words, the beginning of a new story.

It might take one act or it might take a dozen, depending on the length of the narrative, the number of characters, and the complexity of the conflict, but when the discovery is made, the resolution is reached, and you've fulfilled your promises, the story is over.

Q: "What if you're writing a complex story? How do you keep everything straight if you don't outline?"

A: Remind yourself of the context. Some stories are too complex to outline. My novels often involve dozens of characters, multiple plots and subplots, half a dozen point-of-view characters, and single-, double-, or triple-twist endings. Even now that the books are written, if someone asked me to outline one of them, I can't imagine how hard that would be.

Make it easier on yourself, and write organically. Read the context, jot down notes on the characters if you need to, and keep in mind what readers have in mind. Remember, they're not going to have character biographies, outlines, and so on in front of them to help keep everything straight as they read your story, so if you're trying to write one for them that doesn't include or require those things, why would you begin writing the story in such a way that *you* need them?

Q: "But how can you add a twist if you don't outline?"

A: When you understand the dynamics of good storytelling, you can't help but add a twist when you write organically. Remember those three questions from earlier in this chapter? When you let that third one guide you, you'll naturally write scenes and stories that have twists in them. (More on this in Chapter 10.)

The twist will reveal itself to you if you look for it long enough and in the right place by opening your eyes and asking the right questions.

Readers today are narratively astute. Respect them. Assume they're at least as smart as you are. If you're not surprised by the direction the story takes, many of them won't be surprised either.

Q: "When you say to trust the process, how do I gain that intuitive sense of what works? How do I get a sense for these narrative forces you keep talking about?"

A: Read on.

CHAPTER 9

AWARENESS

How Context Determines Content

My oldest daughter has long hair. As she's brushing it, she might not be able to pull the brush all the way through the first time. Rather, she'll brush it until she comes to a snag or tangle, and then, instead of yanking hard to get it out, she'll start over, gently brushing through her hair little by little until she comes to that trouble spot.

Tugging, yanking, forcing the brush through her hair will only make the knots worse.

So, instead, she works through them slowly.

Whenever I'm stuck or having a hard time with a scene, I'll go back and review the previous scenes, brushing through the story until I come to the snag. Usually, I'll be able to untangle a little bit more of the story.

Then, I start brushing through it again from the top.

And little by little the snags come out.

I'm not sure if it's true, but I heard that Ernest Hemingway would re-read the book he was working on all the way through from the first word every morning before he would write another word. Whether that's just literary folklore or not, I can definitely see the practical wisdom in regularly brushing through the whole story to get out the tangles.

My daughter trusts that she'll be able to smooth out her hair if she's patient.

In the same way, writing requires trust in the questions, trust in the process.

Untangle the story one brushstroke at a time.

Your goal: Make your final product appear effortless. Usually, the longer you spend writing a scene, the less time it will take the reader to finish reading it.

Why?

Because you'll have gotten all the tangles out.

CONTENT BOWS TO CONTEXT

You must enter the context to tell the story with the right pace, with the right mood, at the right time.

Remember, what *has* happened informs what *is* happening, and what *is* happening informs what *will*. As you make promises, you'll probably also think of ways that those promises will need to be fulfilled. Because of a story's unity, all of those events are causally related, so the pressure for certain things to happen is made sharper by how distinct each promise is and by the events they ultimately cause.

Context + causality = unity.

So let's say you introduce the villain's martial-arts skills early on. What have you done? Well, you've made a promise that there's going to be a fight scene later, likely at the climax. You might think of ideas for that fight scene—where it will be, what props or weapons might be available, and so on. Then, as you write, you'll keep them in mind, not forcing the story toward that type of fight (because it might change locations as you work the story up until that point) but rather letting it subtly influence your narrative choices.

We write both from and toward—*from* what has previously happened and *toward* the payoff for the promises we've made.

The payoff presses in against the story just as much as the promise does.

As you write, there'll be constant tension between the desire to include material that you think would be good and material that's contextually necessary.

It doesn't matter how clever your descriptions are, how brilliant your dialogue is, or how creepy your graveyard scene is—if it doesn't fit contextually in the story, it needs to go.

Context is tied to brevity. Sometimes words need to go, sometimes paragraphs, sometimes chapters, and sometimes entire storylines.

When I was working on my second novel, I had two storylines—one in Chicago and one in San Diego. Because of the timing of the events in the story, I just couldn't come up with a way to keep them both alive, but boy, did I try.

It felt like two parallel stories rather than one integrated whole. So after struggling with this for more than a month, and with my deadline quickly approaching, I finally made the decision: I needed to cut out the first fifty pages. Slice that entire Chicago storyline from the novel.

Being a responsible novelist, I, of course, put it off as long as I could until I was lying in bed one night and my wife asked me what was wrong.

"I need to rip out the first part of my novel and rewrite the beginning."

A long silence. And there was understanding in it.

"That must be hard."

"You have no idea."

I didn't sleep much that night as I mentally sorted through all the changes I needed to make.

Could I have avoided that by outlining? Absolutely not. It was only because I started with a preconceived idea of what the story needed to contain that I ran into trouble in the first place. Only when I let the interplay of the context and flow inform the story did I actually get things on the right track.

It's terribly painful to perform that kind of surgery on a novel.

But it is necessary.

As you write, you'll undoubtedly come up with dozens, if not hundreds, of ideas that you'll want to use but that just don't seem to fit. Not quite, at least. You'll be tempted to try to find a way to weave them into the story or build a scene around them to get them in.

Always go with what is contextually appropriate over what is brilliant. If it's in the story, it must matter. If it doesn't matter, delete it.

In reference to that overwhelming compulsion to keep the eloquent parts, the clever parts, the funny ones, the ones we've fallen in love with, Annie Dillard points out in *The Writing Life*, "The part you must jettison is not only the best-written part; it is also, oddly, that part which was to have been the very point."

Make sure those scenes you really want to include are not just appropriate but necessary. If not, drop them—as hard as that may be.

Learn to ask, "What do I need to include based on what has just happened and what I've promised will happen?" rather than "What do I need to include based on what I want to happen?"

Ask yourself, "Am I letting the story grow from what's happening, or am I bending it toward where I want it to go?"

It's likely that readers will be able to tell if you let something other than context determine the flow of the story and the content of the scenes.

HAVE I RESHAPED LIFE INTO THE WORLD OF FICTION?

1. **Causality:** Everything follows logically and naturally from what precedes it. Stories contain contingent events rather than random ones. In real life we have coincidences, but including them in your novel will disrupt the fictional world you've created.

2. **Believability:** Everything needs to be believable. It doesn't matter how impossible or improbable an event is. Unbelievable things happen in real life all the time, but everything in fiction needs to fall under the umbrella of believability.

3. **Unity:** Everything matters. In real life we don't always have a sense of unity, of cohesion, but in novels everything ties together in mood, voice, and story movement.

4. **Closure:** Readers are pleased with the resolution rather than irritated by it. The end makes sense when you consider the beginning and vice versa. Closure is something we long for but don't always get in real life. In fiction, if readers don't get it, they'll be disappointed and won't be anxiously awaiting your next book.

PERSPECTIVE AND MOMENTUM

When we edit our stories, there's always a battle going on between freshness and focus.

Let's say you've written most of your novel and you're near the climax. How do you sort out how to write that scene with the right mood, pace, flow, and escalation? Well, the only way is to keep the context in mind.

And the only way to do that is by reading or reviewing the preceding section.

How many pages?

It depends.

It might be a scene, a few scenes, half the book, or the whole thing. When I get close to completing a novel, I'll typically spend the first three or four hours of my workday reviewing the story up until the scene I'm working on.

Let's say you spend just two hours doing that—now you have all that context clearly in mind, but you might be starting to get mentally fatigued or distracted.

So take a break or not?

If you take a break, you'll be able to refresh yourself mentally and perhaps focus better, but you'll also end up stepping out of the story and losing the sense of pace and flow that being right there in the narrative has brought you.

On the other hand, if you keep at it and plow forward, you'll have that vital context in mind and will be able to craft the ending in a way that will require fewer edits, but it's going to get continually harder to concentrate. It's a constant struggle.

By sticking with a scene and diving in headfirst, I can generate momentum that carries me through it—but stepping away gives me new eyes, a more objective view of my work.

On the final pass through my books, I try to read them from start to finish in one day. It usually takes about an hour for every 10,000 words, so some of those days have meant fourteen hours of reviewing, editing, and revising. And then the next day I get to type in my changes and corrections.

Novel writing, in the real world, is terrifically hard work.

Depending on where I am in my manuscript, I might write in complete silence, with familiar music in the background, or with trance or electronic music on. I stand up. I sit. I type. I free write in a notebook. I'll try just about anything to cut down on the hours I spend working on a book.

But of all the shortcuts I've found over the years, I haven't found anything that can replace getting and keeping the context of a story in mind when I'm editing what I've written or when I'm crafting new scenes.

So should you stay in it or step away from it?

I wish I knew the answer.

Try different approaches, and see what helps you. I'm guessing you'll need to move back and forth between the two. I know I do.

Editing is not "keeping the good stuff." It's not "leaving out the bad stuff." Editing is leaving out everything except the *contextually essential* stuff. Most novels are short stories on steroids. They include way too much backstory, fluff, unnecessary scenes, and tangents. While some novels might be too lean, I've never come across one. Most novels need to be slimmed down. Very few need to be fleshed out more.

When I've read the work of some aspiring writers, I've told them, "This is good for an early draft. Now just go through and edit it a couple dozen more times."

And they'll stare at me. "This is the final draft."

I'm tempted to tell them, "Not if you want to get it published," but usually I just say, "Oh. I didn't realize that."

Hemingway acknowledged that he rewrote the first part of *A Farewell to Arms* at least fifty times. I had to do the same with the first chapter of my novel *Placebo*. If you'd rather not have to work and sweat over every sentence, every word, in draft after draft after draft, don't bother. It's probably not worth it. Save the time. Take up golf or skydiving instead.

But don't plan to get published.

Or maybe just self-publish your book. That seems to be the preferred route people are taking today. Put your story through a few drafts, and then send it out into the world.

Ta-da! Look! I'm finished already!

Strive to make your writing exceptional. Put in the extra time.

The truth is, if you like long hours in solitude, emotional turmoil, constant self-criticism, and bouts of heartrending disappointment, you'll make a good writer. And if you can actually tell an engaging story, you might just make a great one.

In the next section, we'll look at how to do precisely that.

PART III

STORY
PROGRESSION

CHAPTER 10

TWISTS

Practical Steps to Pulling the Rug Out

Every great story, regardless of genre, will include a twist.

Why?

Readers want to be both satisfied and surprised. The more they can decipher exactly where a story is going, the more disappointed they'll be. However, if the events of the story aren't causally related, they'll feel just as let down.

Writing instructors and how-to books often encourage authors to "include a good twist at the end of your story." But how do you do that? What are the mechanics of building stories toward that climactic ending that blows readers away?

I've never heard anyone teach how to actually pull that off, so over the years, through trial and error and thousands of pages of manuscript revisions, I've taken note of some practical, easy-to-implement ideas that have worked for me.

Here's what I've picked up.

INCLUDE THE FOUR ELEMENTS OF ALL PLOT TWISTS

For a twist to work, it needs to be (1) unexpected, (2) inevitable, (3) an escalation of what preceded it, and (4) a revelation that adds meaning to what has already occurred.

Put simply, if people aren't surprised by your twist, you need to make it more unpredictable. If they're disappointed by it, you need to make it more believable and climactic.

Too many stories have endings that leave readers wondering, "Where on earth did that come from?"

Others are predictable. Exactly what readers think will happen does. Inevitability and surprise are two sides of the same coin.

Inevitable: There is only one possible conclusion to the story. It's believable to readers, and when they get to it, they see that everything in the story up until then has been pointing toward that ending, rather than the one they were predicting and anticipating. Great twists are more than just believable; they are, in retrospect, the *only possible* ending to that scene, act, or story.

Surprising: It's a conclusion that readers don't see coming but that ends up not only being reasonable but more logical than any other possible ending. It's an ending free of gimmicks, one that both shocks and delights even the most discerning readers.

Flip the coin.

Readers need to see both sides as it rotates through the air.

This insight that stories need to end inevitably and unexpectedly isn't new. It can be traced all the way back to Aristotle's *Poetics*. And it's likely he wasn't the first to notice it either, just the first to articulate it in a manuscript that managed to survive the ages.

Twists are constructed by what you reveal and what you conceal. Remember, every scene is also a mini-story: Something is altered or changed. So as you write, strive to make not only the entire novel end in a way that's unexpected and also inevitable but every scene as well (and every act, if you view your story's progression through the lens of escalating acts).

In essence, twists pull the rug out from under your readers but give them an even better foundation to stand on: You're telling them they're wrong, but you're doing so in a way that pleases them.

A twist doesn't just move the story forward; it unravels it and then rethreads it at the same time, giving more meaning to it. Readers find out that the story is deeper, richer, and more multilayered than they ever imagined.

Satisfying twists are revelatory in the sense that they add new meaning to all that precedes them.

Creating a twist requires (1) managing reader expectations, (2) understanding the importance of buildup, revelation, and payoff, and (3) surprising your readers without cheating.

> Readers want to both guess how things are going to play out and be surprised by how they do.

CREATE MULTIPLE WORLDS OF INEVITABILITY

Apart from the choice or action that initiates the story, all the events in your story are tied inextricably to the ones that precede them. Everything will follow logically. Breakdowns in logic result in breakdowns in both continuity and believability, neither of which will serve your twist.

So the story that precedes the twist will need to stand on its own and not depend on the twist for its meaning, context, or value.

The bigger the twist, the more essential it is that the story makes sense up until that point. The story needs to taste good without the twist. I think of a twist as the icing on the cake, not the icing on the liver.

All of this means that for every twist, you'll need to create a parallel story to the one you're telling on the surface. Then, when the twist occurs, readers will see that the other world actually seems truer to the story events than the one they'd believed was the only thing going on.

Let's say you're writing a mystery without a twist. You'll obviously need to establish that at least one person could believably be responsible for the crime.

If you add a twist, you'll have to make sure that at least two people could be responsible for the crime. (That is, you have two parallel stories, both of which make sense.) If you want a double twist, you'll need to make sure at least three people could've believably committed the crime.

If you shoot for a triple twist, you'll need a story in which four people could all credibly be responsible for the crime. So typically, the more twists you include, the bigger your cast of characters will be, the more clues there will be, and the longer your story will become. (This isn't always true, of course. The opening to the movie *Clay Pigeons* has, according to my count, a triple twist within the first five minutes, with just two characters onscreen.)

Identify the clues that you use to prove the logic and believability of one world, and use them to prove that the second (or third or fourth parallel narrative) makes even more sense—but only *after* the twist is revealed.

TURN EXPECTATIONS ON THEIR HEAD

As we covered earlier, readers approach books with certain expectations.

At first, you'll play to those expectations so readers will think they know where things are going. Then, suddenly, you'll turn those expectations against them to create the twist. For example, let's say the name, cover art, and back-cover copy of your book all set the genre expectation that this is a horror novel about vampires. The name of your book: *I Suck Your Blood.*

Yeah, I think it's pretty safe to say readers will expect certain things out of that story.

Chapter one: A woman is walking home, alone, at night. She doesn't see it, but readers do: There's someone on a branch just above the path. As she passes by, he drops soundlessly to the ground behind her, then moves in closer and closer until all at once he lunges forward and grabs her.

Now, if he's a vampire and bites her, turning her into a vampire, or if he kills her ... yawn. No readers are going to be surprised or blown away. It's just another predictable, by-the-numbers vampire story. Instead, you'll want to twist things so that after your readers have made a prediction, you'll reveal to them that they were wrong, *but you'll satisfy them more than if they were right*.

Maybe the woman pulls out a stake, whips around, and violently drives it through the vampire's heart—oh, she was luring him away from his lair to kill him. Huh. Let's see where this goes.

Or, she snatches the wooden stake from him and then bites *him* on the neck—okay, hmm ... so actually she's the vampire, and he was trying to slay her.

Or, after the vampire bites her, she spins and faces him, and he exclaims, "It's you!" and then keels over and dies—whoa, her blood is lethal to vampires. That's an interesting concept ...

You get the idea.

ELIMINATE THE OBVIOUS

When coming up with the climax to your story, discard every possible solution you can think of for your protagonist to succeed.

Then think of some more.

And discard those, too.

I've had to do this over and over in my books. Whether that's coming up with a clue that readers won't see the significance of right away or coming up with the identity of the final villain, it's never easy. Sometimes it takes months or even a year or more to do, thinking about that story every day.

Remember, you're trying to create an ending that's so unforeseen that if a million people read your book, not one of them would guess how it ends (or how it will get to the end), but when they finally come to it, every one of those people would think, *Yes! That makes perfect sense! Why didn't I see that coming?*

The more impossible the climax is for your protagonist to overcome, the more believable and inevitable the escape or solution needs to be. No reader should anticipate it, but everyone should nod and smile when it happens. No one guesses, everyone nods. That's what you're shooting for.

REDIRECT SUSPICION

As we covered earlier, when you work on your narrative, constantly ask yourself what readers are expecting and hoping for at this moment in the story. Then keep twisting the story into new directions that both shock and delight them.

To keep readers from noticing clues, bury them in the emotion or action of another section. For example, in an adventure novel, offhandedly mention something during a chase scene, while readers' attention is on the action, not the revelation. Use red herrings, dead ends, and foils. Bury clues in discussions of something else.

Conversely, here are three ways to make someone look suspicious. Remember, you're *not* going to make this person guilty in the end. It's all misdirection.

- **Spy/intrigue:** Have him tell your protagonist, "Be careful out there. Don't trust *anyone*." Readers will immediately suspect this guy is the traitor.
- **Comedy/romance:** Have the protagonist suspect that her friend is her secret admirer but then decide that it couldn't possibly be him. The more certain she is that it's not him, the more suspicious your readers will become that it is.
- **Crime/mystery:** Have a person show up all too conveniently at the crime scene (perhaps to write about the murders for the newspaper ... or she's the doctor on call when all three victims' kidneys disappeared ... or he was the custodian cleaning the rep-

tile house when the cobras escaped). Keep him around but on the fringe of the story. Make him innocuous and helpful. The less suspicious you make someone appear, the more readers will think the person is guilty. Use that dynamic to your advantage.

34 THRILLER, MYSTERY, AND HORROR MOVIES (IN NO PARTICULAR ORDER) WITH TWISTS

1. *The Uninvited*
2. *The Book of Eli*
3. *The Others*
4. *The Spanish Prisoner*
5. *The Sixth Sense*
6. *The Prestige*
7. *The Illusionist*
8. *No Way Out*
9. *Sinister*
10. *Drag Me to Hell*
11. *Saw*
12. *Seven*
13. *The Game*
14. *Following*
15. *12 Monkeys*
16. *Gone Baby Gone*
17. *Arlington Road*
18. *Transsiberian*
19. *Blood Simple*
20. *Hard Candy*
21. *Matchstick Men*
22. *Best Laid Plans*
23. *Frequency*
24. *11:14*
25. *Running Scared*
26. *The Perfect Host*
27. *Runaway Jury*
28. *Vanilla Sky*
29. *Primal Fear*
30. *Memento*
31. *Nine Queens*
32. *Deathtrap*
33. *Across the Hall*
34. *The Hidden Face*

AVOID GIMMICKS

Readers want their emotional investment to pay off. The twist should never occur in a way that makes them feel tricked, deceived, or insulted. Great twists always deepen, never cheapen, readers' investment in the story.

This is why dream sequences typically don't work—the protagonist thinks she's in a terrible mess, then wakes up and realizes it was all just a dream. These aren't twists because they almost never escalate the story but often do the very opposite, revealing to readers that things weren't really that bad after all (de-escalation). Showing a character experiencing a harrowing or frightening experience and then having him wake up from a dream is not a twist, it's a tired cliché.

How do you solve this? Simply tell the reader it's a dream beforehand. It can be just as frightening without de-escalating the story's tension, and it can also end in a way that's not predictable.

Another common cliché: writing a scene from a victim's point of view.

A few years ago, someone recommended a book to me. From the back-cover copy, I knew that the story was about a group of rich people who hunt homeless vagrants living in New York City's underground tunnels and sewer systems.

So the book began from a homeless guy's point of view. The author starts the book by giving us the man's life story. I remember thinking, "If he just goes ahead and kills him off, with no twist or anything, I'm putting this book down." Guess what? No twist. Nothing. At the end of the prologue, the homeless man just got murdered by one of the rich people.

Wow. How clever. Didn't see that one coming.

I figured that if the author couldn't even pull off a prologue that didn't surprise me, he wasn't going to be able to pull off a whole novel that did, so I didn't entrust any more of my time to him.

There are five types of plot twists.

1. **Identity:** Your protagonist (or your reader, or both) realizes he's not who he thought he was: He's really the one who's insane, a robot, zombie, werewolf, ghost, clone, or character in someone else's dream, movie, or novel. This discovery could come at the

beginning of your story, setting it up for a redemptive ending, or at the climax, creating a dramatic plunge at the end of your novel.

2. **Awareness:** The world isn't what your protagonist thought it was: He's not on Earth, he's on another planet, or he thinks he's arrived in heaven in the afterlife but discovers he's really in hell.

3. **Complexity:** The heist, confidence game, or sting operation has a whole level of intrigue that wasn't evident throughout the story. (In this case, the protagonist knows something the bad guys and the readers don't. Curiosity about how things will move forward drives readers to keep reading.)

4. **Peril:** The real danger isn't where you thought it was: The hunter is really the hunted; the secret agent's partner is really a double agent; the protagonist's daughter is really the terrorist.

5. **Cleverness:** The detective (or villain) was really one step ahead of the villain (or detective) the whole time and has set a trap that the other guy, and readers, didn't see coming. (Remember: The detective must solve the crime before readers do, or they'll think they're smarter than he is.)

WRITE TOWARD YOUR READERS' REACTION

The way you want your readers to respond will determine the way you set up your twist. Three different types of twists all result in different reactions by readers: (1) "No way!" (2) "Huh. Nice!" and (3) "Oh, yeah!"

When aiming for the "No way!" response, you'll want to lead readers into *certainty*. You want them to think that there's only one possible solution to the story.

The more you can convince them that the story world you've portrayed is exactly as it appears to be—that only one outcome to the novel is possible—the more you'll make their jaws drop when you show them that things were not as they appeared to be at all. If the twist is satisfying, credible, and inevitable based on what has preceded it, readers will gasp and exclaim, "No way! That's awesome! I can't believe he got that one past me."

With the "Huh. Nice!" ending, you want to lead readers into *uncertainty*. Basically, they'll be thinking, "Man, I have no idea where this is going." When writing for this response, you'll create an unbalanced, uncertain world. You don't want readers to suspect only one person as the villain but many people. Only when the true villain is revealed will readers see that everything was pointing in that direction all along.

Finally, if you're shooting for the "Oh, yeah!" reaction, you'll want to emphasize the *cleverness* with which the main character gets out of the seemingly impossible-to-escape-from climax. Often we do that by allowing him to use a special gift, skill, or emblem that has been shown to readers earlier but that they aren't thinking about when they reach the climax. Then, when the protagonist pulls it out, readers remember: "Yes! That's right! He carries a can of shark repellent in his wetsuit! I forgot all about that!"

Relentlessly escalate your story while keeping it believable, surprising, and deeper than it appears.

Include the four elements of all plot twists—surprise, inevitability, escalation, and revelation.

1. Where do I need to shade the details and foreshadowing so the twist is the most credible, inevitable ending to my story?
2. What clues or evidence do I need to include to make the story stand on its own without the twist?
3. Is the story improved by the twist? In other words, is it richer and more meaningful? If not, how can I construct the twist so that it adds depth to the story?
4. How can I use this twist to both turn the story on its head and move it in a more satisfying direction?

Create multiple worlds of inevitability.

1. What do I need to change to create a more believable world for each separate twist I'm including?
2. How can I drop the gimmicks and depend more on the strength of the narrative to build my twist?
3. Will readers have to "put up with" the story that's being told in anticipation of a twist ending, or will they enjoy it even more because of the twist? How can I improve the pretwist story?
4. How can I make better use of the clues that prove the logic of the surface story to create the twist and bring more continuity to the story—but only after the twist is revealed?

Turn expectations on their head.

1. What expectations will readers (or editors/agents) have when they see the packaging of this book (or proposal)?
2. How can I use these expectations to lead readers down one road but then land them on another?
3. Can I have the protagonist make a moral choice at the end that both satisfies readers and surprises them?

Eliminate the obvious.

1. What are all the apparent solutions to the problem posed by the climax? List them. Then think of three more. List those. Then cross them out—they're off limits. Now what ideas present themselves?
2. Based on the protagonist's resources (mentors, tools, helpers, special abilities, etc.) how can I have her resolve the climax in a way that readers won't anticipate? Where do I need to remind readers about these resources?
3. Foreshadowing eliminates coincidence. What do I need to foreshadow to make this ending both inevitable and unexpected?

4. How can I foreshadow any help the protagonist receives on the way to the climactic conclusion and avoid a climax that relies on chance or coincidence?

Redirect suspicion.

1. How can I do a better job of burying the clues readers need to have in order to accept the ending? Where do I need to bring those clues to the surface?
2. How can I play expectations based on genre conventions against readers to get them to suspect the wrong person as the villain or antagonist?

Avoid gimmicks.

1. Will readers feel tricked, deceived, or insulted by this twist? If so, how can I better respect their ability to guess the ending of my story?
2. Have I inadvertently relied on clichés or on any plot turning points that have appeared in other books or movies? How can I recast the story so it's fresh and original?

Write toward your readers' reaction.

1. If I want to shock readers with the twist, have I led them into certainty as they try to predict the ending?
2. If I want readers to suspect a number of different endings, have I satisfactorily built up all the potential outcomes?
3. If I want readers to cheer at the ending, have I (1) created a seemingly impossible situation for the protagonist to escape from or conquer or (2) allowed the protagonist to persevere through wit or grit rather than with the help of someone else (that is, *deus ex machina*)?

At a writers conference, a woman asked me, "What is the absolute worst place to end my book?"

I had to think for a moment. It seemed like she was looking for something specific for her story, which I wasn't familiar with. I really didn't know what to say. Finally, a thought struck me and I said, "Before you've kept all your promises."

I wasn't sure where that answer came from, but I liked it.

When I said it to her, she looked at me in bewilderment, and over the years I've seen that same look from others when I start talking about making and breaking narrative promises. I've come to believe that it's a vital aspect of storytelling, and it surprises me that writing instructors don't spend more time covering it.

Well, let's not make that same mistake.

Flip the page for a detailed look at promises and payoff and how they affect a story's pace and suspense.

CHAPTER 11

PROMISES

The Keys to Building Suspense and Satisfying Your Readers

Stories are built on promises.

If you start a story by showing a grandmother raising a teenage girl who loves her and they're both happy and satisfied and at peace, you've made a promise to readers: Something is going to go wrong and disrupt their lives.

Perhaps the girl will get addicted to drugs or run away, or the grandmother will lose her source of income and that will send them reeling into poverty or homelessness. Whatever it is, something will throw things out of balance. But because of the Ceiling Fan Principle, if you drag the story on too long before keeping the promise you've made by setting things up the way you did, readers will get bored and annoyed.

Remember: The start of your story will set up the overarching promise of the book—will your protagonist have what she desires at the start, lose it, and try to find it again? Will she see it from a distance and pursue it? Or will she be forced to escape what she dreads most?

One of those three scenarios will launch your story and initiate the promises that will guide it.

Foreshadowing is the process of dropping clues in the background to remove coincidences later on. Promise-making is the process of openly telling your readers what's coming or indicating clearly, by the context, what's going to be significant in the story that follows.

You have to let readers know they can trust you. How?

By keeping your promises.

Every word you write about someone is a promise to readers about his significance to the story. If you lure readers into investing their emotions and time into a character who ends up having no other significance to the tale than dying off, you've made readers invest in something meaningless and they won't be happy about it.

Remember narrative weight from Chapter 7? The length of your scenes, the number of words you use to describe a character or an object or a setting, are all in direct proportion to readers' expectations about how important that person, place, or thing will be to the story.

As Renni Browne and Dave King write in *Self-Editing for Fiction Writers*, "However your proportion problems may arise, the most serious effect they can have on your writing is to mislead the reader."

It's a matter of trust. And you'll lose that when you start breaking your promises.

KEEP UP YOUR END OF THE DEAL

Think of your story as a contract with your readers, an agreement that you're going to entertain them, surprise them, satisfy them, and not waste their time.

During the first part of your story, you'll show them the threads that will make up the narrative, and then you'll draw them taut and tie them off at the end.

The more promises you break, the less readers will trust you. And often, when readers put a book down before reaching the end, that's exactly why—they've stopped trusting that the author is going to fulfill the promises he's made.

So how do you fail to fulfill this contract? How do you break promises to your readers?

1. Indicate (by the context, description, or number of words) that something will be important, and then fail to make it significant.
2. Develop conflict, and then don't resolve it in a satisfactory way.
3. Have your characters act in unbelievable ways.
4. Build up a character toward an internal transformation (putty person), and end without letting him have one (staying a pebble person instead).
5. Resolve too much tension too early.
6. Introduce a character, make readers care about her, and then drop her from the story.

The more you tell readers about a character, the more you're promising that he's significant. You break your promise when you (1) never refer to him again, (2) give him a tiny role after setting him up to have a major one, or (3) do the classic share-the-story-of-the-victim's-entire-life-and-then-have-him-get-killed-off-by-the-end-of-the-chapter routine I mentioned earlier in regard to the story with the homeless man.

Just by writing a story, you're promising that it will be believable, it will have escalation, and the events will matter in the life of the protagonist.

The longer and the harder the struggle, the more important it is to keep the promise that there will be some sort of resolution. Once again, the length of every scene is a promise to readers of what is really important to your story. The more time you give something, the more readers will expect it to matter.

What about red herrings—characters or clues in mysteries that are there to throw the reader off track?

Well, if readers end up being thankful for the red herrings, you've succeeded. If they're annoyed and think you didn't keep your promises to them, you've failed.

> Every choice that your characters make has an implication. Every goal they pursue is a promise that some type of resolution will follow. In the end, everything that matters needs to have been promised and every significant promise needs to be fulfilled.

TOO GOOD TO BE TRUE

Just as with everything else, descriptions become promises to readers. Since readers know that something has to go wrong in a story, the more you tell them that a character is good, the less they will believe you.

> "He's the sweetest guy *in the universe*. I mean, he gave me this necklace and he told me how much *he loves me* and we're going out again next week and—I just can't believe how *perfect* he is!"

Readers will immediately suspect that this sweet, perfect, loving guy has ulterior motives. They'll guess that he has some hidden agenda or isn't at all what he appears to be. If he really is as good as you tell readers he is, it might end up feeling like you broke a promise to them.

Remember when the queen in *Hamlet* said, "The lady doth protest too much, methinks"? Well, readers are just as perceptive as that queen was. They know that characters in fiction who are exactly as they appear are cardboard. There's no dimensionality to them. If a character is significant, he will have depth. So the more you tell us how guilty someone looks, the less readers will think he's guilty. The more perfectly happy you make someone appear, the more readers will look for cracks beneath that surface happiness.

The more conflict you include in a scene, the more of a promise you're making that you'll resolve it one way or another, and the more vital it is to have an interlude between it and another scene or action sequence. (More on this in Chapter 12.)

Remember, the bigger the promise, the bigger the payoff. The ultimate payoff is the climax. It's a culmination of all that happens before it. The biggest promise will be made first and fulfilled last. This deals with the central and overriding struggle of your protagonist.

WRITE FROM THE CENTER OF THE PARADOX

Since story events are causally related, each scene is linked to what precedes it and what follows it. Change one stitch in the fabric and you affect every other stitch from there on out, and even the ones you've already stitched and thought were completed may need to be rethreaded.

You cannot know where a story needs to go until you know where it's been, but you cannot know all the places it needs to have been until you know where it's going.

It's a paradox.

And that's part of the fun.

As you work on your book, you'll necessarily have to examine your scenes from both sides—looking at what has caused them and what they are causing. The promises and the payoff, the origins and resolutions of conflict.

As you pay attention to the choices your characters make and you honestly let the implications of their choices transpire on the page, you'll find yourself writing your book forward and backward at the same time, making and keeping promises, weaving in facets of your genre while being informed by the narrative forces that help shape all stories so you can create your work intuitively rather than mechanically.

THE FOUR *R*S

One day I was brainstorming ways that stories flow from conflict to resolution, and I was in an *r* mood (just count the *r* words; you'll see what I mean). I got a little carried away, so take this with a grain of salt, but here are some types of struggles and desires you might think of examining as you work out the forward movement of your story.

1. **Rescue**
- What was lost is recovered.
- What was endangered is protected.
- What was destroyed is rebuilt.
- What was sought is found.

2. **Redemption**
- What was ruined is renewed.
- What was wrecked is repaired.
- What was imprisoned is set free.
- What was dead is reborn.

3. **Revelation**
- What was hidden is revealed.
- What was unknown is discovered.
- What was questioned is answered.
- What was forgotten is remembered.

4. **Reformation**
- What was accepted as the norm is reversed.
- What was unjust is avenged.
- What was wrong is redressed.
- What was overlooked is acknowledged.

SECRETS TO DEVELOPING SUSPENSE

To create suspense, put characters who readers care about in jeopardy.

Four factors are necessary for suspense to occur: reader empathy, reader concern, impending danger, and escalating tension.

As we discussed earlier, writers create reader empathy by giving the character a desire, wound, or internal struggle that readers can identify with. The more readers empathize, the closer and more intimate their emotional connection with the story. Once they care about and identify with a character, they'll be concerned when they see the character struggling to get what he desires most.

We want readers to worry about whether or not the character will get what he wants. Only when they know what the character wants will they know what's at stake, and only when they know what's at stake will they be engaged in the story.

So in every scene you'll need to clarify what a character desires in that scene and perhaps remind readers what he wants from the overarching story as a whole.

Readers experience apprehension when a character they care about is in peril. This doesn't have to be a life-and-death situation. Suspense builds as danger approaches. Depending on your genre, the threat may involve the character's physical, psychological, emotional, spiritual, or relational well-being.

Whatever your genre is, when you show that something terrible is about to happen and then postpone the resolution, you sustain the suspense. Often you can do this by letting readers know something that the characters in the story don't know. For example:

1. Slowly, the bride walks down the aisle, but readers already know that the groom is second-guessing himself. Will he leave her standing at the altar? Draw out the tension with every step she takes as she nears the front of the church.
2. The arsonist thinks the house is empty, but he doesn't know about the eight-year-old girl sleeping upstairs. He splashes the gasoline around the living room, onto the drapes, and on the staircase, and then pulls out a match. He lights it and flicks it onto the gasoline-drenched carpet. He slips outside as flames rage through the room, while upstairs, the girl snuggles up with her teddy bear and rolls over in her sleep.

> To get readers more invested in your novel, clarify (1) what your character desires (love, freedom, adventure, forgiveness, etc.), (2) what's keeping him from getting it, and (3) what terrible consequences will result if he doesn't get it.

We need to escalate the tension in our stories until we reach that satisfying climax. If tension doesn't escalate, the suspense we've been developing will evaporate.

Creating anxiety is like inflating a balloon—you can't let the air out of your story. Instead you keep blowing in more air, tightening the tension until it looks like the balloon is going to pop at any second.

Then add more tension.

And more.

Until readers can hardly stand it.

Incidentally, this is one reason why adding sex scenes to your story is actually counterproductive to building suspense. By releasing all the romantic or sexual tension you've been building, you let air out of the balloon. If you want to titillate, add sex. If you want to build suspense, postpone it.

Apprehension happens in the stillness of your story, in the gaps between the action sequences, in the moments between the promise of something dreadful and its arrival.

Since suspense happens in the space between when the promise is made and when it is kept, suspense-filled stories often require more pages than stories of other genres.

When you write action sequences without promises built in between them, this creates a progression of events that will eventually wear readers out. Readers need the breaks between action sequences to (1) reorient them to what is at stake, (2) remind them what the characters want, (3) keep promises that were made earlier, and (4) make escalating promises that will drive the narrative forward.

When I started my fourth novel, I began with the goal of letting the entire story span only fifty-two hours. I thought that by packing everything into a tight time frame I'd really be able to make the story suspenseful.

Yes, I was trying to use a predetermined, artificial construct.

And as you've probably guessed, my plan didn't turn out very well.

As I worked on the book, I realized that so much needed to happen to build to the climax that if I kept to my fifty-two hour time frame, events would simply occur one after another so quickly that there wouldn't be space for either suspense or romance to realistically develop.

Finally, I added another twenty-four hours to create the opportunity for the promises and payoffs that allowed the story to be suspenseful and also give me the time to believably develop the romance storyline.

Listening to the story saved that novel from becoming a relentless recounting of events.

> Anticipation keeps readers interested, so to draw them into your story, include less action and more promises.

Contrary to what you may have heard, the problem of readers being bored isn't solved by adding *action* but by adding *apprehension*.

Suspense is more about creating worry and anticipation than it is about adding more action sequences.

When readers are bored with a book or when they complain that "nothing's happening," they don't usually mean that nothing is *occurring* but rather that nothing is being promised. Things aren't happening for a good reason—it's just activity without unmet desire driving it forward. The story isn't escalating.

We solve this problem not by adding more action but by making more urgent promises. So we don't increase suspense by "making things happen" but by promising that they will.

Related to this, when readers say, "This story doesn't make sense," they don't necessarily mean that the story is nonsensical or incomprehensible but rather that they don't see the protagonist taking natural, logical steps to solve her struggles.

We fix this by making sure causality and believability are shaping every scene as the characters make choices and take actions to fulfill their unmet desires.

> Since everything in a story points toward the climax, the story's core is not so much "things occurring" as it is the anticipation of those things approaching.
>
> Typically, readers don't get bored because too little is happening but because too little is being promised.

Depending on your genre, promises can be comedic, romantic, horrific, or dramatic, but all stories are built on promises. Either readers can see that something bad is about to happen, or something bad is happening and they can anticipate that it's going to get worse.

For example, two lovers make plans to meet near the stream to elope. That's a promise to readers.

But the young man's rival for the woman's affection has found out and says to himself, "If I can't have her, no one can." He plots to kill her, then heads to the stream and hides behind a tree, waiting for them, dagger drawn.

The lovers arrive, clueless about the danger. They laugh in the moonlight, walking hand in hand along the edge of the stream. They reach the tree where the would-be assassin is waiting. The woman leans her back against it, closes her eyes for a kiss, and then ...

Well, after you make the most of that moment, of the suspense it offers, you better show readers what happens beside that stream.

They don't just want the anticipation, they want the payoff.

KEEP EVERY PROMISE YOU MAKE

Keeping your promises is just as important as making them. The bigger the promise is, the bigger the payoff needs to be.

As we've discussed, in a very real sense, every word in your story is a promise to readers about the significance of that word to the story as a whole. This is where so many authors fumble the ball.

If you spend three paragraphs describing an apartment complex, that building better be vital to the story. If not, you're essentially telling readers, "Oh, by the way, I wasted your time. Yeah, that wasn't important after all. Ha, ha, ha. Didn't I show you?"

Never disrespect your readers like that.

Keep your promises. Build on them. And set up the climax by making more promises or sharpening the ones you've made earlier.

For example, in one of my novels I had the killer tell a woman whom he'd abducted, "Your death will be remembered for decades."

That's a huge promise to readers. I'd better fulfill it by making her death memorable or incredibly terrifying, or else readers will be dissatisfied. In another book I had a character tell the hero that the villain had "a twist waiting for you at the end that you would never expect." Another huge promise. Readers will be thinking, "Okay, buddy. Let's see if you can pull that off."

That's what you want: engaged readers looking forward to fulfilled promises.

Then you'd better step up to the plate and give them what they want.

A promise without fulfillment will always end up disappointing readers.

Make big promises.

Then keep them.

When stories falter it's often because the writers (1) didn't make big enough promises, (2) didn't fulfill them when readers wanted them to be fulfilled, or (3) broke their promises by never fulfilling them at all.

HONING YOUR PROMISES

Let the characters tell readers their plans.

I know, this sounds counterintuitive. Why would we want readers to know what's going to happen? Doesn't that give the ending away?

I'm not talking here about revealing your secrets or letting readers know the twists your story has in store for them. Instead, show them the agenda, and you'll be making a promise that either something will go wrong to disrupt the schedule or the plans will fall into place in a way that drives the story (and the tension) forward in a new direction.

Simply by having your characters tell readers their schedule, you offer a promise that can create anticipation and build suspense.

1. "I'm going to head over to the office to grab my briefcase."
2. "We're planning to meet at Rialto's for supper at eight."
3. "All right, here's what I have lined up for the rest of the morning: Follow up on the fingerprints, track down Barry, and then stop by the prison and have a little chat with Donnie 'The Midnight Slayer' Jackson."

When characters make promises to each other, they also serve as promises to your readers.

1. "I'll see you at the four o'clock briefing."
2. "I promise I'll be waiting for you at the airport when you arrive."
3. "I'll return that necklace to you tomorrow at school."

With these small promises you've dialed in reader expectations and created a rudimentary form of suspense. Readers also know that, given the fact that stories are driven forward by setbacks, something will likely go wrong that'll alter or hinder those plans.

Another way to make promises: Let characters state consequences if their plans don't come together.

1. "If my wife finds out I've been drinking again, I can guarantee you she's going to leave me."
2. "If I don't pass next week's American lit exam, I'm screwed. My dad's gonna make me drop out of basketball."
3. "I know how much this job means to you, but if we can't get some resolution on this thing, I'm going to have to let you go. You know that, right?"

In each case readers know the stakes, and they can anticipate the consequences of the character having to face them.

What promise would be made by beginning a story showing a lonely housewife? A novice lawyer? A series of suspicious deaths at the hospital?

What about the events in *your* story? What promises are you making by starting it where you do, escalating it the way you are, and introducing the characters you have?

To summarize, making promises that matter and then keeping them at the moment in the story when readers expect them to be kept are two keys to great storytelling.

If we make promises and don't keep them, readers will feel frustrated. If we drag out a story after all the promises have been kept, readers will get bored.

So the timing of the payoff needs to fit the readers' expectations of what's coming based on the promises made and the narrative weight of scenes they've already read.

As you analyze your story, ask yourself about those promises: Are they big enough? Have you kept them in ways that surprise readers and still please them? Have you done so at a time and in a way that will make readers clamor for your next book?

So Lakeesha is on her way to college. Based on the context and the story's flow from previous chapters, what nagging questions will readers have? What are they worrying about? What promises have I made about her trip there? Is there a way I can sharpen and clarify them so readers can be more tuned in to what Lakeesha wants and what will happen if she doesn't get it?

Put characters with whom readers identify in peril, make (and keep) promises that create apprehension, show readers what's coming so they can worry about the consequences, continually tighten the tension, and relentlessly escalate to your climax. Do this, and you'll sharpen the suspense, snag readers, and envelop them in your story.

CHAPTER 12

SCENES

Mastering Setbacks, Interludes, and Subtext

A scene is not the same as a chapter. A scene might occur over several chapters, or each chapter might include more than one scene.

A scene is not something that happens in one specific location. A scene might span several locations, and one location might include several scenes.

So what is a scene exactly?

A scene happens when an important aspect of a story is altered. And just like the story as a whole, each scene ends in that unexpected but inevitable way I keep referring to. Something is disrupted, and things don't go as planned. If all goes according to plan—and *exactly* as planned—you have a sequence of events that might be the precursor to a scene, but it's not yet a scene.

Scenes and acts are all mini-stories, but rather than end with closure, they end with a complication that propels the story forward. Stories are not simply sequences of events, and neither are scenes. As you recall, stories include an orientation, a calling or crisis event, escalation of conflict, a choice that leads to a discovery, and a new normal. Scenes do as well.

And so, novels are built scene by escalating scene into cohesive, unified wholes.

PROCESSING OUR STRUGGLES

My friend is a carpenter who creates beautiful, artistic woodwork projects that are functional pieces of art. He often does this without nails, simply by using a special wood glue to hold the pieces together. The merging from one piece of wood to the next is seamless. You don't even notice the change.

If the beautiful pieces of wood are scenes, the adhesive that holds them together are interludes.

A story moves through action sequences to moments of reorientation (I call them interludes) when the characters process what just happened and then make a decision that leads to the next scene. We do this in real life as well—we experience something moving or painful or profound or traumatic, we process it, and then we decide how to respond.

A friend dies; we grieve.

We get laid off; we regroup, pick up the pieces, and try to figure out what happens next.

The grief, the regrouping, the processing of emotions aren't just breaks in the action of our lives, they're essential moments to work through the conflict and setbacks, evaluate the feelings related to them, and make a decision that moves our own personal story logically forward.

The choice might be to retreat into denial or distract ourselves from the pain or disappointment, or it might be the decision to pull ourselves up by the bootstraps and move on.

If a story doesn't include that interlude of reorientation after something significant in that scene is altered, it won't strike readers as true or honest about human nature.

During those moments of reflection, a story can drag and the suspense can be lost, so remember that during every interlude between scenes a promise will either be made or kept.

WHEN TO RENDER,
WHEN TO SUMMARIZE

Scenes need to tilt. If nothing is altered in a scene, summarize it. If something is altered, render it.

For example, I was reading one book about some genetically engineered people-creatures who chase a woman into a laundromat. When she enters it, she starts thinking, "Should I leave or stay here? If I stay here, they might trap me, but if I leave, they might catch me outside. Where am I safest?"

She debates this for several pages, musing about the consequences of each choice, and finally decides to stay in the laundromat. When I was reading the book, I was frustrated that I'd wasted the time reading those pages of internal debate when nothing was altered.

This is an instance where it would have been better not to render the scene but simply to summarize it: "She entered the laundromat and after a few moments of deliberation decided to hide there until morning."

Again, when nothing is altered in a scene, summarize it.

When something is altered, render it.

What can be altered in a scene?

1. Status (the balance of dominance or submission)
2. Stakes
3. Safety
4. Attitude or perspective
5. Relationships
6. Secrets (revealed or concealed)
7. Physical condition

> Scenes are not about events, locations, or discussions. They are about things being altered.

Your protagonist will fail to get what he desires most in every scene except for the final, climactic one. This isn't to say that if he goes into the store to buy a bag of tortilla chips that he won't be able to get them, but if he simply buys them and then leaves the store, (1) the scene would need to be about something *else* being altered, (2) purchasing the chips has to escalate the tension somehow and make it harder for him to get what he desires most, or (3) the subtext needs to embody the truer, deeper meaning of the scene.

If you allow your character to find resolution before the climax of your story, readers will lose interest. Remember that a story is about a character who wants something but cannot get it. Whether it's stopping a terrorist, saving his marriage, or discovering the meaning of life, he'll be striving to resolve this crisis as the story progresses. And he won't achieve his objective (or ultimately fail in his attempt to do so) until the end of the story.

In other words, he never fulfills his deepest desire (that is, gets what he wants most in relation to his internal, external, and interpersonal struggles) until the last scene.

I've heard several other authors refer to this process as one in which the protagonist "fails his way to success." I like that phrase.

So the majority of a story is about how a character is failing his way through escalating setbacks and struggles until all seems lost, and then, at the climax, he overcomes or is overcome by the struggle.

For example, the detective chases the villain through the streets but doesn't catch him. Frustrated, she goes back to her house, and while she's taking off her shoes, she rubs her feet and remembers the chase.

While doing so, she realizes that the villain was limping as he ran. That motivates her to drive across town and accuse her friend, who recently sprained his ankle, of the crime.

Her friend is angry and shows her that he's limping on the left leg rather than the right one. He's so offended that she would accuse him of the terrible crime that he says he never wants to see her again. He slams the door in her face, and she returns home, dejected.

There are three scenes in this plot summary: the chase scene, the short scene in the house, and the detective's encounter with her friend. The house scene contains an interlude as our protagonist processes what just happened and makes a decision that leads to the next scene.

This interlude between the two other scenes serves as a transition but also reorients the character and the readers to the new state of affairs in the story and the specific goal of the next scene. Her choice then moves the story forward.

Notice how the detective fails in both the chase scene and the encounter with her friend and how those failures serve to escalate the tension of the story, making things worse and worse: Not only does she fail to catch the killer, but now she has lost her friend.

However, each of these failures also serves as a step toward her eventual success because now she knows two things she did not know earlier: (1) the villain limps, and (2) her friend is not the villain (unless of course he's faking his limp as a red herring).

Things are getting worse for her.

But also, in a sense, getting better.

Why?

Because these failures propel the narrative forward.

As Carolyn Wheat notes in *How to Write Killer Fiction*, "A character wants something, something concrete in the here-and-now. Will he get it? There are four possible outcomes: 'Yes,' 'No,' 'No, and furthermore,' and 'Yes, but.' The first two outcomes *do absolutely nothing to move the plot.* [emphasis in the original]"

If the answer is "Yes" and the character gets what he wants, you don't have a story, you have an event—the detective catches the killer. The end.

If the answer is "No," the story goes nowhere. It's over. Done. She fails to catch the killer and ... well ... nothing. The end.

If the answer is "No, and furthermore," you have escalation of an existing struggle. That's good. In the scenes in our example, the detective doesn't catch the killer, and guess what? Now she has lost her friend as well.

If the answer is "Yes, but," you have the introduction of a new struggle. In this case, she might have caught the killer during that chase scene but then he announces that he has buried someone alive and will only tell where the person is if the charges against him are dropped. Things have just gotten much, much worse.

There is one other way to move the story forward.

Sometimes characters will find something that adds intrigue, deepens the suspense, or makes a promise that will be important to the rest of the story. For example, remember Ruth and Naomi from earlier? When Naomi sent Ruth to the field to find grain, she met up with Boaz and that set the rest of the story into motion. Her meeting was a promise that ended up being significant to the story.

So your character might find a clue, uncover something vital, solve a coded message, and so on. When you reach a dead end, remember to use "No, and furthermore" and "Yes, but" and to ask, "How can I take things deeper?"

PROCESSING EMOTIONS

Just as the number of acts will differ with each story, so the number of scenes in an act will vary depending on the narrative weight of the acts, the flow of the story, and the progression of the narrative.

What's the difference between a scene and an act?

An act is a series of scenes that builds to a climax greater than that of any of the scenes. Each act serves to escalate the story as a whole.

Remember how stories begin with an orientation to the world of that story? Well, so do scenes. Interludes allow you to reorient the story characters and the readers to get ready for the next scene. During the interlude you might have two characters process what just happened.

1. "So where are we at with the case?'"
2. "How did that talk with your dad go last night?"
3. "Fill me in. What do we know?"
4. "Okay, so what was all that about?"

In his book *Scene & Structure*, Jack M. Bickham does a good job of describing this processing of events that happens during an interlude (which he calls a "sequel." See Chapter 7: "Linking Your Scene: The Structure of Sequel" for detailed ideas on how to handle these sections).

> As you create scenes and build your story, ask what's at stake. Try to answer why it's imperative that the character achieves what he has set out to achieve in each scene.
>
> Remember, readers want to worry about your protagonist, and they only do that when: (1) they care about him and (2) they know what he wants.

Contrary to what some writing instructors teach, the interlude might happen internally, that is, solely within the thoughts of a character.

Fiction writers have the inner world of the characters at our disposal. So scenes in novels don't need to be entirely external, action oriented, or visible to the story characters and to the reader, as if they were happening on the stage of a play. Interludes can include the internal reflection that reorients readers, and story characters, to the world of the story in preparation for the next scene.

Scenes can be processed through the character's thoughts, through dialogue, or through actions that express that character's feelings. After all, thoughts can motivate us to act just as much as external events can.

Action, emotion, and thoughts all intertwine in a story just as they do in real life. And they all affect each other—actions cause us to think and feel; feelings cause us to think and act; thoughts cause us to act and feel. Don't discount any of these and their relationships to each other as you develop your scenes and interludes.

Look for ways your characters can physically express their feelings. Avoid having them simply emote on the page.

So Jeremy's son runs away. That makes him angry and hurt and afraid. He tries to find his son but fails. Rather than focusing on explaining how he feels, how can I show what's going on inside of him by what's going on outside of him, through how he acts? How can I externalize his feelings—as raw and real as they are— by showing the way he responds to other characters, objects nearby him, and his environment? What will he do now? What actions will he take?

In each scene the protagonist will move from goal to setback(s) to a decision that drives things forward. Your character will seek something, fail in a way that makes things worse, process what just happened, and then proceed into the next scene of the story.

Four steps: seek, fail, process, proceed.

As the character responds naturally and believably to the setback, choosing a course that he thinks will lead him closer to the goal or objective of the story (what he believes will ultimately bring him happiness) or farther from the danger pursuing him, the scene develops and then progresses.

This is how stories move forward. Remember, for readers to know what the scene is about, they need to know what the character's goal is— his driving, unmet desire. So constantly ask yourself—what does this character want? What will happen if she doesn't get it? How far is she willing to go to get what she desires?

A character in conflict will feel emotion. When readers identify with that character, they'll feel that emotion as well. The more they identify with the struggle of the character, the more they'll be impacted by his transformation.

So each scene should show this process—development or portrayal of the character's desire, a struggle that ensues as he tries to achieve it, and, finally, a crisis or setback that interferes with him achieving that goal. If your scene ends with resolution, it'll need to introduce a new conflict before the chapter or section break.

Seek, fail, process, proceed.

And each scene will contribute to the transformation of the protagonist, the escalation of the plot, or the deepening of the story's internal, external, or interpersonal struggles.

> So we're at the castle, the fight scene is over, and the king is meeting with his advisors. Does this scene have an ending that drives the story forward or one that just falls flat? Is something meaningful altered, and if not, how do I need to change things around to fix it—or do I need to drop this scene altogether? How does my character seek, fail, process, and proceed?

DEFINING THE GOAL

The flow of a story is closely related to the narrative forces of believability and motivation, so our characters need to have clearly defined goals in each scene.

Genre, the importance of the scene to the overall plot, and the narrative weight of the scene dictate the length of the interlude following it.

For example, in a techno-thriller, the characters might regroup, quickly review where they're at in their pursuit of the terrorists, and then immediately move into position to go after them with a new strategy. The genre dictates that things move swiftly.

However, in a relationship-centered story, the emotional processing will take a lot more space: She had a good time on the date, and the next day she tries to decide if she should call the guy—if she does, she might seem too forward, but if she doesn't, he might think she's not interested. What should she do? This deliberation serves as the interlude and may go on for some time. Readers in this genre expect this.

Usually, the more time you've spent making a promise, the more time it'll take to process the emotions after that scene or act. Since acts contain the closure of a number of scenes, they will usually require a longer interlude.

Think about your genre and your readers' expectations about how much processing will be needed throughout the novel to weave together the scenes and acts that build the story.

Just as we won't know what the story as a whole is about until we know what the character wants to achieve, obtain, or accomplish, we won't know what the scene is about until we know what the character wants in that scene.

The clearer the goal, the more readers will be able to worry about whether the character gets it.

How do we clarify that to readers?

Here are six ways.

1. **Have the character state what he wants.**
   - "I'm here to find out everything I can about the murder."
   - "I just wish I could convince her that I forgive her."
   - "Come to London, honey. I want to spend time with you."
2. **Indicate it indirectly.**
   - "Man, am I hungry. When are we gonna eat?" (In essence he's saying, "I want to eat.")

- "So this device, are you going to tell me what it's for or not?" (In essence: "I want to know what this device is for.")
- "I'm going to stop praying for healing. God's not answering my prayers." (In essence: "I want to be healed, and I'm frustrated that God hasn't healed me.")

3. **Have another character ask the person what he wants.**
   - "What are you doing here? What is it you want from me, anyway?"
   - "I'm not sure I understand what you're saying. What is it, precisely, that you're asking me to do?"
   - "So why are you going to visit the warehouse? What do you hope to find there?"

4. **Reveal what the character wants through his thoughts.**
   - *Easy, now. Be calm. Once you get past security you'll be home free.*
   - *I swear to God I'll get revenge.*
   - *Focus. Just two more sutures and you're done.*

5. **Simply tell readers.**
   - Jacob wanted to save Monica no matter what, and he was going to do whatever it took to find her kidnappers.
   - He went to the house for one reason: to get the $5,000 David owed him.
   - She desired him. And as she fantasized about spending another night with him, she felt her heart race with wild, unbridled anticipation.

6. **Show readers the goal through the character's actions.**
   - He threw the car into reverse, punched the gas, and rocketed out of the parking lot.
   - She dug her phone out of her purse and stared at it for a long time. No messages. She checked to confirm that the ringer was turned on. It was. Finally, with a sigh, she slipped it back into her pocket.

- Jamaal narrowed his eyes, handed the basketball to the older boy, and said, "Alright. Bring it on."

We are a desire-driven species. Even if we don't know exactly *why* we do the things we do, something motivates our actions. Our interactions with other people are always influenced by these desires. Characterization is revealed as a person pursues the things he wants.

All of this means that you won't use a "scene" simply for characterization, that is, to show what a character is like, as some writing instructors will suggest. Without a setback or complication in the story, you will quickly lose your readers.

And you won't use dialogue simply as a means of exposition, as all too many novelists end up doing. Usually when this happens, a writer has realized he needs to get a certain amount of information to his readers. He doesn't want to just dump it into the story, so he decides he'll slip it in by adding a "scene" of having two characters discussing it.

You'll be tempted to do this. Trust me, you will. Resist the urge. Info-dumping will stall out your story, bore readers, and weaken the narrative.

> A problem that can be solved with one action isn't a struggle. A conflict that can be resolved with one choice isn't a story. Don't try to make it into a scene. Don't try to force it into bearing the weight that only a transformative moment can bear.

RATCHETING UP YOUR CHAPTER ENDINGS

Use the end of your chapters as places to turbo-boost your story's forward movement. Don't think of chapter endings as places to let readers pause and relax or places to put on the brakes. Think of them instead as places where you hit the gas to accelerate the narrative.

Since we want readers to stay in the world of our stories, we don't want to give them any reason to put our novels down. So rather than providing resolution at the end of a chapter, we insert a revelation, choice, conflict, or action that will motivate the reader to flip to the next chapter. For the most part, I prefer short chapters in the novels I write and read. I believe it helps with the pace. Also, readers will see that the chapter ends in a few pages and will think, "I'll set the book down then." But they don't realize that I'm doing all I can to make them decide to go ahead and read one more chapter.

And then one more.

And, oh look, the next one's not too long. I guess I'll read that, too.

That's how you keep people up all night.

So end your chapters and section breaks with forward movement rather than moments of resolution.

And please don't end your chapters with The Big Problem That Turns Out To Be Not Such A Big Thing After All or the teaser that just ends up being annoying: "He heard footsteps and spun around, gun in hand. A person stepped out of the shadows."

End chapter.

And the next one begins, "It was his daughter."

No. Don't do that. It de-escalates the story and will annoy readers.

But if you wrote it like this, they would definitely keep reading.

> He heard footsteps and spun around, gun in hand. A person stepped out of the shadows.
> He fired and heard a body drop to the ground.
> In the dim light, he edged forward to see if it was the kidnapper.
> But it wasn't.
> It was his daughter.

End chapter.

Yeah, now you've got your readers right where you want them.

When looking at your chapter breaks and the length of your chapters, ask yourself:

- Does this chapter break serve to move the story forward?
- Does it deepen the tension or include too much resolution?
- Is this chapter's length appropriate for its placement in the book, considering the context and pace at this moment of the story?

The impetus for moving to a new chapter (or even a scene) may be caused by an event, a choice, an interruption, or a revelation, but don't overuse any of them. Especially avoid the most common ways of ending a scene and moving on to another one: Someone shows up at the door, a phone rings, a text message comes in, or another person interrupts the conversation.

MINING THE DEPTHS OF SUBTEXT

Dialogue is a lot more than what people say.

The story that readers experience is more than the text you write.

If your scene appears to be about two people carrying on a conversation about chicken fajitas, it might actually be (and nearly always is) about something deeper. The truth of the scene often lies beneath what is said and even beneath what is done.

Subtext is the substrata of your story.

Maybe the chicken fajita discussion is really about how the two people talking are vying for power. Or trying to impress each other. Or each guy is trying to control the other, or intimidate him, or flatter him, or take revenge on him, or negotiate a deal.

That's subtext.

So whenever two characters are carrying on a conversation, ask yourself:

- What does each character want out of this discussion? Why can't he get it? How will he try to get it?

- How can I show this goal to readers through language choice, body language, posture, action, and reaction?
- Is this the appropriate amount of subtext for this scene and this genre?
- How does his status in this situation influence the story? (More on status in Chapter 21.)

Sometimes subtext becomes a distraction and can get in the way of the story. Genre and context dictate how much subtext each scene will contain. A horror story, thriller, action adventure, or comedy may have very little subtext, but a drama, romance, coming-of-age story, or self-realization story will often have deeper subtext. In those cases, what readers see on the page is only a window into what's really going on between the lines.

Scenes in which you're showing romantic tension are the most common places for subtext to appear.

- He has his arms around her, but he's not just helping her with her golf swing.
- She isn't just at the art gallery to look at the paintings; she's really visiting to get the attention of that cute security guard who works there. When she asks him about the Renoir, she doesn't really care about the painting as much as she does about getting and keeping his attention.

In film, actors can show tension and subtext through facial expressions, glances, gestures, and so on to convey what novelists have to express through writing—but we have to be careful not to get bogged down with too much description, or the story will suffer.

We need to express as much meaning as possible in as few words as we can.

Take the following bit of dialogue for example.

"I saw you at the game."

"Yeah, I was there."

"I thought you were going to be at—"

"I was. My priorities changed."

Now, reread the dialogue with the following substrata of the story in mind.

1. The first speaker is a father who's talking to his teenage son. He's upset at his boy for not being at home cleaning his room. His son is defiant.
2. The first speaker is a college-age guy, and the second is a young lady he wants to ask out. They're both flirting with each other.
3. The first speaker is a mob boss, the second an assassin who has been hired to kill him.
4. The first speaker is a woman, and she's talking to her estranged husband with whom she's trying to reestablish a relationship. First, imagine that he doesn't want to get back together with her, and then reread the dialogue again, imagining that he does.

See? The subtext could carry the tone of defiance, flirtation, menace, forgiveness, and more. And that's all from only four lines of dialogue. When the context and backstory are clear to your readers, they'll catch hold of the subtext and take away more from a scene than the words you've used to cast it.

Remember, in a scene, a character is trying to accomplish something, not just explain something. Readers need to know what's at stake if the character doesn't get what he wants. How will he suffer? What will he lose? How will he be set back in his pursuit of happiness? The more that's at stake for a character, the more readers will be engaged in the story.

CREATING MUTUALLY EXCLUSIVE GOALS

Scenes can often be strengthened (1) when the two people carrying on the conversation desire different things, specifically objectives that are in conflict with each other, or (2) when they desire the same thing but must work together to overcome something that's currently keeping them both from accomplishing it.

If you and I are playing a game of chess, my success depends on your failure and vice versa. If we're rock climbing, however, my success depends on your success. In each case, something is at stake—bragging rights or our lives. We each have a clearly defined goal—to win, to reach the top of the mountain.

So consider putting characters in a scene where they have *mutually exclusive goals*, like they would when playing the game of chess.

Or, give them a *mutually beneficial goal* in which they have to work together—like climbing that mountain. In either case, the task is clear, the consequences are clear, tension is present, and the reader can worry about the scene.

Sometimes you'll have cohorts and sidekicks who all share the same goal in a scene, like the two rock climbers do. Even then, in their conversations, look for ways to give people different views or attitudes so you can create tension and avoid situations where you dump information on your readers without including conflict.

When I was writing my first novel, I needed to get a great deal of information and background to readers about the Jonestown massacre in South America back in 1978. There are a lot of misconceptions about what happened there, and I wanted to bring those up in a way that informed readers without just unloading the facts on them or making them feel stupid or uninformed for not knowing those things already.

In my first draft, I just had one person explain it all.

Three thousand words of explanatory dialogue with the sole purpose of exposition.

A tension-killing scenario.

After several rewrites, I finally fixed this problem by writing a scene that put two characters at odds with each other. One was skeptical, and the other tried to get through to him, bring him up to speed, and inform him of what really happened in Jonestown, allowing me to do the same with my readers.

Besides making someone overcome the skepticism of others as I just described, here are five other ways to get information to your readers without having characters lecture each other.

- Give characters opposing views, and have them try to convince each other that they're right or that there's something different they need to do. Let them spar with words.
- Let your character verbally sort out for himself what's going on. He might change his mind in the end, but in either case, as he thinks things through, your readers will be able to do so as well.
- Give your protagonist an obstacle to overcome as he tries to get the information out: There's too much background noise, everyone is hungry, or there are endless interruptions.
- Lower the status of the character who's giving the information.
- Put your character on the stand in a courtroom, and have her try to convince the jury (and, vicariously, readers) of her point.

Earlier we discussed a number of the narrative forces that press in upon a story. Over the last eighteen years of writing professionally, I've come to believe that understanding those forces is one of the keys to producing quality stories in less time.

In the next section, we'll take an in-depth look at some of the most vital forces that shape the stories we tell.

Some you may have heard of before, but others may surprise you.

I know they surprised me.

PART IV

THE NARRATIVE
FORCES
THAT SHAPE OUR STORIES

CHAPTER 13

CAUSALITY

How the Contingent Nature of Stories Affects Every Sentence You Write

Causality is the chain that holds a story together.

Everything that happens in a story is caused by the thing that precedes it. Therefore, a novel moves forward from cause to effect, not effect to cause.

I know this sounds like an embarrassingly obvious observation, and when I mention it in my writing seminars I don't usually see people furiously taking notes, muttering, "Man, are you getting this stuff? This is *amazing*! Things in a story are *caused*; they're not *random*!"

Though it seems simplistic, truly mastering the implementation of this principle will transform your writing forever.

If there are any cardinal sins of fiction writing, I'd say writing in a way that drives readers out of the world of the story would be at the top of the list.

Instead, we strive to do the opposite—make it as hard as possible for people to put our books down.

As a storyteller, you want readers to always be emotionally present in the narrative. However, if they're forced to guess why something happened (or didn't happen), it causes them to intellectually disengage and distances them from the story. Rather than remain present, they'll begin to analyze or question the story's progression. They might think, *I don't get it. Did I miss something? This just isn't making sense.*

Apart from a few exceptions detailed later in this chapter, when you're trying to engage your readers emotionally, making them ask "Why?" is one of the worst things you can do. As soon as you cause them to ask that, you create a barrier between them and their engagement with the story.

Be sure actions are caused. Avoid times in which actions occur or characters make decisions for no apparent reason, leaving readers lost—even if it's only for a moment.

Why is cause and effect so important? If you move from effect to cause for no good reason:

1. Readers will stumble as they try to figure out why something just happened the way it did.
2. They'll be confused about character intention and desire.
3. It'll kill the pace of the story.
4. It'll undermine believability.
5. It'll reveal your weakness as a writer.

When everything that happens in a story follows logically from what precedes it, cause to effect, readers will stay immersed in the narrative.

Okay, so how does all this play out on the page?

Let's say you're writing a horror story, and the protagonist is at home alone. You might write, "With trembling fingers Stacy locked the door. The killer was on the other side."

But no. You wouldn't write it like that.

If you did, you would disrupt, just for a moment, your readers' emotional engagement with the story. They'll wonder, "Why does she reach out and lock the door?" Then they read on. "Oh, I see, the killer is on the other side."

Here's the difference: If you find that one sentence is serving to explain what happened in the sentence that precedes it (effect to cause), you can almost always improve the writing by reversing the order of the sentences so you render rather than explain the action (cause to effect).

It's stronger to write, "The killer was on the other side of the door. Stacy reached out with trembling fingers to lock it."

Cause: The killer is on the other side of the door.

Effect: She locks it.

Think of it this way: If you can theoretically connect the events of the story with the word *because*, you can typically improve the scene by framing it so the events could be connected with the word *so*.

For example (you wouldn't write it like this, but this is, in essence, what each sentence is saying):

1. "Stacy locked the door BECAUSE she knew the killer was on the other side." If written in this order, the sentence moves from effect (her response) to cause (the stimulus that initiated it).

2. "Stacy knew the killer was on the other side of the door, SO she locked it." Here the cause, or stimulus, leads directly to the effect (her response).

Realizations and discoveries happen after actions, not before them. Don't tell readers what a character realizes and then tell them why she realizes it. For example, "She finally understood who the kidnapper was when she read the letter." Rather, render the scene, "When she read the letter, she finally understood who the kidnapper was."

Think action/reaction, not reaction/action.

Think stimulus/response, not response/stimulus.

One thing leads naturally to the next, and that leads to the next, and so on.

In the following example, the woman's response precedes the stimulus that creates that reaction.

"How could you do this to me!" she screamed when he told her he was in love with another woman.

You could improve it by writing:

> He told her he was in love with another woman.
> "How could you do this to me!" she screamed.

(Incidentally, you might not need to include the words *she screamed* because the context and exclamation point make her tone of voice all too clear.)

Always build on what was said or done. Don't lay the foundation after the idea is built. Try to continually move the story forward rather than forcing yourself to flip backward to give the reason why things occurred. So you wouldn't write, "We need to get out of here. This guy is making me suspicious," but rather, "This guy is making me suspicious. We need to get out of here."

Or how about this: "Alice walked past the strange-looking man and began to run. A tremor rippled down her spine." There are three things that happen. Simply put them in the correct order: "Alice walked past the strange-looking man. A tremor rippled down her spine. She began to run."

In the same way, in the examples below, follow the thought progression of the spy as he evaluates how to respond in a scene leading up to a chase sequence. Which of these six possible sentence orders actually moves from cause to effect, with one event causing the next, then causing the next? (Hint: Try inserting the word *so* between each of the sentences, and you'll see that only one series makes sense.)

> He's injured. Marianne shot him. You can catch him.
>
> He's injured. You can catch him. Marianne shot him.
>
> Marianne shot him. He's injured. You can catch him.
>
> Marianne shot him. You can catch him. He's injured.
>
> You can catch him. He's injured. Marianne shot him.
>
> You can catch him. Marianne shot him. He's injured.

See how the third example follows the natural progression of events? The man is shot; therefore he's injured; therefore our protagonist can catch him.

But things are not always quite that simple and clear-cut.

Think about the progression of events in the following two examples. How well do they flow? Which is better? Could a different order be even more effective?

> 1. She looked at her watch, promptly rose, and strode toward the door. "Let's go. Their office is close, but the meeting starts in fifteen minutes and I don't want to be late."

> 2. She looked at her watch and promptly rose. "The meeting starts in fifteen minutes. Their office is close, but I don't want to be late." She strode for the door. "Let's go."

Which example follows cause/effect and makes the most sense?

To figure that out, ask yourself, "What does looking at her watch cause her to do? What causes her to decide to leave? What does that decision cause?" Would she say, "Let's go" and then explain why they need to leave or explain why they need to leave and then round everyone up and tell them it's time to go?

In this case there's no right answer. The order of events would depend on the characters' quirks and personalities and on the broader context of what's happening in the story rather than the connection of a few sentences.

If you were shaping that paragraph, the narrative forces of flow, pace, and characterization would all influence your choices as you craft the sentences and take a close look at what causes what. Whatever you choose should be done purposefully, remembering that every event is caused by the one that precedes it.

Don't give readers time to analyze what's happening or why. Actions should follow each other naturally and immediately. At the moment when the stimulus occurs, readers want to see the character's reaction to it or the character's emotional response.

If there's a gap in time between the stimulus and the response, readers will wonder why it's there, why the character didn't respond right away. This will push readers out of the story, so have your characters respond immediately and believably to the stimulus events.

One of my writing students once had me critique the opening to a novel he was working on. On the first page, his protagonist felt his heart sink, then he rebuked himself for giving in to fear, then felt apathy, then courage, then shame, then apathy again, then hatred. All on one page and *all from the same event.*

This is disorienting to readers. The initial response is fine, but something must cause the character to have each of those subsequent emotions.

Can an emotion cause another emotion?

Sure, but make it clear by the context that the character's progression of emotions is logical.

As we examined in the last chapter, actions, emotions, and thoughts all affect each other. Keen psychologists know this and realize that changing a person's behavior will change his thoughts and emotions, changing his emotions will affect his thoughts and actions, and changing the way he thinks (about the world or about himself) will subsequently alter his emotions and his actions.

Just as the best therapists realize this, so do the best storytellers.

Remember that every change in thought, emotion, and action needs to be caused. Don't fluctuate between emotions (or thoughts or actions) without good reason.

By the way, characters cannot help but respond to the things that happen to them (either in their thoughts, feelings, or actions). Repressing your feelings or ignoring someone or pretending not to respond is still a response—whether that's a thought, action, or emotion. There's no such thing as "lack of a response." You, as the author, just need to figure out what that response is and clearly communicate it to your readers.

Sometimes, if context dictates it, you can start a sentence with the word *because* or *since* and keep the order moving from cause to effect. All of these would work:

> 1. Because of the stab wound in his jaw, I expected his words to be raspy or coarse.
>
> 2. Since he'd been stabbed in the jaw, I expected his words to be raspy or coarse.
>
> 3. He'd been stabbed in the jaw, so I expected his words to be raspy or coarse.

Okay, one last example.

> Greg sat bored in the writers workshop. He began to doodle. He'd heard all this stuff before. Suddenly he gulped and stared around the room, embarrassed, when the teacher called on him to explain cause-and-effect usage.

As it stands, at least seven events occur in the paragraph above, and none are in their proper and logical placement in the text. Here they are in the order in which they actually happened.

1. Greg sits in the workshop.
2. He realizes he's heard all this before.
3. Boredom
4. Doodling
5. Getting called on
6. Embarrassment
7. Gulping and staring around the room

Each event causes the one that follows it. (Incidentally, since readers will be able to tell from the context that he was bored and embarrassed, we don't need to tell them that.) Here it is, untangled.

> Greg sat in the writers workshop. He'd heard all this stuff before and began to doodle. When the teacher called on him to explain cause-and-effect usage, he gulped and stared around the room.

The old adage "show, don't tell" applies in the case of causality. When you go from effect to cause, you're telling (writing something and then explaining it) rather than showing (rendering the scene as it unfolds).

Remember, you don't want to tell readers something and then explain why it happened. Rather, you'll want to render the scene so the forward movement of the story isn't lost and readers don't have to constantly flip mentally backward for an explanation of, or motivation for, events.

Your writing will be more effective if you show readers what's happening as it happens rather than continually explaining what just happened.

That said, since story trumps structure and context so strongly affects a story's flow, there are a number of times when it's acceptable, even preferable, to move from effect to cause.

1. **In chapter or section breaks.** Taking the example from earlier, you might begin a section by writing, "'How could you do this to me!' she screamed."

   Immediately, readers will be curious who's screaming, who she's screaming at, and why she's responding that way. This could make a good hook. During a hook you want readers to ask, "Why?" but in the middle of a scene, you don't.

2. **When one action causes two or more simultaneous reactions.** In the paragraph about Greg, when he's called on, he gulps and stares around the room. Since his embarrassment causes him to respond by both gulping and looking around the room, the order in which you tell readers that he did those two things could go either way.

3. **When writing a scene in which your investigator shows his prowess by deducing something readers haven't yet concluded.** Think of Sherlock Holmes staring at the back of an envelope, cleaning out the drainpipe, brushing off a nearby tree branch, and then announcing that he's solved the case. Readers are thinking, "Huh? How did he do that?"

   Their curiosity is sparked, and later when he explains his deductive process, they see that everything followed logically from the preceding events. But if you have a detective follow this process, readers need to trust that you'll eventually give them the cause for his actions. If you never do, they'll be disappointed and frustrated.

The next few exceptions deal with context and happen most often in dialogue in order to create a higher level of verisimilitude.

You might move from effect to cause when something vitally important is being revealed and the flow dictates that an answer has to be given immediately, at the beginning of a sentence or paragraph. For example, "Dr. Fromke, the child is still alive! He was seen in the slums leaving one of the huts!"

Cause to effect would read, "Dr. Fromke, the child was seen leaving one of the huts! He's still alive!" But in real life, a person would likely emphasize the most important news first—that the child is alive—and then go on with the less important explanation of how she knows that—he was seen leaving the hut.

Remember to ask what the natural reaction would be. What's the most believable response for this character to have at this moment?

Sometimes, just like in real life, (1) characters will reverse the order as they sort out their thoughts, or, (2) for impact, we might want to put more emphasis on the last thing listed, even though it moves from effect to cause: "He knew he needed to focus, to stay alert. It might end up being a long night—especially if he had to use the blowtorch he'd brought along for the interrogation."

The impact of hearing about the blowtorch is accentuated by including it toward the end. Cause to effect makes sense but doesn't carry quite the same impact: "It might end up being a long night—especially if he had to use the blowtorch he'd brought along for the interrogation. He knew he needed to focus, to stay alert."

> Reverse cause and effect only if you want readers to ask "Why?" or if the context requires that you do so in the service of believability.

Analyze every scene, every paragraph, every sentence in your story to make sure that it's moving from cause to effect or, if not, that you have a good reason to reverse the order to better serve your readers.

Tied closely to causality is the believable response of characters to the stimuli in the story. In the next few pages, we'll take a careful look at believability and how it works hand in hand with causality to help form evocative, smooth-flowing stories.

CHAPTER 14

BELIEVABILITY

Removing Coincidences and Sustaining Belief

In writing circles it's common to speak about the suspension of disbelief, but that phrase bothers me because it seems to imply that readers approach stories wanting to disbelieve them and that they need to somehow set that attitude aside in order to engage with the story.

But precisely the opposite is true.

Readers approach stories wanting to believe them. Readers have both the intention and desire to enter a story in which everything that happens within the narrative world that governs that story is believable.

As writers, our goal isn't to convince readers to suspend their disbelief but rather to give them what they want by continually sustaining their belief in the story.

It's not suspension of disbelief, it's retention of belief.

The distinction isn't just a matter of semantics, it's a matter of understanding the mindset and expectations of your readers. Readers want to immerse themselves in deep belief. We need to respect them enough to keep that belief alive throughout our stories.

All else being equal, as soon as readers stop believing your story, they'll stop caring about your story—and readers stop believing stories when things don't follow logically or when characters act inexplicably.

At one of my novel-writing intensive weekends, a woman shared a story she'd written about a National Transportation Safety Board investigator looking into a plane crash.

The investigator arrived at the scene and started holding press conferences and making phone calls and chatting with people.

I wasn't sure how to help her improve the scene without hurting her feelings. Finally, I just asked her to talk me through what her investigator would naturally do at the crash site.

She thought about it. "Well, she would put on gloves so she doesn't leave fingerprints or DNA over everything, she would make sure they looked for survivors, she'd take pictures, and she'd analyze the wreckage, things like that."

She already knew what her protagonist would do; she just needed to write the scene that way. After all, those were the same things readers would expect, the very things they would *want* to see.

I encouraged that author to let her character do those things, and the story improved dramatically.

Ask yourself: Is this really the way this character would react, or are you just making him act this way because of something you need to have happen later in the story? An agenda to "move the plot along" will usually encroach on the believability of a scene. Keeping your story believable is one way of keeping your promises to your readers.

Since believability is so central to fiction, you don't want a character to do something unbelievable without giving readers a legitimate reason why. Also, since stories consist of contingent events, you can't expect readers to stay engaged when you make things happen for no reason.

As I mentioned earlier, as organic writers shape stories, we continually ask ourselves, "What would this character naturally do in this situation?"

And then we let him do it.

Always.

Why?

Because readers, whether they're conscious of it or not, are asking the same question, and as soon as a character acts in a way that isn't believable, either in reference to his characterization or intention, or to story progression, readers lose faith in the writer's ability to tell the story.

If a character acts in an unbelievable way, you'll need to give readers a reason why—and it'd better be a good one.

In fiction, no matter how impossible something is, it must be believable. The narrative world is shattered when an action becomes unbelievable.

If a reader has to ask why an event took place, who a character is, or what exactly is happening (because it's too difficult to picture or too confusing), they'll end up disengaging from the story. They might think things like:

- *She's an office intern, how does she suddenly know how to handle a machine gun?*
- *Where did he get that flashlight from?*
- *How come the wizard doesn't just cast a spell on them?*
- *I don't get it. Where did that person come from all of a sudden?*

Your story doesn't have to be possible, but it must be believable. Coincidence is the enemy of believability.

Here are ten ways to remove coincidences from your narrative.

1. **Set expectations.** The world you've oriented your readers to at the beginning of the story will set their expectations about what's going to be believable throughout the rest of the story. If animals need to talk later in the story, foreshadow early on that they'll be able to do so.

Once you've set reader expectations regarding the world of your story, keep that world consistent.

2. **Recast the scene to make it believable.** For example, people don't usually stop to study themselves in the mirror and internally describe what they look like, but this happens frequently in fiction, especially when the author is trying to find a way to describe the character's physical appearance to readers.

Also, people don't usually talk to themselves. They think to themselves.

It's pretty unlikely that someone would stand in his living room and say to himself, "I am going to find my wife's killer, and I'm not going to stop until I've done to him what he did to her."

He might think that, sure. But say it? Probably not.

When you find unbelievable events like these, simply fix them.

In this case, just tell readers his thoughts or show his response by his actions.

3. **Show skills and characteristics early.** You can't introduce a skill at the time it's needed late in the story. That's coincidence. That's cheating. Introduce it earlier, and it'll feel natural to bring it back into the story later on when it's put to the test.

4. **Remember cause and effect.** As we discussed in the last chapter, causality is a major narrative force that will shape your story. If one action doesn't follow naturally from what preceded it, the believability of your story will suffer.

Check to make sure that the stimulus is sufficient for your character's response. So if someone slaps your protagonist's cheek and she responds by pulling out a handgun and shooting him in the chest, is that believable? Would she really respond with that violent a reaction? Perhaps. But make sure it's the *only* reaction that makes sense for her within the context of that scene.

> *So I'm writing the scene where my protagonist comes back from war and meets his wife at the airport. What happens next? Do they go home? Out to eat? Are there other people there? Whatever happens, is there a cause for the progression of events that makes sense based on who the characters are, their backstory, the context, and the scene's subtext?*

5. **Foreshadow important events.** When you've finished going through your manuscript, go back and reseed it, foreshadowing revelations and insights. As you do, flesh out the most important scenes to increase their narrative weight so it correlates with the promises you're trying to weave in and the payoff you've included. Plant clues or red herrings, and make sure the things that have a big payoff have been promised in the appropriate ways.

   Also, by scheduling events, they won't seem as contrived when they happen. For instance, rather than having a character just show up at a briefing, foreshadow that she will.

> "Ariel's on her way. When will she get here?"
> "She should be here in the next ten minutes or so."

   Or, rather than writing "It's noon. Time for our meeting" out of nowhere, let characters remind each other about the upcoming meeting throughout the morning so readers expect it when it arrives.

6. **Pace your transitions.** Don't let the timing of transitions intrude on your story's believability.

   Whenever you use phrases such as "just then" or "as we were," you run the risk of including a coincidence that doesn't need to appear in your story. Readers might think, *Oh, how convenient, just as you're discussing him, he walks through the door.* Or, *Just then the police arrive? Really? Just in the nick of time?*

Solve this by letting some time pass between events. Something along the lines of: "A few minutes later ..." or "I'd lost track of how long I'd been reviewing the files when I heard a knock at the door."

7. **Have an expert refute your premise.** In his book *Writing the Breakout Novel*, Donald Maass points out that in *Jurassic Park*, Michael Crichton acknowledged how implausible the premise of his book was by using characters who were experts point that out. It's a great example.

Since readers know that things in a story are not always what they appear to be, if you have an authority in a certain field argue *against* the believability of something that's implausible, readers will actually find it *more* believable than if he argued *for* its believability. In fact, the more skeptical an expert is that something extraordinary or seemingly impossible will work, the more readers will believe that it could. Use this dynamic to your advantage.

Related to this: Don't have experts explain things to experts. Having a character interrupt someone in mid-explanation to finish the explanation for him is one way to handle getting the information to readers without lecturing them.

> I started an explanation of cognitive mapping, and she cut in, "I know all that—people's lack of familiarity with an area skews the mental maps they form in their mind. I told you I read that article, remember?"
>
> "I'm sorry, you're right. I forgot. I'm just a little overwhelmed by all of this."
>
> "That makes two of us."

A short exchange like this would add a touch of tension to the scene and allow you to share the information you're trying to get to your readers without having one expert explain it to another (which kills the scene's believability).

8. **Make something believable by stating that it's a little-known fact.** For example, "Most people don't realize it, but there are six holding cells located beneath the parking garage under FBI Headquarters in downtown DC."

Are there really holding cells there? If so, are there six? Who knows? Readers accept it even if they haven't heard about them before—after all, since you've mentioned that *most* people don't know about the cells, it's completely reasonable that the reader is one of those people. Readers will accept it as true simply because you said it's not common knowledge. This can be a sly little fix, but don't overdo it.

9. **Present the chain of evidence that would lead to that inescapable conclusion.** If you're writing a medical thriller, you could show that scientists can change the genetic coding of rats to increase their lifespans by 80 percent. So, sure, why couldn't they do it for humans as well? If your science is sound, the conclusion will seem valid even if it's not possible—yet.

Show the science behind something until readers not only believe it's possible, but inevitable. Don't just try to make something plausible. You don't want readers to be thinking, *Yeah, okay. I suppose that could happen.* You want to get them to the point of thinking, *Oh, my gosh. That's probably happening in a secret lab somewhere right now!*

10. **Point out the problem to readers.** Simply have a character tell readers that things aren't believable.

There are two ways to do this.

First, compare the fictional event to something unbelievable in real life. So you might have a story character say, "I heard about a parachutist whose chute didn't open. He fell 7,000 feet and survived. I guess I can accept that the Ranger fell eighty feet from that helicopter and walked away with only a broken rib."

Second, point out the story's plot flaws. Have your character say something like, "I couldn't believe she would do such a thing. It just didn't compute." Readers will keep reading (as long as you've been keeping your promises so far), trusting that eventually things will compute. The more you admit that the scene has a believability problem, the less readers will hold you accountable for it.

So when something unbelievable or odd happens, don't be afraid to let your character notice and respond.

- "I had no idea why she stomped out of the room, but I could tell something big was up."
- "All right, that was unexpected. Why would she say that anyway?"
- "Huh? That doesn't even make any sense."
- "Obviously, there's more going on here than I thought when I first found the necklace."
- "As strange as it seemed, she didn't give in. Knowing her, I could hardly believe it."
- "She was surprised to hear that Francine hadn't ordered the investigation. It really threw her for a loop to hear that Internal Affairs was behind it."
- "He glanced at Amy. He could see by the look on her face that she was as confused as he was about their son's behavior."

Imagine your CIA agent in an espionage thriller arrives at the site of a terrorist bus bombing right after it occurs. Write down three things he would naturally do. What about the terrorist who set off the explosion? Let's say he's there in the crowd watching—what would he do next? What about the family member of a victim? What are three things she would do?

Then, think about your work in progress. Focus on the natural reactions of your characters. Allow the people to be themselves on the page, and don't try to rein them in. Where in your story have you constrained your character from acting naturally because you were trying to include something to move the plot forward?

Remember those three vital questions we studied in Chapter 8.

1. "What would this character naturally do in this situation?"
2. "How can I make things worse?"
3. "How can I end this in a way that's unexpected and inevitable?"

They focus on believability and causality (question 1), escalation (question 2), and twists (question 3), and are some of the most important narrative forces that shape stories.

All of them interrelate with each other.

When every event is naturally caused by the one that precedes it, the story makes sense.

As characters act in ways that are credible and convincing in their quest for their goal, the story remains believable. The deepening tension and struggles of the story will keep readers caring about what's happening as well as interested in what's going to happen next.

And when the twist comes, it floors readers, blows them away, not just because they didn't see it coming but because they feel like, of all possible endings, this is the most logical one.

By consistently driving your story forward through action that follows naturally, characters who act believably, tension that tightens exponentially, and twists that grow logically from the texture of the story, you'll keep readers engrossed in your story.

In the following chapter, we'll take a brief tour through five genres and show how each of them can help improve your story, whatever type of fiction you might be working on.

CHAPTER 15

EXPECTATIONS

Working with Overlapping Genres

Reader expectations affect where you begin your story, where you take it, and the outcome that will be most satisfying to them.

They desire and expect different things at different points in a story. They want everything to make sense, to flow, and to be believable. They want you to play fair, to entertain them, and to tell the truth about the world rather than promote a certain agenda.

Readers start out trusting you with their time.

Don't make them regret that.

To tell how much trust readers have in an author, look at their reaction to the character's decisions. When a character does something stupid, do readers get mad at the character or at the author?

If they blame you, you don't have their trust.

If they blame the character, you do.

The reader should be thinking, *Okay, this author is good. He knows what he's doing, so this character must have a reason for doing that. I'm sure it'll be explained later.*

They should not be thinking, *I have no idea what's going on here. This author's an idiot.*

Readers don't want antics and games with language. They simply want a strong story that will resonate with them and speak to them deeply.

But all too many writers forget that.

Choose what you would rather have—praise from critics who look for gimmicks or passionate readers who just can't put your book down.

To make your work seem literary and important, don't finish the story. End it before your climax, and make sure you fail to fulfill all your promises.

Bring the story to the point where readers say, "Huh? What? I don't get it?" They'll be confused, but the literary elite will effuse over your book, admiring how it didn't stoop to the level of marketable fiction.

But if you want to sell your story, give readers what they want: entertainment, satisfaction, and fulfilled promises.

GENRE AFFECTS READER EXPECTATIONS AND STORY PROGRESSION

Have you ever flipped to the back cover of a feel-good romance and the copy reads something like, "When Amy's husband leaves her for another woman, her world is shattered. Will she find true love again?"

Um.

Let's see.

How about ... yes?

Or a techno-thriller—"Will Special Agent Jameson stop the terrorist cell before they blow up the Pentagon?"

Or psychological suspense—"Will Cherise track down the kidnapper before he takes the life of her only daughter?"

Or a cozy mystery—"Will Inspector Grayson untangle the clues and figure out who the diamond thief really is?"

Or an inspirational novel—"Will despair consume Andrea, or will she find the hope and peace she's longing for most?"

The people who write that copy can't really be serious.

Most of the time the questions are moot. They're answered by the genre. Case closed.

If it's a cozy mystery, of course the detective will figure out who the bad guy is. And in an inspirational novel, readers know there'll be a happy ending before they even crack open the book.

Uncertainty about the story's outcome might have been the norm in the past, with different societal literary expectations, but today, for the most part, it's no longer the case. Today, readers can guess pretty accurately what kind of ending the story will have based on the story's genre, author, or packaging.

When readers pick up a novel and find out that it's the third in a series, and if they notice that the next one will be released next summer, they're not going to be too worried that the protagonist will survive the book, no matter how many times he's endangered.

And since this is an ongoing series, they'll anticipate that the protagonist's nemesis will in all likelihood survive so he can return in a future installment.

Most of the time, the genre answers the "narrative question" or "story question" or "dramatic if" or whatever it's being called these days.

> The question for almost all novels today is not *will* this or that happen but *how* will it happen.

No story falls into only one genre.

A spy story might also include a romance and a coming-of-age storyline.

A dystopian novel might be intertwined with a mystery.

A fantasy story could also be a political/conspiracy thriller.

But if no story falls into one genre, how do we write toward our readers' expectations?

Good question.

Do your best to understand what your readers are looking for, and worry more about writing great stories than about pigeonholing them into one category. Tell stories so powerful that they end up reshaping readers' views of what that genre (or those overlapping genres) should contain.

You can break any genre norms if it means telling a more impactful and emotionally resonant story.

Besides, genre categorizations themselves are arbitrary.

Is it a crime story? A mystery? A detective novel? A police procedural? Suspense? Who knows? Maybe it's all of them.

Genres even differ in regard to the art form we're engaged in. For example, in fiction we have the genre category "romantic suspense." But have you ever heard of a movie being advertised as "romantic suspense"? I haven't. It's a genre that apparently doesn't exist in film.

So set your readers' expectations through your title, voice, mood, and all of those things we covered in Chapter 2 when we examined the orientation of your story. And then work to meet them.

BRINGING DIFFERENT GENRES INTO YOUR STORY

Stories satisfy readers in different ways. Readers might be looking for intellectual stimulation, an escape from everyday life, a deep exploration into human nature, an emotional thrill ride, or a light-hearted retreat from the stress of their jobs.

They might want to laugh or shiver or cry. You need to deliver.

Genre dictates the amount of intellectual or emotional engagement your reader expects to have. Some genres are more emotive (romance, thriller, suspense), and some are more reflective (cozy mysteries, literary novels).

Some rely on comedy, others on horror.

Most stories, however, are improved with touches of humor and with a love element (it doesn't have to be romantic love; it could be sacrificial love). Additionally, since the pathway to the story's outcome remains in question, stories of every genre will have some mystery in them. Also, all stories contain suspense as readers worry about how the protagonist will achieve his goal or overcome his hardship, whatever that might be.

Finally, many stories have horrific moments where narrative forces of desire and danger converge to form terrifying, unsettling, or unforgettable scenes.

Writing toward your readers' expectations involves crafting scenes that include these five elements—humor, love, mystery, suspense, and horror—in the right amount, at the right time.

Love

Love can be erotic, romantic, platonic, familial, sacrificial, or some combination of the above. It appears in nearly every story, and it makes stories of nearly every genre better.

TYPE OF LOVE	WHAT YOU'LL EMPHASIZE	WHAT'S AT STAKE
Erotic love	Sensuality	Sex
Romantic love	Intimacy	A long-term relationship
Platonic love	Companionship	Friendship
Familial love	Loyalty	Harmony in the family
Sacrificial love	Selflessness	A giving of self—maybe even the lover laying down his life for the beloved

The anonymously written book *Go Ask Alice* tells the story of a runaway teenage girl who is addicted to drugs and living on the street. It's written as a diary, and one of the most memorable scenes occurs in the middle of the story when she finally contacts her parents again.

In this entry she doesn't even know what day it is. Here's what she writes.

Another Day

I finally talked to an old priest who really understands young people. We had an endlessly long talk about why young people leave home, then he called my Mom and Dad. While I waited for him to get the call through I looked at myself in the mirror. I can't believe that I have changed so little. I expected to look old and hollow and gray, but I guess it's only me on the inside that has shriveled and deteriorated. Mom answered the phone in the family room, and Dad ran upstairs to get the extension, and the three of us almost drowned out the connection. I can't understand how they can possibly still love me and still want me but they do! They do! They do! They were glad to hear from me and to know I am all right. And there were no recriminations or scoldings or lectures or anything. It's strange that when something happens to me Dad always leaves everything in the whole world and comes. I think if he were a peace mission involving all humanity in all the galaxies he would leave to come to me. He loves me! He loves me! He loves me! He truly does!

The powerful love of a father for his daughter, and her realization of that love, creates a stirring and poignant moment in the story.

Incidentally, most readers aren't looking for sappy, contrived love stories. Emotion on the part of your readers cannot be manufactured or commanded; it must grow out of empathy and concern for the story's characters.

Regardless of the type of love you're exploring, things going wrong in the relationship or misunderstandings between the people who care so much about each other will propel the story forward.

When in doubt, add conflict.

And since most marketable stories will have a happy ending (Tolkien called it a eucatastrophe, the opposite of a catastrophe), the love will win out in a way that emerges naturally from all that precedes it.

Humor

When my daughter was in second grade, she told me this joke.

Q: What's the difference between boogers and broccoli?
A: Kids won't eat their broccoli.

The joke made me smile because it's true. Just like a good story, it ends in a way that makes sense but it isn't an ending we necessarily see coming.

Humor is truth no one has noticed. It often involves telling or showing people something they're familiar with but haven't viewed from that perspective before.

A lot of humor in fiction comes from misunderstandings. This is common in romance stories—he thinks she's thinking one thing, she thinks he's thinking another, and comedic consequences take off from there.

While humor on stage and screen can be physical and slapstick, humor that works best in print is often truth exaggerated, absurdity, irony, and callbacks.

- **Truth exaggerated:** Often the funniest stories are ones that take truth and play it out to the extreme. Readers don't get the impression that the author is trying to be funny, but rather they sense that, in her own way, the author is trying to tell the truth about the world through hyperbole.
- **Absurdity:** Situations get more and more ludicrous and often create the impetus for exploring truth from a unique vantage point. Readers look forward to the moments of comedic misunderstanding, the clash between enigmatic characters, and the bizarre situations that result.
- **Irony:** This often grows from the idiosyncrasies of a character: The Army Ranger likes to use pillow mist; the coffee snob is forced to drink truck stop coffee; the edgy, gothic teenage girl sleeps with a teddy bear.
- **Callbacks:** Readers see that the exaggeration, absurdity, or irony is going to be cycled back to and referred to later in the story.

Self-effacing humor also works well in print. This is most easily done when writing in first-person point of view. It typically comes when a character is naive or overconfident and faces the humorous results of his naivety. For example, "I knew I was going to have a wonderful marriage as soon as I got done changing my wife." Immediately, readers will be thinking, *Oh, man. This guy is in for it big time.*

Be aware that if readers feel like you're not from their subculture and think you're making fun of them, they won't find what you're writing very funny. In a humorous story, no one gets hurt—including readers.

Be wary of puns. They can be useful for showing characterization—say, of someone who is trying to be funny—but they don't usually make readers laugh and they can backfire and distract from the story.

Some writers shoot for humor by using speaker attributions like "she joked," "he quipped," "she mentioned in her usual fun-loving way," and so on. Don't go there. If your story is funny, you don't need to tell your readers. If it's not funny, you don't need to draw attention to that fact.

Mystery, Horror, and Suspense

Reader expectations and the depth and breadth of what's at stake in the story will determine the amount of mystery, horror, or suspense you'll want to include. It's vital that as a writer you become aware of how you shape those sequences to create the desired effect on your reader—curiosity, dread, or apprehension.

Suspense is always emotional. It appeals to the concern of readers for the wellbeing of the characters. In suspense, readers are afraid to look away. In horror, they're afraid to look. In mystery, they're not afraid at all. They're inquisitive.

When readers care about a character and that character is put in peril (emotional, physical, psychological, etc.), suspense is born. So a murder is not suspense. An abduction with the threat of a murder is.

Regardless of the genre, the more violence there is, the less impact each violent act will have on readers. Violence numbs us. Better one scene where it is implied than a dozen generic murders where it's shown.

Make readers worry through anticipation and imagination. Often it's more terrifying to imagine violence than to see it. Set it up, then show the aftermath.

The scariest stories aren't necessarily the bloodiest, and the most suspenseful aren't necessarily the most violent. For example, *The Silence of the Lambs* had very little on-screen violence but is considered one of the scariest movies of all time—scarier than most slasher movies.

Incidentally, in comedy, the amount of violence doesn't matter so much as the amount of pain. You can have all sorts of cartoonish violence, but when characters start to really get killed or hurt or tortured, it stops the humor right in its tracks.

So even if you're writing a dark comedy, be aware of the interplay of violence as opposed to pain (in whatever form that may come—physical, emotional, or relational).

In a mystery, a victim might have been beheaded before the book begins and the detective (or team of detectives) must work to solve the crime. In a horror story, you might show the beheading in all of its grisly detail. In suspense, readers learn that someone is going to be beheaded and the protagonist must try to stop the crime before it occurs.

	MYSTERY	HORROR	SUSPENSE
TIMING OF CRIME OR CRISIS EVENT	The violence occurs before the story begins. (Solve it.)	Readers witness it as it happens. (See it.)	Readers anticipate that it will happen. (Stop it.)
READERS WONDER:	Who was responsible for the crisis/crime?	How will the character suffer?	How can the crisis or impending crime be averted?
READER ORIENTA-TION	Readers often lag behind the detective in comprehending the importance of clues.	Readers view the action. They're in on the secret.	Readers know about danger that the characters in the story do not.
APPEALS MORE TO:	Head (intellectual curiosity)	Gut (visceral reaction)	Heart (worry and concern)

We might use a crime to intrigue (mystery), to gross out (horror), or to frighten (suspense). In mystery, readers are curious. In horror, they're shocked. In suspense, they're anxious.

But what about other genres? How do these three narrative forms relate to different types of stories?

The chart below is by no means comprehensive, but it will give you an idea for how mystery, horror, and suspense might fit into the story you're working on.

GENRE	MYSTERY	HORROR	SUSPENSE
HISTORICAL/ MEDIEVAL	Who in the queen's entourage is the traitor?	Carnage: Readers see the gruesome bodies left in the field after the battle.	The encroaching army has surrounded the castle and given the people inside twenty-four hours to surrender. How will they prevent the oncoming slaughter?
YOUNG ADULT	Did the boy drown, or was he killed?	Terror: a flashback or dream sequence from his point of view as he drowns	Someone has tweeted that he's going to strike again at 8:00 P.M., that another boy will die. Who sent the tweet? How will the protagonist stop him?
ROMANCE	Who left the flowers and note at her desk at work?	Shock: She finds her boyfriend in bed with another woman.	What will her blind date be like? Will he be someone she can trust?
MEDICAL THRILLER	Where are the four sets of lungs that were supposed to have been delivered to the organ bank?	Gore: The autopsy or surgery happens on the pages of the book, with all of the blood and reek made plain to the readers.	The virus completely paralyzes people, and they subsequently awaken, unable to move during their autopsies. How will the protagonist find the next victim before the autopsy begins?

Think of a wave rising behind a surfer. If he catches it at just the right instant, it will carry him forward by its own energy and momentum.

The wave is the story.

The surfer is the reader.

That momentum builds as promises are made, tension escalates, and the timeframe available to solve the problems shrinks.

Let's take a close look at how the momentum of the wave can carry readers past plot incongruities.

CHAPTER 16

CONTINUITY

How Narrative Momentum Carries Stories Forward

Readers can become so invested in seeing the promises kept, so engrossed in the story, that they don't notice the narrative glitches that have found their way into the tale.

That happened with my third novel.

Only when I was reading it through on the final pass before it was going to be sent to the printers did I notice the plot hole—one big enough to drive a dump truck through.

It was too much to fix and too late to fix it. I had to send it to press knowing that hole was there.

Yet, to this day, no readers have complained to me about the plot hole. I don't think most of them even noticed it.

Why? Well, first let's look at the scenario.

In the story, the villain is planning to bury the hero alive. Throughout the book that's his goal, and as the story builds to the climax, readers know that the climactic encounter is going to occur in an abandoned gold mine west of Denver.

Well, just before the climax, there's a helicopter chase, and the bad guy leaves two rattlesnakes on the helicopter that the protagonist is riding in. The pilot gets bitten and they almost crash, but the hero survives. When they land, he rushes to the mine to try to save a hostage whom the villain has taken.

Okay. So if the antagonist wanted so badly to bury the hero alive, why on earth would he have left two rattlesnakes that could have killed the guy or the pilot, causing the chopper to crash?

Plot-hole alert.

It just didn't make any sense.

But why didn't readers notice?

Well, I think it's for the same reason that I didn't notice it—even though I'd been through that book more than a dozen times while editing it.

We knew that the requisite climactic scene needed to occur in the abandoned gold mine. And when the helicopter chase begins, we have nearly 400 pages of momentum carrying us forward.

Rather than stopping to look closely at the logic of the scene or taking the time to analyze what was going on, at that point we were so focused on the coming climax that we didn't notice the plot flaw.

The wave we were riding carried us right into the climax.

When you're making promises in the first part of a book, it's vital that you build readers' trust so that later, when you're keeping those promises, you can rely on that as well as on the narrative momentum of the story's escalation to help you rush past plot holes before readers notice them. (For more on fixing plot problems, see Part VI.)

WEAVING IN SUBPLOTS WITHOUT KILLING MOMENTUM

Subplots are inseparable from the main storyline.

As you recall, when you introduce a character, every word you write about him adds to the promise you're making that he'll be significant to the story.

So in essence, when you introduce a character, you inevitably introduce the potential for a subplot.

There's a tendency to view subplots as their own stories rather than as dimensions of the main narrative. However, if you can remove a subplot without changing the outcome of the story, it's not a subplot—it's a distraction.

Recast it or delete it.

You can't just decide that you want to add a subplot. It should be so inextricably tied to the main plot that it can't be removed without altering the main plot in irrevocable ways.

Parallel storylines don't create subplots; they create separate and distinct stories. Interweave them so that one informs the resolution of the other, or remove one of them and write a different book with it.

Don't ask yourself, "Should I include a subplot?" but, "How best does this story need to be told?" If you can even *identify* a subplot, it's likely it hasn't been woven into the story well enough.

Multiple storylines should meet without coincidence being the thing that brings them together. For example, one storyline has the hero of our legal thriller trying to solve his first big case and take down a mob boss involved with human trafficking in Las Vegas. Another storyline revolves around the protagonist's niece's disappearance in Connecticut. Guess what? She just happens to be one of the girls the mobster's people have lured to Vegas.

So the story has unity, right?

Well, unless you can foreshadow things so that all of this is inevitable, you really have two separate storylines and readers won't buy it that the two stories just happen to be so closely tied together.

How do the storylines all meet and inform the resolution of each other? Every person who has a relationship with the main character affects the movement of the main plot.

As you recall, all storytelling is built on promises, whether they are stated directly or simply implied. The more words you pour into every storyline (that is, subplot), the bigger the promise you're making to readers about its significance.

We'll look carefully at status in Chapter 21, but for now remember that different levels of status create opportunities for subplots. So if you have an action hero who always has the same status throughout the story, it will be harder to develop subplots.

Bringing all the storylines together creates cohesiveness in the story. A tale that flows seamlessly from scene to scene and has an appropriate pace and mood has good fluidity, the next narrative force.

CHAPTER 17

FLUIDITY

The Interplay of Pace, Flow, Narrative Time, and Flashbacks

Pace is how quickly (or slowly) the story progresses. Flow is how smoothly it does so.

A fast-paced story might have a choppy flow, while a story that flows well might have a slower pace. Whatever the pace is, you'll want the story to flow in a way that keeps readers enthralled.

Problems come when a story's pace is too slow for readers to stay interested, when it's too fast for them to stay focused, or when it doesn't match the story's mood.

For example, creating a moody, atmospheric ghost story that's as fast-paced as an action thriller might not work. Or, a light, airy comedy might get dragged down by too slow of a pace.

Escalation directly affects pace. As you escalate the story, you'll ratchet up the pace. So regardless of genre, the pace leading up to the climax of your story will be the briskest section of your book.

Often I've found that, as I'm working on my story, I get ideas for climactic scenes or sequences. Following the threads of the story, I write up those scenes. They look good in isolation—but when I'm editing the book, I inevitably find that the pace of those sections is off. It might be too slow or too descriptive or maybe too cryptic, and the only way for me to get the right feel for it is to keep the context in mind.

Editing a scene without taking context into account will backfire and cause you more work in the long run because:

1. You won't craft the scene with the right mood, pace, flow, and length.
2. You won't balance out that scene with the ones on either side of it.
3. You won't know what promises to keep at the right time or in the right way.
4. You won't have in mind what readers want at that moment in the story.

The momentum of the story that precedes every scene needs to inform the content and pace of that scene.

We face a challenge of balancing two things: creating mystery and grounding readers. As a story progresses, it should solve mysteries even as it introduces new ones. It's great to make promises and create a sense of unbalance, but as the story progresses, readers need to feel like they're being filled in at the appropriate times.

There's no set rule for this except to anticipate the questions readers will ask and then address them at the point in the manuscript where they would most naturally come up. As soon as readers start thinking, *Enough already!* (annoyance) or *I'm just not getting this* (confusion), you've lost them.

Don't leave too many unanswered questions hanging out there. I once read a book in which the author withheld important information from readers. When I asked him about it, he told me it was "to create suspense." But failing to give readers what they want doesn't create suspense; it only leads to dissatisfaction.

So answer readers' questions as they arise.

Since readers need to know the stakes if they are going to be concerned about the outcome of a scene, suspense actually requires that we reveal, not conceal, information.

Additionally, there's a fine line between building the suspense and irritating readers. There are two key questions to ask: Does the danger escalate? Is the outcome unknown?

If you're trying to draw something out and readers know what's going to happen, it won't work. For example, don't spend ten pages having someone who's tied to a chair wriggle free from her bonds when readers already know, from the context, that the person will get free.

However, when you have a scene that the readers won't be able to guess the outcome of, you can milk the suspense.

Many times, the parts of the story that the writer stretches out are the very parts that should be shrunk, and the parts that should be shrunk are the parts the author ends up stretching out.

As best-selling novelist Lee Child says, "Write the slow parts fast and the fast parts slow." In other words, spend more time drawing out the tension-filled sections, but condense the other sections—the descriptions and so on.

Flow is closely related to causality. If there are disruptions in the cause/effect movement of your story, it'll also disrupt the flow of your story. The techniques for handling cause and effect issues (explored in Chapter 13) will also improve your story's flow.

> Make it as easy as possible for your reader to follow your story. You do the hard work so they don't have to.

THE IMPORTANCE OF NARRATIVE TIME

Unless you're writing a story about time travel, in a fictional story, just as in real life, time moves forward for all of the characters at the same speed.

I was listening to an audiobook of a best-selling novel, and at the climax the protagonist is in a room with his son and the villain. Meanwhile, there are a couple of other characters locked outside the far end of the building. The author is flipping back and forth between the storylines.

Okay, no problem there.

But here's the sequence. And remember, this is the climax of the novel. A *thriller*.

The hero shoves his son into the corridor out of the antagonist's line of sight. The bad guy aims his gun at the protagonist, who springs into action to bolt across the room and get the gun from him to prevent his son from being harmed.

He knows he might very well get shot in the process.

Alright, no problem there either.

So the hero used to be a professional athlete. He's in good shape. It should only take him a second or two to cross the room.

Well, he starts on his way, thinking he's going to get killed. As he moves forward, he reflects on his son and how much he loves him. This is fine, but it goes on and on, taking longer to think through than anyone could possibly have time to do while sprinting across a room—and definitely longer than we would want for a story's climax.

And then, while he's still on his way across the room, the author flips to the storyline of the guy's buddies outside. The men are chatting about how to get into the building, trying to figure out the pass code to get past the locked door. They discuss this and then finally decide on a password they want to try. In the audiobook, this sequence takes thirty seconds. (No, I'm not kidding.)

All the while the bad guy has the hero in his sights. Nothing is holding him back from firing.

Back to our hero.

He's still on his way across the room.

Must be a big room.

He reflects some more. Runs some more.

In reality, by the time he's done with all this pondering about his relationship to his son and those other two guys are done with the lock, our hero would either be long since dead or he could have disarmed the guy, handcuffed him to a pipe, and been on his way out for some pistachio nut ice cream with his boy.

Instead, he's still on his way across the room.

Honestly, when I was listening to the story, I burst out laughing. I couldn't help it. That scene was supposed to be the climax of a thriller, but it was so absurd and ludicrous that it became a joke.

Because of the narrative force of escalation, as a story nears its climax, your characters aren't going to pause and reflect on life in a way that would take longer than the timing of the events in the story would allow.

Also, use caution when flipping to different point-of-view characters during the climax. What happens in one point-of-view scene has to happen in the same amount of time that elapses in all the other storylines.

Let's say at your climax you're flipping through three point-of-view characters, Francine, Reggie, and Aneesh.

Francine falls in a river, and it's sweeping her toward the waterfall.

Reggie jumps in to save her.

Aneesh rushes ahead of them to toss a rope into the water for them to grab hold of.

- **Sequence A:** Francine falls in, goes under, tries to swim toward shore. (Span of time: about six seconds)
- **Sequence B:** Reggie sees her trying to get to shore and jumps in, swimming toward her. (Notice that the moment we leave Francine's storyline we pick up Reggie's. We stick with him for about nine seconds.)
- **Sequence C:** While Reggie is swimming toward Francine, Aneesh runs downstream and pulls out the rope. (Nine seconds or so)
- **Sequence D:** Back to Francine. Eighteen seconds have passed for her (and for everyone else) since we've left her storyline. So when we pick it up again, she's eighteen seconds closer to the waterfall, Reggie is still trying to save her, and she can see Aneesh pulling out the rope.

CHARACTERS	SECONDS		
	1 . . . 5 . . . 10 . . . 15 . . . 20 . . . 25 . . . 30		
FRANCINE	⊢A⊣ ⊢D⊣		
REGGIE	⊢——B——⊣		
ANEESH	⊢——C——⊣		

When using point-of-view flips, remember, that (1) time passes at the same pace for everyone in the story, (2) we pick up the story at the moment we left it off, and (3) whatever happens during a character's point-of-view section must feasibly be able to happen within that allotted amount of time.

Also, keep in mind the time it would realistically take to complete that task and the length of time it's going to take readers to read about it. If there's a jarring discrepancy in either area, it'll distract readers and negatively affect the flow.

As you flip point of views, readers need to stay oriented to what's happening, how much time is elapsing, and what the characters have been doing in the meantime.

Remember, (1) the more time your story spans, the less urgency it will contain, and (2) since we pick up each storyline where we dropped the characters off, the more point-of-view characters you include, the less time your novel can span.

Here's another surefire way to annoy readers: Leave a point-of-view character while you're in the middle of an action sequence.

For example, in a chase scene, if you write (about your protagonist), "She careened around the bend and crashed into the cement pylon jutting up from the side of the road," and then you close your chapter, readers will obviously want to find out if the woman is conscious, injured, dead, etc.

But some writers will then jump to another point-of-view character, often in a less stressful situation, and then return to the woman in the car (or maybe she's in the hospital by then) a chapter or two (or more) later.

Me? I'd just skip those chapters to get back to the injured woman's storyline.

Don't tempt your readers to skip chapters. Instead, make them afraid they'll miss something vital if they skip ahead at all. Strive to make every chapter intriguing and unskippable.

Stay with the character, and avoid changing the point of view until there's a span of time during which he's not doing anything significant. For example, he might be spending an hour researching a project, driving across town, taking a nap, etc. While he does so, flip to the other storyline.

All point-of-view storylines must escalate concurrently so that when the story reaches the climax for one character, it simultaneously reaches the climax for the other point-of-view characters.

WHEN TO CONDENSE TIME AND WHEN TO EXPAND IT

The passage of time is elastic in novels. One sentence can summarize the passage of a century, while in the climax, a minute might take an entire page or more to render.

Think of it this way—at the beginning of the book and during less intense sections, you'll cover more time with fewer words. In climactic sequences, you'll cover less time with more words.

By expanding time too much at the beginning of a story, you can end up making everything top-heavy, causing the story to lag and making readers impatient for it to move forward.

You'll expand the time toward the end of the novel as things escalate on their way to the climax, then condense it again in the denouement (if you have one).

Early on you might write, "Twenty minutes later we were still in the waiting room."

Later in the story, it might be, "Five seconds passed. Another five. 'Let's go. Let's go!' I cried, 'He's bleeding out!'"

But we wouldn't reverse the order and let the twenty minutes of time pass like that at the climax.

What if you wanted to write an entire novel that only spans a single hour? Will readers accept it?

Perhaps. But whenever I've tried reading novels that use this type of gimmick, I simply got bored at a certain point. I just wanted the story characters to get on with life and accomplish something.

We are all time-constrained creatures. We know that things take a certain amount of time to happen in real life, and sometimes when we're reading we just want things to progress. Keep that desire, that dynamic, in mind as you shape your stories.

HOW TO HANDLE FLASHBACKS

Flashbacks disrupt the flow of novels.

Think of driving through town. You come to a stoplight that's green, and rather than keep going, you pull to an abrupt stop and turn off the engine. After a moment you start the car again and turn right, make a series of right turns that brings you back to the same intersection, and then finally you drive forward again.

Flashbacks halt the story. When you include them, you're stopping the forward movement of the narrative completely, taking a detour, and then picking up the story again where you left off earlier.

It's usually better to glance in the rearview mirror once in a while as you finesse your story forward. For example, you're telling the tale of a boy who was made fun of and called names as a child. Now he's working in an office as an adult. He hears the boss call him an "inept moron," and it all comes back to him: the days in the schoolyard, the cruel names the other children used, all of it. He feels his hands tighten into fists.

Now.

Do you flip back and tell readers the whole story of one of those teasings, or is this enough?

Context will inform you, but as a rule of thumb, be wary of flashbacks.

Remember, they kill the forward movement of the story. I've read books where I'll skip entire chapters because the flashbacks weren't essential. Use flashbacks only if they:

- inject more conflict and tension.
- provide essential information that readers need to know at that specific point in the story.
- answer a nagging question.
- bring to light a hidden secret at just the right time.
- provide vital information that helps tie the story together.

If you do use a flashback, you'll typically include only one major flashback in a novel. In film, since viewers can almost instantaneously be reoriented to the setting (in time and place), it's easier to include multiple flashbacks. On the page, it's tough; on the screen, not so bad.

Ask yourself if the flashback is truly essential. Does it serve the forward movement of the story or end up disrupting the flow? Is the information only important for you, the author, to know, or is it vital for your readers to know as well?

If you're skimming over some sections of your book to get to the good stuff, readers will probably be doing the same thing. Be merciless in your self-editing. As Elmore Leonard said, "When I write I always try to leave out the parts readers skip."

Write so that readers can't skip to the good stuff because every word is the good stuff.

You accomplish this by polishing your work—which is what we'll look at next.

CHAPTER 18

POLISH

Touching Up Your Story

An engaging story has closure, and all of its pieces fit together to form a completed whole. The action intensifies, more setbacks occur, and then at the climax, the conflict reaches a satisfying resolution or conclusion. Everything in a cohesive story is tied together: the action, emotion, desire, and dilemma.

When polishing a story, take a close look at the interplay of brevity, specificity, subtlety, and mood.

When you write a story, every word is auditioning for a part.

Every word must matter.

So not only will you want to remove any unnecessary scenes (those in which nothing is altered, which you'll summarize rather than render), but also every unnecessary word.

Here are three ways to write more concisely.

1. Delete or shrink strings of prepositions: "He walked over toward me" becomes "He approached me." "He went out of the building" becomes "He left." "I went back over the details of the crime" becomes "I reviewed the details of the crime."
2. Combine verbs and adverbs into one, more specific verb: "He ran quickly" becomes "He bolted." "She called loudly" becomes "She shouted."
3. Don't show readers something and then tell them what you just showed them: "Angelina's eyes grew large, and she eased away

from the man and clung to her mother's skirt. The man made her nervous." Readers will understand that the man made her nervous from seeing Angelina's actions. They don't need to be told what they already know.

Your book should be only as long as it needs to be to tell your story and not one word longer. Tighten the language whenever possible. Look for more concise, unique, and memorable descriptions and details. As *New York Times* best-selling author Robert Dugoni says, "If it can be presumed, it can be cut."

That said, the book should also be long enough to provide your readers with the experience they're seeking. Fantasy, science fiction, and suspense novels are often longer than mysteries or romance novels because they're creating a unique, coherent world. And as I mentioned earlier, they provide an immersive experience. So you'll need more words to tell the stories of those complex worlds.

If you tell your story well enough, readers won't notice or care about the length. Some 200-page novels seem way too long, while some 500-page novels seem much too short.

THERE'S NO SUCH THING AS A SYNONYM

Every word means something slightly different.

Running is different from jogging and sprinting and ambling and bolting. Juicy is different from succulent. Slender is different from skinny. A criminal who slaughters people is not quite the same as one who murders people.

Be specific. Use the right word.

This is also true about character descriptions.

Even if you're writing about a static character (a pebble person) who plays a minimal role in the story (a street vendor, flight attendant, coffeehouse barista, etc.), you're not writing about a generic twenty-something woman or an elderly man or a little kid.

Think in more specific terms.

- The waiter turned to me, tilted his head, offered a fabricated smile. He might have been a robot. "And you, sir?"
- She wore a perky little skirt and moved in a way that showed she knew what guys like.
- She touched back a strand of her impossibly straight, rodent-colored hair and glared at me.

The more specific we can be, the more universal the story will feel. So if you're striving to write about a grand, sweeping concept like guilt, make it guilt over a single choice. With war, focus on one soldier. With healthcare, tell the story of one patient. With love, explore one person's relationships.

HINT AT YOUR CHARACTER'S EMOTIONS

Err on the side of understatement. When it comes to conveying emotion, subtlety is key.

Rather than telling readers how lonely someone is, let them follow the downward glance of her eye. Let them see the slouching of her shoulders. Let them feel the tension in her throat.

Your word choice for describing the actions of your characters can serve as a powerful key to creating depth and emotion in the minds of your readers.

Think of a vagrant going through a dumpster. How would you describe this simple action? Would you say, "He slid his hand into the throat of the dumpster," "He snaked his arm under the lid," or, "He gingerly picked up a piece of bread"?

A homeless person who gingerly picks up his food isn't used to being homeless. That tells us a lot about him. He's new to the streets. "Snaking" your arm "under the lid" brings something sinister to mind. And sliding your hand into the dumpster's "throat" further accentuates the man's own hunger.

Hesitancy, evil, and desperation can all be conveyed by the words you choose to describe the simple action of picking something up.

MOOD IS MORE THAN HOW YOU FEEL

Picture sunlight on the ocean. Is it dancing on the waves? Piercing them? Caressing them? Embracing them? Sliding across them? Leaping from them?

"The waves glistened in the sunlight" is much different than "The waves swallowed the sunlight." One of them shows hope ("glistened"), while the other implies danger ("swallowed").

Think of a description of a cave. Is it spacious or cavernous? Well, it depends on the mood you're trying to convey in that sentence. *Spacious* is a more positive term than *cavernous*. And that mood should match (1) the attitude your character has toward being in the cave and (2) the overall atmosphere of your novel.

Don't let the mood be undermined by the descriptions you use. I once read a book in which a character was flinging back her hair (a carefree gesture) while at a crime scene speaking with the press about the nineteen victims. That one little authorial stumble jarred me right out of the story, and I never found my way back into it.

Keeping in mind issues of brevity and unity in your story will help you snip off extraneous threads. Zeroing in on specific details will help crystallize the scene. And creating a consistent, unified mood through the subtle use of language will strengthen your narrative.

Most fiction authors have heard that having our characters face difficult decisions will improve our stories.

And it's true.

But how do we do that? What are the secrets to weaving believable moral predicaments into our novels?

Moving forward, let's explore some practical, easy-to-implement steps to creating gripping moral dilemmas that will intrigue and rivet your readers.

CHAPTER 19

DILEMMAS

Creating Moral Quandaries
for Your Characters

Before our characters can face difficult moral decisions, we need to give them beliefs that matter: The assassin has his own moral code—he will not harm women or children. The missionary would rather die than renounce his faith. The father would sacrifice everything to pay the ransom to save his daughter.

A character without an attitude, without a spine, without convictions, is one who'll be hard for readers to cheer for and easy for them to forget.

So to create an intriguing character who faces meaningful and difficult choices, give her *two equally strong convictions* that can be placed in opposition to each other.

For example: A woman wants (1) peace in her home and (2) openness between herself and her husband. So when she begins to suspect that he's cheating on her, she'll struggle to decide whether or not to confront him about it.

If she *only* wanted peace, she could ignore the problem; if she *only* wanted openness, she would bring it up regardless of the results. But her dueling desires won't allow her such a simple solution.

That creates tension.

Which drives the story forward.

Find two things that your character is dedicated to, and then make him choose between them. Look for ways to use his two desires to force him into doing something he doesn't want to do.

For instance, a Mennonite pastor's daughter is killed by a drunk driver. When the man is released on a technicality, does the minister forgive him (and what would that even look like?) or does he take justice into his own hands? In this case, his pacifist beliefs are in conflict with his desire for justice. What does he do?

Good question.

Good tension.

Good drama.

Another example: Your protagonist believes that cultures should be allowed to define their own subjective morality but also that women should be treated with the same dignity and respect as men. She can't stand the thought of women being oppressed by the cultures of certain Middle-Eastern countries, but she also can't stand the thought of imposing her values on someone else. What does she do?

See? You're trying to construct situations in which your character's equally strong convictions are in opposition to each other. That's what will create occasions for thorny moral choices.

PUT YOUR CHARACTER'S CONVICTIONS TO THE TEST

We don't usually think of it this way, but in essence, to bribe someone is to pay her to go against her beliefs. To extort her is to threaten her unless she goes against them.

For example:

- How much would you have to pay the vegan animal rights activist to eat a steak (bribery)? Or, how would you need to threaten him to coerce him into doing it (extortion)?
- What would it cost to get the loving, dedicated couple to agree never to see each other again (bribery)? Or, how would you need to threaten them to get them to do so (extortion)?

- What would you need to pay the pregnant teenage Catholic girl to convince her to have an abortion (bribery)? What threat could you use to get her to do it (extortion)?

Look for ways to bribe and extort your characters. Don't be easy on them. And don't be afraid to take them to the brink.

As writers we sometimes care about our characters so much that we don't want them to suffer. Consequently, we might shy away from putting them into difficult situations.

Guess what?

That's the exact opposite of what needs to occur.

What's the worst thing you can think of happening to your character, contextually, within this story? Now, challenge yourself—try to think of something just as bad and force your character to decide between those two scenarios.

Plumb the depths of your character's convictions by asking, "How far will he go to …?" and "What would it take for him to …?" (Note: The first question deals with the character's dedication to a single cause, and the second pits two strong desires against each other.)

1. How far will Frank go to protect the one he loves?
2. What would it take for him to stand by and watch the one he loves die when he has the power to save her?

1. How far will Angie go to find freedom?
2. What would it take for her to choose to be buried alive?

1. How far will Detective Rodriguez go to pursue justice?
2. What would it take for him to commit perjury to set a rapist free?

Ask yourself: What does my character believe in? What priorities does she have? What prejudices does she need to overcome?

Then, press her to the breaking point to make her truest desires and priorities come to the surface.

Try challenging yourself to examine moral dilemmas more deeply by asking, "When is it right to _____ ?" "When is it better to _____ than to _____?" or "When is _____ a gift?"

Fill in the blanks with something appropriate for your story. For example: "When is it right to kill?" "When is it better to break the law than to obey it?" "When is a lie a gift?"

STICK YOUR CHARACTER BETWEEN A ROCK AND A HARD PLACE

Don't give him an easy out. Don't give him any wiggle room. Force him to make a choice, to act. He cannot abstain. Take him through the process of dilemma, choice, action, and consequence.

1. Something that matters must be at stake.
2. There's no easy solution, no easy way out.
3. Your character must make a choice. He must act.
4. That choice will deepen the tension and propel the story forward.
5. The character must live with the consequences of his decisions and actions.

If there's an easy solution, there's no dilemma. Don't make one of the choices "the lesser of two evils." After all, if one is lesser, it makes the decision all that much easier.

Here's the truth: Easy choices make for weak fiction. Instead of having your hero choose between a good thing and a bad thing (in which there is no drama), or even two good things (in which nothing vital is at stake), let him choose between two bad things.

Consider forcing your character to choose between honoring equal obligations. For example, he could be caught between loyalty to two parties or perhaps be torn between his family obligations and his job responsibilities. Then raise the stakes—his marriage is at stake and so is his job, but he can't save them both. What does he do?

The more imminent you make the choice and the higher the stakes that decision carries, the sharper the dramatic tension and the greater your readers' emotional engagement.

Ask, "What if?" and the questions that naturally follow.

- What if she knows that being with the man she loves will cause him to lose his career? How much of her lover's happiness would she be willing to sacrifice to be with him?
- What if an attorney finds herself defending someone she knows is guilty? What does she do? What if that person is her best friend?
- What if your character has to choose between killing himself or letting someone else die? What about killing himself or being forced to watch his friend get tortured?

Make your character reevaluate her beliefs, question her assumptions, and justify her choices. Ask yourself, "How is she going to get out of this? What will she have to give up (something precious) or take upon herself (something painful) in the process?"

Explore those slippery slopes. Delve into those gray areas. Avoid questions that elicit a *yes* or *no* answer, such as: "Is killing the innocent ever justified?" Instead, frame the question in a way that forces you to take things to the next level: "When is killing the innocent justified?" Rather than ask, "Does the end justify the means?" ask yourself, "When does the end justify the means?"

Here are four simple ways to create moral dilemmas.

1. **Reverse expectations.** Take common assumptions, and turn them on their head. Make people think about issues from a unique perspective and evaluate things they've simply accepted but never really considered before.
   - Does altruism exist, or are all of our motives marred with self-interest?

- When is torture justified?
- Is getting all you wish for a curse or a blessing?

2. **Start with a question rather than an answer.** Since drama depends on tension, it's better to work from the center of a dilemma than from a solution.

   - What's more powerful, hatred or love? How is apathy the opposite of love? How is it the opposite of both love and hatred?
   - Is preemptive justice really justice? If you can be convicted of conspiracy to commit murder, are you being judged by your thoughts or your actions?
   - Most people seem to cringe in the face of the truths about themselves, and yet we claim we want to hear the truth. Do we really desire truth, or do we prefer illusion?

3. **Explore an abstract idea.** Don't try to express a theme, but rather use thematic concepts as a starting place to build the dilemmas of your story. Let tension, rather than an agenda, drive your narrative.

   - **Guilt:** Perhaps in your story, one person accepts it, another is consumed by guilt and it drives her to suicide, and another continues to live in denial of what she did.
   - **Accountability:** Despite our upbringing and genetics, at what point are we morally responsible for our choices? What if someone is genetically predisposed to be psychopathic? Should we hold those people to the same degree of accountability for morality as we do others?
   - **Love:** What is the true cost of love? What does it require of us? What is more important, love or freedom?

4. **Examine hot-button issues.** Bring up polarizing issues, and try to get readers to think about them in ways they hadn't before. Play devil's advocate. Whether that's cloning, bioengineering, wealth redistribution, or any other contemporary, morally divisive topic, let your characters wrestle with it even as you do.

- **Abortion:** If "every child should be a wanted child," as some people claim, why stop at birth? Why not allow infanticide? What is the difference between partial-birth abortion and infanticide?
- **Security:** How much collateral damage (the unintended killing of innocent civilians) is justified in the name of national security?
- **Poverty:** In our world, millions of people eat themselves into obesity while millions of others starve to death. How much governmental action is justified in changing this in the name of human rights for the poverty stricken?

THREE WAYS TO FORCE THE ISSUE

Make characters choose between two bad things.

- He must decide between letting two guilty people go free or imprisoning one innocent person for life. What does he do? Why?
- A woman is giving birth, and your protagonist is the only one there to help. He can only save the mother or the baby. Which does he choose? Why?

Make them give up a good thing.

- Happiness or freedom? His choice: He can live in a virtual world where his every desire is fulfilled, where he will never grow old, never suffer, never die, or he can live in the real world and be free—but face suffering and eventual death. He can either have happiness (without freedom) or freedom (without happiness). What does he choose? Why?
- Comfort or truth? Her choice: She can either live with the illusion that she's loved or find out the truth even though it might hurt. What would she prefer? Why?

Make them draw the line.

- What factors determine if someone is a freedom fighter or a terrorist? A traitor or a whistleblower? Greedy or simply ambitious?
- At what point are we responsible for our choices? When should teenagers (or younger) be tried by our justice system as adults? What would it take to make the punishments meted out truly fit the crime?

LET THE DILEMMAS GROW FROM THE GENRE

Examine your genre, and allow it to influence the choices your character must face. For instance, crime stories naturally lend themselves to exploring issues of justice and injustice: At what point do revenge and justice converge? What does that require of this character? When should we take justice into our own hands? When shouldn't we?

Love, romance, and relationship stories often deal with questions of faithfulness and betrayal: When is it better to hide the truth than to share it? How far can you shade the truth before it becomes a lie? When do you tell someone a secret that would hurt him? For example, your protagonist, a young bride-to-be, has a one-night stand. She feels terrible because she loves her fiancé. Should she tell him what happened and shatter him—and perhaps lose him—or keep the truth hidden?

Fantasy, myth, and science fiction are good venues for exploring issues of consciousness, humanity, and morality: How self-aware does something need to be (an animal, a computer) before it should be afforded the same rights as humans? At what point does destroying an AI computer become murder? Do we really have free will, or are our choices determined by our genetic makeup and environmental cues?

LOOK FOR THE THIRD WAY

You want your readers to be thinking, "I have no idea how this is going to play out." And then, when they see where things go, you want them to be satisfied.

There's a story in the Bible about a time when the religious leaders caught a woman committing adultery and brought her to Jesus. In those days, in that culture, adultery was an offense punishable by death. The men asked Jesus what they should do with this woman.

Now, if Jesus had told them to simply let her go free, he would have been contravening the law. However, if he told them to put her to death, he would have undermined his message of mercy and forgiveness.

It seemed like a pretty good trap until he said, "Whoever is without sin among you, let him cast the first stone."

Nicely done.

I call this finding the Third Way. It's a solution that's consistent with the character's attitude, beliefs, and priorities while also being logical *and* surprising.

Present your hero with a seemingly impossible conundrum.

And then help him find the Third Way out.

Every one of us tries to find meaning in our experiences. We look for the deeper truth lying beneath the surface events of our lives.

Stories reflect that innate desire to derive meaning from existence.

The stories we tell will always reflect a search for or an attitude about meaning, and a story that boldly tells the truth about the world is a story that can impact readers forever.

And that's where we turn our attention next.

CHAPTER 20

MEANING

Telling the Truth About the World

Novelist and short story writer Flannery O'Connor wrote, "When you can state the theme of a story, when you can separate it from the story itself, then you can be sure the story is not a very good one. The meaning of a story has to be embodied in it, has to be made concrete in it. A story is a way to say something that can't be said any other way, and it takes every word in the story to say what the meaning is."

According to O'Connor, the more clearly you can define your theme, the shallower your story is.

And yet, it seems that most English teachers and writing instructors are deeply invested in this idea of coming up with a story's theme when you write or deciphering the theme of the stories you read.

I remember my high school literature teachers and college professors dissecting poems for us, looking for the themes, turning the poems into lessons. They did it with fiction as well. All we had left were corpses of words. That affected me deeply. It drained the power, ripped out the mystery, turned me away from my love of language, poetry, and story—and these were the very teachers who should have been fostering my love of literature, not stifling it.

If you craft a story simply to teach a lesson, the story will always be subservient to the single idea you're trying to express.

One of the most famous stories ever told is "Cinderella." The young woman, Ella, must clean the fireplace and becomes scarred from the cinders, causing her to be derisively nicknamed "Cinder-Ella" by her evil stepsisters. She receives help from a supernatural source, meets the prince of the land, and, though she is separated from him because of her carelessness, he seeks her out and finds her. Together they live happily ever after.

So what's the theme?

The story deals with injustice and compassion, hopes and dreams, heartache and loss, choices and consequences, good and evil, selfishness and selflessness, and more.

But what is the theme?

Well, all of them are.

In truth, the only way to know what the story of Cinderella is about is to experience the story.

And that's just a short story that might take a few minutes to tell. What about a novel? If you can summarize your novel in a theme statement or sentence, why on earth would you spend a year or a decade crafting a 500-page book? It would not only be a colossal waste of your time, but a waste of your readers' time as well.

In a very real sense, if your story can be summarized, it need not be told.

If you can identify the imagery, symbolism, and so on, expect that readers will be able to as well. And as soon as they do, they'll be distracted from the story itself. In *The 38 Most Common Fiction Writing Mistakes (and How to Avoid Them)*, Jack M. Bickham noted, "Fiction does not exist primarily to convince anybody of anything; it exists to tell a story, and by so doing to illuminate the human condition."

So stop trying to define your theme. Write a story to tell the truth about human nature or our relationship to eternity and to the divine, and your story will say more than any theme statement ever could.

Good fiction holds up a mirror for readers to better see themselves.

Sometimes people ask me what message my books are trying to convey or what takeaway I want people to have after they've read one of my novels.

When they ask me that, it makes me think of a story I heard about a dancer who danced an incredible program. After she finished, one of the women from the audience approached her. "That was an amazing dance!" she said. "I was moved to tears, but I just have one question— what did your dance mean?" And the dancer replied, "If I could tell you what it meant, I wouldn't have had to dance it."

If I could tell you what my novels mean, I wouldn't have to write them.

The poet Donald Hall wrote, "The unsayable builds a secret room in the best poems."

It's true of stories as well.

A few years ago, I picked up a literary novel that everyone was talking about. In chapter after chapter someone was getting baptized or crying or washing dishes or it was raining outside, and I remember thinking, "Okay, I get it. Your image is water. Your theme is cleansing. Now get on with the story."

And from that point on, guess what I was doing?

Exactly.

Looking for the next place the writer was going to weave a water image into her novel. And she delivered, in scene after predictable scene.

I was no longer wrapped up in the world of the story. I'd become a critic, an observer. And that's the last thing we want to happen to our readers.

As soon as they notice your use of imagery, they'll begin looking at the story from the outside in, keeping an eye out for the next symbol, motif, or theme. And when they do that, you've allowed them to pull back emotionally from the narrative and start analyzing it, poking around it with their questions from a safe, objective distance.

The risk of using symbolism typically outweighs the potential benefits that it might lend to the story. Why work so hard at putting something into a novel, all the while hoping that no one will notice it, and running the risk that if they do, the story will lose its impact?

Why play games in which the most observant readers end up being the least satisfied?

Why on earth would anyone do that?

Why not just tell the story?

So rather than building your story around a theme (love, forgiveness, freedom) or advice ("Follow your dreams," "Be true to your heart") or a cliché ("Every cloud has a silver lining," "Time heals all wounds"), drive your narrative forward through tension and the kind of moral predicaments we've been exploring.

- Instead of using the theme of "justice," let the story ask the question "What's more important: truth or justice?"
- Rather than giving advice such as "You should forgive others," let your story probe the dilemma "How do I forgive someone who has done the unthinkable to someone I love?"
- Let your story do more than reiterate the cliché "The needs of the many outweigh the needs of the few." Instead, challenge that axiom by asking, "When do the needs of the few outweigh the needs of the many?"

Write from the center of your questions rather than your answers.

Drama depends on tension, so as soon as you start with an answer, you've short-circuited the story because you're beginning with something other than tension, something other than drama. You run the risk of making your story didactic, moralistic, and predictable.

As we examined in the last chapter, start instead with the abrasion of ideas, with significant moral dilemmas. Create situations in which your character needs to (1) be in two places at once, (2) keep two conflicting promises at the same time, or (3) follow two strong convictions that aren't compatible with each other.

For example, does the man who discovers he has terminal cancer tell his family (honesty) or keep his condition a secret and suffer privately (to protect them from worrying about him)? Honesty or protecting loved ones? Which is more important?

That's not an easy question.

And that's why it might make for a good story.

Don't let anything get in the way of your readers' engagement with the story. As soon as readers figure out your literary games of theme and imagery, they'll start looking for the different ways you play, and the whole time they're doing that, they're not immersed in the narrative world you've worked so hard to create.

THE ARTIST'S CALLING

There's an inherent problem in using fiction to try to convey a message: The book can easily turn into propaganda.

For instance, let's say you're writing about a hot-topic issue such as the death penalty—should it be legal or not? If you present the story in such a way that readers get the impression that you're trying to push an agenda—whatever that might be—they'll be distracted from the story: "Okay, I get it, you're against the death penalty. Whatever. Just get on with the story already."

The impact is lost as soon as your agenda interrupts the story and becomes evident to readers.

Propaganda is when a viewpoint is promoted regardless of truth. Art is when truth is rendered regardless of agenda. Art rips the veil away, revealing reality in a way we cannot ignore. It forces us to see the world as it is, to see ourselves as we truly are, and to embrace once again the deep actualities about human nature that we know but so easily forget. Within art, truth touches time, debate becomes irrelevant, and thematic summaries are unnecessary.

Every story happens within a distinct moral universe. There may be immoral stories, but there are no amoral stories. They're all told from a certain worldview, from a specific moral perspective. Every story is based on perceptions of right and wrong, good and evil, life and death.

They all come from a set of beliefs and assumptions about the world and about what matters.

Or, perhaps, that nothing ultimately matters.

That God doesn't exist.

That he does.

That he's in control.

That he's not.

That he cares about you.

That he doesn't.

Do our choices really make a difference, or, at the end of the day, are our lives inconsequential in the big scheme of things? Will justice prevail, or is it an illusion? All of these questions and issues matter, and the views of the author will affect how they are approached.

There's a difference between a story's moral fabric and your own moral agenda. Strive to let your fiction depict the truth of the world as it really is, rather than how you wish it were.

Let the story offer readers perspectives about reality that so often get drowned out in the hum and hustle of daily life.

> "Story is a vessel for carrying meaning. It is the currency of human interchange, the net we cast to capture fugitive truths and the darting rabbits of emotion."
> —Daniel Taylor in *Tell Me a Story: The Life-Shaping Power of Our Stories*

Keep in mind that every story worth telling will offend someone. The truth makes people uncomfortable. If you try to please everyone, you'll end up writing trite, mealy little stories that don't impact anyone. Instead, let the truth stretch out its wings in your stories. Let it resonate in your readers' lives.

You may not have thought about it this way before, but to be a fiction writer, you also need to be a psychologist (understanding people's personalities and intentions), a philosopher (asking big questions about meaning and human nature), and a poet (breathing life into your words and the spaces between them).

To write fiction, you must be intimately familiar with the ragged landscape of the human heart. And you must be willing to explore that territory.

OUR AGATHOKAKOLOGICAL PLANET

A number of years ago, my daughter, who was in sixth grade at the time, was studying for a spelling bee, and one of the advanced words was *agathokakological*. I'd never heard of it before. When I looked it up, I discovered it means "consisting of both good and evil." What a fabulous word: *agathokakological*.

We humans have agathokakological hearts, motives, dreams, passions.

The next day I told my youngest daughter to inform her first-grade teacher that we are an agathokakological species. I wish I could have seen her teacher's expression when she told her that.

Philosophers have long wondered how we fit into this world, somewhere between the apes and the angels. To make us into one or the other is to deny the full reality of who we are, because we have both animal instincts and divine desires. Pascal wrote, "Man must not think that he is on a level either with the brutes or with the angels, nor must he be ignorant of both sides of his nature; but he must know both."

We are an odd race capable of both martyrdom and murder, poetry and rape, worship and genocide. We're from below and from above, bestial and celestial, children of the earth and offspring of the stars.

Agathokakological.

Our world is both more evil than we care to admit and more filled with breathtaking wonder and glory than we dare to imagine.

I'll bet you know some people who only see the agony and not the beauty. Over time they've become skeptical, cynical, jaded. You can see it in their eyes and in the flatness of their smiles, hear it in the thin edge of their laughter.

Other people ignore the pain and pretend there's always a bright side of life. They're the ones who think if we're just nice enough to the terrorists, they'll be nice to us in return. Maybe we can all join hands and dance around the campfire singing, "Give Peace a Chance." But the problem is, right in the middle of the hugfest, someone's going to sneak up from behind with a stiletto and slit your throat. Because that's the kind of world we live in, too. Full of both good and evil.

And the unsettling truth is that we are both the dancers by the fire and the assassins with knives drawn, lurking in the shadows.

We are the ones who make the world the way it is.

Sometimes denial—in one direction or the other—seems like the only way to make sense of things. After all, how could life have so much hope *and* pain?

But if denial doesn't work, we might try to turn down the volume of both the horror and the glory. Go for a middle-of-the-road approach. By muting both the sharpest screams and the wildest laughter we can pretend things aren't nearly as bad or as good as they seem.

It just doesn't make sense that life could be both this magnificent and this terrible, but yet it is. People really do live in palaces. People really do live in garbage dumps. Those of us who reside in middle-class America tend to believe the illusion that this is a middle-class world, but it is not. It is a world of great poverty and great wealth, great pain and great peace. Ecstasy and oblivion.

Consisting of both good and evil.

Agathokakological.

The only option left is to accept the truth that our planet is somehow full of tear stains and giggles, delight and despair. Fiction rips the masks away and allows people to see the stunning, breathtaking, heart-rending realities of life.

The poet Robert Bly beautifully noted the paradox of this world's sadness and splendor when he wrote of "the puzzled grief we all feel at being appointed to do mysterious tasks here, on this planet, among mountain meadows and falling stars."

How do we keep from weeping every hour?

How do we keep from falling to our knees in marvel and amazement?

How do we so blithely go about our daily lives without doing both?

In the end, the glass isn't half empty or half full. It's not half anything. It's an all-of-the-above world. Life is both more full than you'd ever expect and more empty than you can imagine. Lift the strange cup of reality to your lips, look closely at the world for yourself, and you'll see what I mean.

When you write, don't romanticize either wishful thinking or violence.

Don't make light of the evil of the world.

And make a commitment to never silence the joy.

How have I presented evil? Have I glamorized it and made it look alluring or portrayed it as disturbing and repugnant? What about at the other end of the spectrum? Does the story offer hope? Is it redemptive? Is it honest about the paradoxical extremes of our world?

Passion and truth are two clarion attributes of great writing—passion that embraces both the wounds and dreams of life, both the glory and the pain, and truth that guides readers toward experiencing life more fully.

Our stories should (1) tell the truth about the world—exposing the anguish and terror as well as championing the hope and joy; (2) honestly portray the threads of evil, both in our world and in our own hearts;

(3) celebrate love, virtue, and beauty; and (4) uphold the dignity and worth of human life.

Art of any lasting value honestly explores the profound enigma of the human condition and the questions that influence our lives and our destinies. This is the type of writing that honest authors strive to produce.

Rage against mediocrity.

Imbue your fiction with truth.

We are artists. We are writers—slightly neurotic and probably addicted to coffee, late nights, sunsets, laughter, tears, and heartache. Creativity is our drug. We lose ourselves in the smell of old books. We're bewildered by how we can live in a world this full of glory and grief and not be awestruck every moment. And we write stories to help wake people up before they fall asleep for good.

PART V

SUBTLETIES OF
CHARACTERIZATION

CHAPTER 21

STATUS

What No One Is Teaching You
About Characterization

One of the most effective ways of creating unforgettable characters is something that most writers have never even heard of.

Managing status.

I first learned about status years ago while studying physical comedy, mime, and improvisation. I remember listening to acting instructor Keith Johnstone (author of *Impro* and *Impro for Storytellers*) explain how dominance and submission affect actors on stage and how stillness raises status. As he spoke, I kept thinking of how essential it is for writers to capture the same characterizations on the page.

Since then, I've been on the lookout for ways to fine-tune the status of my characters. Here are four essential principles I've discovered.

VARIABLE STATUS IS THE KEY TO DIMENSIONALITY

So what exactly is status?

Simply put, in every social interaction, one person has (or attempts to have) a more dominant role. Those in authority or those who want to exert authority use a collection of verbal and nonverbal cues to gain and maintain higher status. But it's not just authority figures who do this. In daily life all of us are constantly adjusting and negotiating the amount of status we portray as we face different situations and interact with different people.

Novelists have the daunting task of showing this dynamic of shifting submission and dominance through dialogue, posture, pauses, communication patterns, body language, action, and, when applicable, the character's thoughts.

- Dominant individuals have confidence, a relaxed demeanor, loose and easy gestures and gait. Submissive people constrict themselves—their stride, voice, posture, gestures.
- Typically, the closer a person's hand is to his mouth during a conversation, the less status he has. Looking down, crossing your legs, biting your lip, and holding your hands in front of your face are all ways of hiding. Concealment lowers status.
- Eye contact is a powerful way of maintaining dominance. Although cultures differ, in North America we make prolonged eye contact when we wish to intimidate, control, threaten, or seduce.
- Stillness is power. Dominant people delay before replying to questions, not because they can't think of anything to say but to control the conversation. They blink less frequently than submissive people and keep their heads still as they speak. The more fidgety, bedraggled, or frazzled a person is, the less status he has. In movies the protagonist will often smoke so he or she has an excuse to be slow in answering questions as he pauses to take a drag from his cigarette—a high-status play.
- Submissive people apologize more and agree more than dominant people. They try to please and placate and are easily intimidated. To act as if I need something from you lowers my status. To let you know that you can be helpful to me raises my status.
- The most effective negotiators tend to mirror the status of the people with whom they're doing business. This way they neither appear too aggressive (intimidatingly high status) or too willing to give in and compromise (unimpressively low status).

Think about the roles you play in relating to your boss, your lover, your children, the bellhop you meet at the hotel. You step onto the court of your son's basketball game to be a referee and you enter one role; you go on a date with your spouse and enter another. Golfing with your buddies, visiting your mother at the nursing home, giving that big presentation at work—all of these situations require a certain set of behaviors and call forth differing degrees of confidence and status.

As an interesting exercise in evaluating status, watch a presidential debate with the sound turned off. If you're like most people, you'll be able to start reading signs of status quite easily when you begin to look for them in other people.

Status varies with respect to three things: relationship (a father has higher relational status than his ten-year-old daughter), position (a boss has higher positional status than her employees), and situation (if you're attacked by a team of highly trained ninjas and you've never studied martial arts, you'd have quite a bit lower situational status than your nunchucks-wielding assailants). Banter between friends and mutual sarcasm are signs of equal status. Vying for power in the relationship is not.

Although the level of relational, positional, and situational status might be out of our hands, our response to it is not. Status can be shown through tension, how characters handle setbacks, or just in how they deal with everyday encounters with other people. The daughter might manipulate her father, the employee might quit, and you might summon up enough moxie to frighten off those ninjas.

So in determining status, choices matter more than circumstances.

> Stillness, confidence, courage, and moral groundedness all raise status.

When readers complain that a character is one-dimensional, flat, or "cardboard," they may not realize it but they're actually noting that the character—regardless of the social context in which she appears—always has the same degree of status. She might always be angry or ruthless or heroic or any number of things, but the more uniformly she responds to everyone and everything, the less interesting she'll be to readers.

People in real life are complex.

Fictional characters need to be as well.

We understand a person's characterization, whether in real life or in fiction, by seeing how that person responds in different situations to different people.

So what's the key to a well-rounded character?

Simple: She doesn't have the same status in every situation.

To create a fascinating and memorable protagonist, readers must see her status vary as she interacts with the other characters in the story.

Dimensionality is brought out by showing the subtle shifts in status as the character relates to others within different contexts. To show complexity of characterization, we need to see the character in a variety of relationships or conversations.

In my novels featuring FBI Special Agent Patrick Bowers, whenever he's at a crime scene or standing up to a bad guy, he always has the highest status. He will never back down, he will never give in, he will never give up.

However, to have dimensionality he also needs relationships in which he has *low* status. As a single dad, he struggles with knowing how to handle his sharp-witted and surly teenage daughter, and, lacking some social graces, he fumbles for the right things to say to the women he's attracted to. Without his daughter or a love interest to reveal those *low-status* aspects of his characterization, he would be one-dimensional and certainly not engaging enough to build a series around.

If you want readers to emotionally invest in your protagonist, you'll need to find some areas of his life where he has a weakness, low status, or something to overcome. Remember, even Indiana Jones was afraid of snakes and Superman—the highest-status superhero ever created—is defenseless against Kryptonite.

WORD CHOICE DETERMINES CHARACTERIZATION

In theatre the phrase "stealing the scene" refers to instances in which another person upstages the star. Actually, it's just another way of saying that the star (or protagonist) no longer has the highest status.

When this happens onstage, it'll annoy the star.

When it happens in your novel, it'll turn off your readers.

You can shatter hundreds of pages of careful characterization with one poorly chosen word.

A person with high status might shout, holler, call, or yell, but if he screams, screeches, bawls, or squeals, his status is lowered. Similarly, a character who quivers, trembles, whines, or pleads has lower status than one who tries to control the pain. For example:

> 1. Parker drew the blade across Sylvia's arm. She shrieked and begged him to stop.
> 2. Parker drew the blade across Sylvia's arm. She clenched her teeth, refusing to give him the satisfaction of seeing her cry.

In the first example, Sylvia's uncontrolled reaction lowers her status beneath that of her assailant. In the second, however, her resolve raises her status above that of Parker, who has evidently failed to intimidate her. Rather than appearing victimized, she has become heroic: Yes, he could make her bleed, but he could not make her cry. That's a woman with high status.

While an antagonist might have higher situational, relational, or positional status, your protagonist must never *act* in a way (that is, make choices) that lowers his status below that of the antagonist.

Take a moment to let that sink in.

You might find it helpful to imagine high-status movie stars playing the part of your protagonist. I'm not sure about you, but I have a hard time imagining Liam Neeson, Jason Statham, or Bruce Willis pleading for mercy or screaming for help.

Choices, more than anything else, will determine status.

So while editing your story, continually ask yourself what you want readers to feel about each character. Do you want them to be on this character's side? To cheer for him? Fear him? Despise him? Discount him? Every action, every word of dialogue, every gesture—even every speaker attribution—communicates a certain level of status.

Make sure the words you choose support the impression you're trying to make. Don't undermine all of your efforts to create a strong protagonist by using the wrong verb. If Betty *stomps* across the floor (showing lack of self-control) or *struts* across it (implying the need for attention) she'll have lower status than someone who *strides* across it (showing composure and confidence).

Even punctuation affects status.

> 1. "I know you heard me! Move away from Anna! If you lay a hand on her, I guarantee you will regret it!"
> 2. "I know you heard me. Move away from Anna. If you lay a hand on her, I guarantee you will regret it."

In the first example, the exclamation points cause the speaker to come across as frantic or desperate. In the second, the periods show him to be controlled, measured, authoritative. That's how a hero responds.

A wimpy protagonist isn't interesting.

A wimpy antagonist isn't frightening.

In marketable fiction, both heroes and villains need high status. When villains aren't frightening or heroes aren't inspiring, it's almost always because the author has let them act in a way that undermines their status.

PROTAGONISTS NEED OPPORTUNITIES TO BE HEROIC

When I was writing my second novel, one section gave me a particularly difficult time. Agent Bowers is at the scene of a suicide when Detective Dunn, a street-smart local homicide cop, shows up. Dunn is tough. He's used to calling the shots, to having the highest status.

In this scene, he makes an aggressive high-status move by getting in Bowers' face and then taunting him. I struggled with showing that, as bold and brash as Dunn is, my hero still has higher status. After thrashing through numerous drafts, here's how the encounter finally played out (from Bowers' point of view).

> Dunn stepped close enough for me to smell his garlicky breath.
>
> "This is my city. The next time you and your pencil-pushing lawyer buddies from Quantico decide to stick your nose into an ongoing investigation, at least have the courtesy to go through the proper channels."
>
> "I'd suggest you back away," I said. "Now."
>
> He backed up slowly.

Agent Bowers refuses to be baited and isn't intimidated by Dunn's aggressive posturing. If he was, readers would lose faith in him and side with Dunn. Instead, Bowers remains calm and, by exhibiting poise and self-control, induces Dunn's submission. (Incidentally, by adding the speaker attribution "I said," I inserted a slight pause in Bowers' response, subtly adding to his status even more. To see the difference, read the sentence aloud with and without the pause.)

At the end of the scene, when Dunn steps back, there's no doubt in the mind of the readers who is in charge.

Readers won't empathize with a weak protagonist. They expect protagonists who have strength of conviction, moral courage, and noble aspirations. It's true, of course, that during the story the protagonist might be struggling to grow in these areas, but readers need to see her as someone worth cheering for along the way. If you're grappling with how to do that, try one of these three ways.

1. **Have your protagonist sacrifice for the good of others.** This might come in the form of a physical sacrifice (stepping in front of a bullet), a financial sacrifice (anonymously paying another's debt), a material sacrifice (volunteering for the Peace Corps), or an emotional sacrifice (forgiving someone for a deep offense).

2. **Have her stand up for the oppressed.** I've noticed that some authors try to show how "tough" their protagonist is by portraying her as cold or unfeeling—especially at a crime scene. Bad idea. Most of the time, readers want the hero (or heroine) to be compassionate and life-affirming.

    Let's say your medical examiner is at that crime scene and one of the other cops gestures toward the corpse and quips, "They stab 'em, you slab 'em." Your protagonist needs to uphold the value of human life. She might reproach the cop or remind him of the victim's grieving family. Conversely, if you had her say those words and make light of something as precious as life itself and she gets rebuked by someone else, you'll end up devastating her status.

3. **Have her turn the other cheek.** If someone slaps your protagonist and she refuses to fight back, her self-control raises her status above that of the attacker. Strength isn't only shown by what a person can do but by what she *could do* but *refrains from doing*. Self-restraint always raises status.

STATUS CRYSTALLIZES AS THE STORY ESCALATES

As your story builds toward its climax, the status of both your hero and your villain will also rise. The bad guy will become more and more cold-hearted or unstoppable, and the good guy will need to summon unprecedented strength or courage to save the day.

Status has more to do with actions than motives, so even though the hero and villain have completely different agendas, you can raise the status of either of them by giving him more self-control, courage, and resolve.

Remember, stillness is power, so to make a villain more imposing, let him slow down. Show readers that he's in no hurry to commit his evil deed—he has such high status that he can walk slowly and still catch the person fleeing frantically through the woods.

Those with high status accomplish the most with the least amount of effort.

A terrifying villain doesn't violently yank someone's hair back and twist her head around to make her look him in the eye. Instead, he might entwine his hand in her hair and slowly force her to look at him, even as she struggles to get free. But for him it is no effort. Yes, he could jerk her head back, but he chooses not to. Instead, slowly and methodically he forces her to submit.

Villains are less frightening when they're self-congratulatory, impressed with their own plans, swaggering, or showing off, because all of these actions lower their status.

You actually *lower* a villain's status by giving him the need to prove himself. Sadistic, chortling, hand-wringing villains aren't nearly as unnerving as calm, relentless ones who are simply indifferent to the suffering of others. The more they admire themselves, the lower their status becomes.

Villains are made more believable and more frightening when they don't find pleasure in other people's pain but treat the suffering of others with indifference.

If your story calls for multiple villains, stagger their status so the top-tier bad guy has the highest status and is therefore the most threatening and dangerous person for your protagonist to encounter at the story's climax.

To summarize: Think of every relationship and social encounter as a transaction of status. Give your protagonist a variety of relationships that reveal different status dynamics and bring out deeper dimensionality. Be sure to sharpen status differentiations as your story progresses and build toward that satisfying and surprising climax.

Are there any places where I've undermined the status of my protagonist? Is the status of each of the characters consistent within specific relationships or social contexts? Have I intentionally decreased the status of unimportant characters to flatten them out and give them less dimensionality?

STATUS AT A GLANCE	
LOW STATUS	HIGH STATUS
- Arrogance	+ Confidence
- Loss of control	+ Self-control
- Crying or weeping often	+ Reserved, might cry over the death of a loved one
- Screaming	+ Shouting, calling, speaking calmly
- Quivering, trembling, begging	+ Resisting giving in to the pain, never begs
- Slouching	+ Good posture
- Tense	+ At ease, relaxed
- Averts eye contact	+ Steady gaze
- Postures, shows off	+ Exhibits poise, feels no need to impress others

LOW STATUS	HIGH STATUS
- Brags, narcissistic	+ Doesn't draw attention to self, humble
- Shrinks from danger	+ Rises to the occasion
- Cowardly	+ Courageous
- Shy	+ Outgoing
- Self-congratulatory	+ Self-effacing
- Needy	+ Self-reliant
- Argumentative, interrupts others	+ Listens attentively
- Tries to be cool	+ Can't help but be cool
- Worries about reputation	+ Cares more about ideals
- Dependent	+ Independent but also relational
- Vies for control	+ Naturally has control
- Gives in to pressure, conforms	+ Sets trends
- Makes threats	+ Takes action
- Impressed with himself, self-congratulatory	+ Lifts up and encourages others
- Worried about what others think	+ Doesn't care what others think
- Sadistic	+ Compassionate

CHAPTER 22

ATTITUDE

Quirks, Idiosyncrasies, and the Difference
Between Intention and Motivation

Whether the protagonist is admirable or not, readers have to be on his
side. Our goal: Create a character who readers are interested enough in
to worry about *and* to want to spend the next two—or ten or twenty—
hours of their lives alone with. If they don't care whether or not he succeeds, they won't care about the story and they won't recommend the
book to others—if they even finish it themselves.

Readers need to desire the protagonist's ultimate happiness or success, but that might not always come in the way the character anticipates.

If he wants something that readers know isn't good for him—for
example, fame and fortune at the cost of his marriage—they might actually be worried that he *will* get what he wants because they know that
in the end the character ultimately desires happiness but is mistaken
or deceived about how to get it. In that case, readers would want him
to *fail* to get what he thinks he wants so he can *succeed* at getting what
he really needs.

However, as writers, we need to be honest and let the character live
out the consequences of his choices without intruding on the story by
placing an agenda on his growth or manipulating the story toward a
cheesy, contrived ending.

Two of my novels terrified me when I was writing them. Both gave
me nightmares. It wore me out emotionally. I didn't want to tell such
dark stories, but those were the dinosaurs that I was uncovering. I

couldn't just tidy them up and make them safe and neat and clean and harmless. In *Writing in a Convertible with the Top Down* Sheila Bender claimed, "We can't write meaningfully if we are trying to be nice." I think she's right on the money.

Let the story kick and scream and bleed if it must. Don't tame it. Don't remove its claws and fangs, or you won't be as honest with it as your art form demands.

Asking me to censor the character's actions or change them because they made me feel uncomfortable would be like telling a ballet dancer, "Hey, why don't you jump in the middle of that dance?" If the jump doesn't fit naturally in the dance at that point, it wouldn't look right when she performed it.

A dancer's moves must grow from her emotional connection to the music.

A character's choices must grow from his pursuit of his unmet desires.

Sometimes you need to ask where the darkness is rearing its head in your story.

And then look it directly in the eye, and write what you see.

THE UNIVERSAL PURSUIT OF HAPPINESS

All fictional characters, just like real people, desire happiness. As philosophers throughout the ages have pointed out, happiness is the end to which we all aspire. After all, nobody pursues happiness so he can get money and power; he pursues money and power so he can get happiness.

The route the character takes in his pursuit of happiness might be one that readers know is bad (alcoholism, drug addiction) or one they respect (volunteering to help AIDS patients, donating to charity).

If you're writing a scene about a fifth-grade girl's soccer team, make it clear to your readers what your protagonist wants. Is it to win the game? Show off? Be popular? Make a friend? Prove something? All of these are valid. But whatever you choose will need to be contextually appropriate. Stay focused on one intention so readers can dial into it and worry about whether she ends up getting what she wants (the good thing) or if they should cheer for her to fail (to get a better thing).

INTRIGUING CHARACTERS HAVE IDIOSYNCRASIES

Readers want contradictions within a character but consistency in how she responds to similar situations. Here are four ways to do that.

1. **Quirks:** Give your character a flaw, weakness, wound, or incongruity. For example, she could struggle with anger (flaw), have asthma (weakness), be recovering from grieving a lost loved one (wound), or be emotionally needy but also intellectually acute (incongruity).

2. **Reversals:** Give a trait, characteristic, or attribute to someone readers wouldn't expect. For example, they might not be surprised that a motorcycle-gang member gets a skull tattoo on his neck, but what if the conservative Baptist preacher does?

3. **Habits and hobbies:** Is he a beer snob? Does she always talk about herself in the third person? Does he collect model airplanes? Does she make sure the morsels of food on her plate never touch each other? Does he only set his alarm clock to prime numbers? Give your characters a unique and memorable habit or pastime.

4. **Introversion and extroversion:** The typical introvert/extrovert paradigm isn't robust enough for authors because it doesn't take social context into consideration.

   Every one of us is outgoing in some areas of life but not in others. Status affects this. So does the situation. Your protagonist might be reserved at his accounting firm, boisterous and jovial watching the football game with his buddies, sensitive to his wife, goofy with his kids. A character can recharge his batteries and act in contextually appropriate but multivariate ways and remain consistent. That's what we're shooting for.

> Does each main character have a peculiarity, foible, special skill, or emblem that represents something significant in his life? Remember to keep in mind:
>
> 1. Status
> 2. Quirks
> 3. Inconsistencies
> 4. Desires

When trying to create empathy for a character who's unlikable but with whom you need your readers to identify, give her a wound we all share—perhaps a memory that haunts her, a shattered dream she can't get over, or grief over losing someone precious to her.

Avoid the clichéd archetypes that some writing instructors encourage authors to use (the Hero, the Trickster, the Mentor, the Nemesis, and so on ...) and instead develop your own unique characters that fit integrally with the story you're trying to tell.

Explore your character's fears and phobias. (Phobias are irrational fears. So to be afraid of a cobra is not a phobia, but to be afraid of all snakes is.) Most people are afraid of helplessness in the face of danger (for example, being buried alive). Many are afraid of needles, the dark, drowning, rats, heights, closed spaces, and so on. Think of the things that frighten you the most. It's likely that many of your readers will fear them as well.

Look at the doubts, shame, secrets, and desires of your character but also at what those emotions and reactions reveal about him.

- Doubts are often the result of wounds. Where does he hurt? What kind of healing does he hope for? How is he trapped by the past? What causes him to doubt his core beliefs?
- Shame reveals a person's values. What is your character ashamed of? What does that tell you about what she considers virtuous be-

havior? What steps has she taken to overcome her shame/guilt? What happened as a result?

- Fear comes from encountering things that we believe can injure us (physically, emotionally, psychologically, socially). What we desire is inextricably tied to what we fear. So if we desire freedom, we'll fear imprisonment. If we desire adventure, we'll fear monotony. When you know someone's deepest desire, you'll also know his greatest fear.

- Frustration happens when something interferes with us reaching our goals. What frustrates your character the most? What does that tell you about her priorities?

- Secrets show us what a person is striving to protect. What secrets does he have? Why has he kept those things to himself? What would happen if his secrets were made known? What steps is he willing to take to hide them?

- Passion elicits an ardent response. What makes her weep or pound the table? What dreams does she have? Why might she be afraid of pursuing some of them?

- Anger is the cousin of love. When you know what your character loves, you know what will enrage him (when that thing is threatened). Does he love his pet dog? He'll be angry when someone tries to poison her. Does he love unborn children? He'll be furious about abortion. Does he love the environment? He'll be enraged about pollution.

BACKGROUND HISTORIES ARE OVERRATED

Many writing books and instructors encourage aspiring writers to write up a detailed background synopsis of main characters. Books and websites offer complex worksheets for this: Where did your character go to college? What's her favorite food? Color? Outfit? The templates include places to insert favorite sayings, work history, parents' names, and so on.

Filling out those detailed character histories and personality profiles is most often simply a waste of time.

I don't know where my best friend went to high school or his favorite band when he was in college or where he lived when he was ten, but I know what he's passionate about, what he likes to do in his spare time, what makes him furious and happy and thankful. Those are the things that matter—not the movie he took his first date to, or his favorite snack food when he was eleven, or his nickname for his cat.

Just like with outlining, if you spend a chunk of time coming up with this type of material, you'll be tempted to use it. Readers don't need all of that background information. If you choose to dump it on them, they'll resent having to wade through it.

A character with an attitude is always more interesting than a character with a history.

Details need to serve the broader scope of the story. Honestly, most readers don't care if a character is wearing a "dun-colored, virgin-wool cardigan sweater." They want to know what this sweater-wearing person is doing in the story in the first place. What does she want? What is she trying to accomplish, obtain, or avoid?

Spend less time telling us about the character's background and more time depicting her quest to fulfill her dream or overcome the obstacle that's keeping her from what she desires most.

Just like real people, interesting fictional characters have different goals, attitudes, and histories with regard to the other people they meet.

As we explored in the last chapter, characterization is brought out by showing how a character acts in relationship to others. By showing your character's quirks, fears, hopes, priorities, and attitudes in relation to her environment and to other people, you'll render her both memorable and realistic.

She might be trying to seduce her co-worker.

Or use him to get ahead.

Or help him succeed.

But whatever she wants from him or for him will shape every interaction she has with him. Every bit of dialogue. Every gesture. Every aspect of body language and inflection.

A character's history with another character might be very brief or virtually nonexistent: Your protagonist approaches the hotel registration desk to get a room and chats with the desk clerk, or he might hail a cab and tell the driver an address—but in each case he wants something from the other character.

Scenes in which you have three, four, or more characters become exponentially difficult to craft because every character's response to every other character needs to be natural and will reflect that person's goal, history, and attitude toward him or her.

For example, imagine four people go out for supper: Janie, Andrew, Kim, and Russell.

Janie

- Has been dating Andrew for five months, is deeply in love with him, and is hoping he'll ask her to move in with him
- Doesn't know Kim very well and would like to get to know her better but is also jealous of her stunning good looks
- Is intimidated by Russell because he holds her lover's career in his hands

Andrew

- Is dating Janie but is losing interest in her. He knows he needs to end the relationship but doesn't know how to do it in a way that's sensitive to her feelings.
- Is angry at Kim for running over his dog
- Is good friends with Russell but also works for him. He feels tension between his personal and professional obligations.

Kim

- Covets Janie's financial success
- Wishes Andrew would forgive her and patch up their relationship
- Hates Russell because he fired her last year

Russell
- Knows he needs to fire Andrew and is distancing himself from him so it will be easier
- Is annoyed by Janie's vanity
- Has fallen in love with Kim and is divorcing his wife, who is dying of cancer, so he can pursue her

Now, give this group either a decision that needs to be made or something controversial to discuss, and see what happens.

With all those attitudes and goals jockeying for position, would this scene be a difficult one to write?

Absolutely.

Well, guess what?

That's what you'll be doing in every chapter, in every scene, in every bit of dialogue you write.

You'll need to keep in mind every character's goal, attitude, and history concerning every other character and balance that with everyone's relational, situational, and positional status.

Tough?

Oh, yeah.

That's one reason it's so hard to write good fiction, and that's one reason why so many characters fall flat and why you'll find so many novels in which everyone acts and talks pretty much the same.

INTENTION DIFFERS FROM MOTIVATION

Intention is what the character is trying to accomplish. Motive is why he's trying to accomplish it.

So I might be hungry and looking for something to eat. My intention is to find food. My motivation is my hunger.

Simple enough.

But they seem to get easily mixed up.

In the theatrical world, many times when an actor asks, "What's my motivation?" he really means, "What's my intention?"

Problems come when we confuse these two aspects of characterization. Just as in real life, story characters will always want certain things and take concrete steps to achieve them. However, just as in real life, when we're not always aware of why we want something, story characters might not always be aware of their motivation either.

Additionally, a character might think he knows why he's pursuing some goal, but he might be wrong. However, that doesn't change how active he is in trying to accomplish that objective.

"What do I want?" is a far different and far easier question to answer than, "Why do I want it?"

After all, every action we take is shaded by a thousand "whys." Even though police officers and lawyers might make a big deal out of "proving motive," that's actually impossible to do. After all, how could we prove a motive that the person committing the crime might not have even been aware of, and how could we be so presumptuous as to boil it down to one word like *greed* or *hate* or *revenge*?

As an author, it might be helpful for you to understand a character's motive, but it's far more important for you to clarify, in the minds of your readers, her intention.

Often motive doesn't make one iota of difference to the forward movement of the story—only the way in which your character pursues the object of her desire matters. As Jerome Stern writes in *Making Shapely Fiction*, "The actions you give your characters should be densely informative."

Every choice reveals.

Every action exposes.

Let's say you're writing a political intrigue novel. There's a ruthless politician vying for power. Why is he doing it? Well, he obviously gets some satisfaction from it, but why does he get satisfaction from it? Who knows. Nature? Nurture? A mixture of both?

Or imagine a master criminal who wants to take over the world. Why? Maybe he's power hungry. Maybe he's bored. Maybe he thinks it's the best thing that could happen to humankind. It could be a mid-life crisis, and world domination seems more attractive to him than buying a red convertible. Or maybe all of the above. Move past that, and ask, "What steps does he take in his quest to take over the world?" Ah, now you're getting to the heart of the story.

We run the risk of making him too one-dimensional when we try to define motive too narrowly.

Why? Because readers know that people in real life act for reasons that aren't so simple and clear-cut. Why do people get a divorce? Maybe because they're angry, disappointed, frustrated, hurt, facing financial difficulties, resentful, disillusioned, hopeless, have fallen out of love with each other, are in love with someone else, or any combination of those reasons—and others.

Most of the time, it would be futile to try to pinpoint which of the many complex factors was the one that finally contributed to the death of the marriage. Making it seem as if there is only one reason could also alienate readers because it would strike them as too simplistic.

Yes, you could try to show the genesis of a killer by showing that his mother punished him for bedwetting until he was ten or that the boys in his seventh grade class called him names. If this ties in and informs the current story without being offered as a simplistic explanation for his complex sociopathic behavior, then go for it. But usually, the more you try to convince readers that *one* thing created the motive behind *everything*, the less they will believe you.

Life is complex. The reasons that lie behind our intentions are not always clear. (If they were, an awful lot of psychiatrists and therapists would be out of jobs.)

To create believable, three-dimensional characters, stop trying to distill their motivations down into one word or idea.

However, intention is another story.

In the case of showing intention to readers, the more specific you can be, the better.

The character goes into the kitchen. What does he want? To find the checkbook? To get a bagel with cream cheese? To fix the sink? If you want to make your readers worry about whether he gets what he wants, they'll obviously need to know what that object of desire is.

A character's motives might be multidimensional and open for debate, but his intent in each scene needs to be crystal clear.

And remember, he might think he knows why he wants certain things, but just as in real life, he might be wrong.

He might be under the impression that he wants to coach his son's football team so he can help his boy succeed, but it might be clear to readers that he's really doing it to avoid spending time with his wife.

Hidden desires run beneath the surface of our lives—subtext we don't even realize is there.

And it's going to be that way in our stories as well.

You might try to accomplish something both for selfish reasons and unselfish ones at the same time. For example, I might be writing this book to earn money to pay for my daughter's college education (an unselfish reason) but also to impress you with how smart I am (a selfish reason), or to help you become a better writer (unselfish), or to finally organize more than a decade's worth of notes on writing (selfish), and so on.

So readers need to know the intention of each character in each scene, but they won't always know the motive behind the intention. Make the intention clear through action, dialogue, body language, and so on, or simply have the character state his desire.

To summarize: An action that the character takes in pursuit of a goal is not his motivation. His motivation is why he would ever pursue that goal in the first place. Motive is the reason behind the intention. Intention is the reason behind the action. Motive might remain unknown to you and your readers. Intention should be evident to your readers, or they'll be confused about what the scene is primarily about.

When you're writing, remember that:
- Variable status develops dimensionality.
- Contradictions create depth.
- Believability facilitates empathy.
- Intention drives action.

SETTING IS NOT JUST A LOCATION

Treat setting as a character in your story rather than simply the back-drop of your story.

Just as your characters will have specific goals, attitudes, and histo-ries with the other characters in the story, they'll also have these (at least to some degree) with regard to the setting of the story.

As Donald Maass points out in *Writing the Breakout Novel*, "How does your setting make people feel? That is the key, not how a place looks but its psychological effect on the characters in your novel."

When your protagonist visits the beach, it might bring back mem-ories of the time when he was ten and his brother drowned or his ex-periences skinny-dipping out here with his girlfriend when he was in college—two vastly different emotional responses. Whatever that loca-tion brings to the surface, whatever feelings it calls forth, it will affect his actions, mood, and demeanor.

Perhaps the garden she's in brings her a sense of peace and security.

Or the dark woods give her chills.

Or the busy street corner disorients her.

Or her desk at work reminds her of how unhappy she is in her job.

Two people are making their way through an abandoned gold mine—how does that make each person feel? Claustrophobic? Ner-vous? Adventurous?

They're at the opera—are they bored? Intrigued? Impressed? Confused?

How does the setting affect the psychology of the characters? How do they interact with it? How does it make them feel? Let them express this in the way they respond to the situation and to the other characters within that environment.

Our characters shouldn't just exist as one-dimensional cutouts dropped into different environments. They should have an active relationship and attitude about each location.

Is the relationship between my characters and the story environment clear? How does the setting affect their psychology? How do they interact with it? What annoys them about this environment? What gets in the way of them reaching their goals? What disadvantages does the setting cause them? What assets does it provide? Are there ways I can reshape the story to make the setting more significant to the plot?

Also, try giving your character an attitude toward an object—he's afraid of guns; seeing blood makes him faint; black leather boots turn him on. Whatever.

Giving your character an attitude toward people, objects, and settings will help bring his characterization to life.

Next we'll explore the debate about whether stories exist to alter characters or to reveal them. It's not an easy question, but understanding the issues revolving around it will help you create more memorable and well-rounded characters to populate the stories you tell.

CHAPTER 23

DEPTH

Revelation vs. Transformation

A number of years ago, I was speaking at an event to train ministers on more effective storytelling techniques. When I was done, one of them called me aside and told me about a teenage boy named Phil from their church.

Apparently, the young man's father told the boy all the time that he was worthless and no good. Well, the night before, Phil had taken a razor blade and carved the word *worthless* into one of his forearms and the words *no good* into the other. Now he was in the hospital, and the pastor was on the way to visit him. He was trying to figure out what to say to him, and he wanted to see if I had any ideas.

I'll never forget that conversation as we tried to figure out what he could tell Phil to affirm that he truly was precious. The events involving Phil's choice undoubtedly affected him, as well as his father and that minister, for a long time.

Phil's decision to carve those words in his arms didn't just show us what he was like, it also affected the direction his life was taking in a very real and concrete way.

INNER STRUGGLE, INNER CHANGE

There's some disagreement among story theorists about the relationship of characters to stories. Some people teach that stories exist simply to reveal characterizations, to show readers what that character is really like inside. Others believe stories are there to transform characters.

They refer to "character arcs" and point out how the struggles of the story change the character.

So does a character need to change? Are stories just there to reveal characteristics or also to shape characters?

Putty people and pebble people.

Where do you stand?

Remember the three types of struggles that characters face in stories: internal, external, and interpersonal. The pathway through each struggle toward its resolution affects characters in different ways.

The more profound the internal struggle, the more profound the change in the character. As writers, we can't just generate empathy and concern toward our characters and then fail to deliver a satisfying emotional payoff.

As I mentioned in Chapter 3, often in stories that deal with external struggles, either justice or survival (physical, spiritual, psychological) is at stake. Think of a crime story (in which justice is at stake) or a horror story (where survival is).

If the struggle is primarily external, the character might remain essentially the same but the situation will be transformed. If the struggle is primarily internal or interpersonal, the character will be transformed and the situation might remain essentially the same.

CONFLICT SHAPES CHARACTERS

In real life when we're faced with a struggle, change is inevitable—we'll either overcome or be overcome, grow or crumble, engage more in life or retreat more from it. We won't come out of the struggle the same as we entered it.

Getting or not getting what we want affects us in real ways, so it needs to affect characters in fiction. It's not just if the character gets what he wants but how that closure, that new normal, affects him. The journey through conflict always changes us, at least to some degree.

The conflict serves to develop the characters and is significant to their growth or peace. If they have learned nothing and acquired no new knowledge or skills, the story has essentially done nothing for them.

Think of it this way: Even in a story centered on external struggles, at the end of the narrative, the main character will have matured and grown more aware of her recourses or acquired more insights or acumen to face the future. The master spy will be better prepared for his next mission or adventure, the detective more experienced, the stunt car driver more adept and responsive.

It's naive to think that a character who faces a struggle isn't shaped by the experience, that the character's entire personality is intact and is simply brought to the surface during the struggle of encountering the dilemma of the book.

Two summers ago I was driving a rental car and was in an accident with another vehicle. The car I was driving got smashed up pretty badly. Thankfully, no one was hurt, but our insurance company then informed us we were not covered under our current policy.

Talk about being thrown into a difficult situation.

In the end, the credit card company paid for the damage, so there was a happy ending, but the experience didn't just reveal who I was or what I would do in that situation—it also affected me for months, making me nervous about driving rental cars.

That misadventure changed me.

The more the story relates to internal and interpersonal struggles, the more transformation or change. The more it focuses on external struggles, the more revelation. But think about it: Surviving a hurricane, saving a drowning child, killing someone in self-defense—all of these things would deeply affect you if you experienced them. Traumatic experiences not only reveal, they also impact.

Those who believe stories are simply there to reveal characterization claim that people in real life don't change that much.

But in real life, people *are* altered by their circumstances—they convert to a new religion; they get a brain tumor and reevaluate their lives; a friendship disintegrates, and they learn lessons about themselves and how they relate to other people.

They carve the words *worthless* and *no good* into their arms.

That choice affects them, alters the trajectory of their lives.

Sometimes for the better, sometimes for the worse.

Does your response to conflict reveal what you're like? Sure. And does it shape who you're becoming? Of course. We repress, we try to ignore, we drink ourselves into oblivion, we find a spiritual awakening, but we are dynamic people. After all, if conflict only serves to reveal characteristics about a person, what could it possibly be that shapes or changes us?

We are always being impacted by the struggles we face.

So are our story characters.

The question isn't just, "What does this situation reveal about him?" but, "What does it call forth from him that he would not have been capable of without experiencing the conflict of the story?"

The genre and the character's primary struggle determine how much revelation and how much transformation occur. But once the struggle becomes personal, change is inevitable.

Stories aren't just here for us to see what the characters are made of but to make those characters into more than they are. Readers aren't simply interested in what this character is capable of doing but in who this character is capable of becoming. Conflicts don't just reveal characterizations; they also develop characters.

Choice precedes change. If your protagonist changes in a significant way just because another character told him he should, the story will suffer.

Give your protagonist something to overcome and a significant decision to make on the journey toward that goal.

At the end of all stories, there is some degree of either redemption/ renewal or some loss of hope. The end of a story is intimately tied to the escalation of the protagonist's struggle. Will he succeed? Find freedom? Give up? Commit suicide?

A deepening self-awareness always requires a response. That response might be acceptance, the courage to pursue new dreams, denial or distraction, or any number of things. To some degree, internal growth is a subplot of all meaningful stories.

If readers care about a series character, they want him to become more fleshed out and to do more than just rise to the challenge—they also want him to learn so that in each progressive episode he can rise to another even greater challenge. That's the difference between a chronicle of events and a story. Events reveal traits. Stories develop characters.

So look at the physical, emotional, psychological, intellectual, interpersonal, and spiritual aspects of the character's life, and brainstorm ways to show how the struggles have informed him or equipped him to better face the future.

Here are four questions to consider as you evaluate your protagonist's relationship to your story.

- Does this character become more complex as a result of this story, or does he remain unchanged? Is that what this story demands or requires of him?
- Does this story show what the character is capable of doing or who he's on his way to becoming? Is the story primarily here to explore the character's depths or expand them? How does it end up doing both?
- What does this struggle draw out of him, and what does it pour into him?
- What effect would this event have on this character's personality? Dreams? Aspirations? Self-esteem? Self-confidence?

> When thinking about your characters' struggles, remember that readers want a series of progressively worse things to happen to (or within) the protagonist.

While it's exciting to experience a good spy novel, unless there's an internal struggle we can identify with or a love story (interpersonal struggle) to engage our emotions, we might appreciate the story but will probably not be moved by it. So to create more reader empathy, include more internal struggles that readers can emotionally identify with.

These last few chapters have covered a lot of ground regarding characterization. Before closing up this section, let's have a short Q & A time about characters.

Q: "How many characters should you include?"

A: The fewest possible to tell your story well.

Q: "How many point-of-view characters can you use?"

A: It depends on the story. As I was reading one novel, I stopped keeping track after the author reached nineteen point-of-view characters. It split my empathy so much that I was no longer emotionally engaged in the story.

Most stories have fewer than five or six.

By the way, make sure your point-of-view characters or other major characters haven't gotten lost in the shuffle as the story progresses. If you made them important enough to have a point of view, you've made a promise to your readers that these characters are significant to the story. Keep the important ones onstage in the narrative, and don't forget about them.

Q: "Can you have a story with multiple protagonists? For example, in romance stories in which you're telling the story of both lovers or an action story where you have a team of Navy SEALs, are they all protagonists?"

A: Theoretically, yes—although I honestly can't think of any examples of stories that truly have two (or more) equally delineated and developed protagonists.

Even with stories that have multiple protagonists, one of them almost always emerges as the central character. When there's a team of protagonists, they usually play the role of one protagonist, as if they are multiple aspects of, or exhibit different characteristics of, one person.

The more protagonists you use, the more you will split your readers' empathy.

For example, if you have five elite military personnel all playing the same role, readers won't know who to cheer for *specifically*. Instead, they'll start to be on the side of the team, but their empathy will be split five ways instead of centered on one individual.

It's very hard to write a story with multiple protagonists. You risk losing or splintering reader engagement.

To see if one protagonist rises to the forefront, ask:

- Who is in the first and last scene?
- Who is the putty person? Who changes the most?
- Who makes the most significant sacrifice to save others on his team?

You can use the dynamic of multiple protagonists to your advantage, but here's the kicker—to increase the tension, give them mutually exclusive goals as we discussed earlier. For one to succeed, the other must fail—like in the multiple-protagonist films *The Fugitive* and *House of Sand and Fog* (although, even these examples have one primary protagonist).

Q: "Can you switch protagonists partway through a story?"

A: Yes. When trying to pull this off, you'll typically allow readers to sympathize with (feel emotion *for*) or empathize with (feel emotion *along with*) one character and then turn the tables and show readers that the person they thought was the protagonist was really a villain in disguise. As soon as this happens, you'll need to have readers switch to feeling sympathy for or empathy toward the other character. This is tricky, but it is possible.

The indie thriller movie *Hard Candy* plays with the audience's empathy and moves this dynamic back and forth between the two main characters, at one point creating empathy for one of them, and then for the other. It's a very interesting dynamic and not easy to pull off.

In the story, after a flirty encounter, a fourteen-year-old girl goes home with a thirty-something guy she met online. But then, when the tables are turned, you see that she might not be so young and helpless after all. The hunter becomes the hunted ... or maybe not. That's for you to decide as your empathy is twisted around itself in ways you never see coming.

Q: "Can the protagonist and antagonist be the same person?"

A: Yes. In stories with an unreliable narrator, this might happen. For example, the main character, because of his split personality, doesn't realize that he's really the killer.

An unreliable narrator might be deceiving us, or he might be deceived himself.

In a sense, each section of this book has been leading up to here.

From the ingredients of a story to the principles and practice of organic writing, to the narrative forces that press in upon the tales we are striving to tell, to the intricacies of character development, everything revolves around telling great stories that resonate with our readers.

But something can get in the way of that. As you work on your book, you'll inevitably find problems with your plot. In the next and final section, we'll explore what causes them and examine specific ways for removing or resolving them.

PART VI

PLOT FLAWS
AND HOW TO
FIX THEM

CHAPTER 24

INCONGRUITIES

How to Tackle Problem Spots in Your Fiction

A plot flaw is either a glitch in causality or believability.

And every story has them.

When a character acts in a way that doesn't make sense (a problem with believability) or when a scene doesn't naturally follow from the one that precedes it (that is, there's no contingent relationship), readers will stumble and start to lose faith in the world of the story or in the storyteller's ability to uphold the belief that they've put in the narrative.

Anything that's inexplicable to readers will create a momentary gap between them and their engagement with the story.

We all know it when we come across it—that unbelievable jump in logic, often a coincidence that the author is using to drive the story forward.

If things happen for no reason—plot flaw.

If there isn't enough stimulus to elicit that response—plot flaw.

Imagine that your protagonist hears that a killer is in the neighborhood and she decides to go upstairs and take a shower. Readers will think, "What?! Why doesn't she lock the door, or call the police, or run to her car and get out of the area?"

At the very moment in your story where you want your readers to be drawn deeper into the narrative, they'll pull away and start to question your character's actions, and to some extent, your storytelling ability.

Unless there's a specific reason to keep readers asking, "Why?" you'll want to make it as hard as possible for them to be confused or wonder what's going on.

Remember, the more you fulfill the promises you made earlier in your story, the more readers will trust you with the questions they might have about what's happening now. This will, in some cases, give you more flexibility to breeze past some plot flaws toward the end of your story because narrative momentum will be pressing in on the clay.

Make sure your reader trusts you, and then trust your reader.

But keep a close eye on your story. Blatant mistakes will jar and distract readers.

In the first printing of my novel *The Pawn*, I made the mistake of having the antagonist step onto a porch and then three pages later open the front door and step outside.

Oops.

A mistake like that will confuse readers and cause them to page back through the book to see if they remember things correctly or not. And of course, that'll drive them out of being present in the story.

Errors in fact-checking will also distract readers from your story. If you mention a woman's sable hair after you've referred to her as a blond earlier in the book, or if you get a date wrong, or someone's age is off, or you refer to the wrong way to use or hold a certain type of gun, readers will rightfully take you to task.

When a story lags, it's often because of missing tension (there's no unmet desire on the part of the characters) or lack of escalation (there's too much repetition). To fix this, show us how deeply the character wants something but cannot get it, and escalate the story by making sure that thing is even harder to get.

Don't leave readers confused. If someone picks up something, he needs to put it down. If he opens a door and it's freezing outside, he needs to (or someone else needs to) close that door.

If you leave actions incomplete, you'll cause readers to stumble. For example, the character answers the phone but then never puts it away: *What? He jumped into the pool? The last I heard, he was talking on the phone. Did he take his cell with him into the water?*

To ratchet up the tension of the story, don't default to simply adding more action. When a story begins to stall out, tighten the screws to increase the escalation or:
- Remind readers what the protagonist wants.
- Look carefully at the dialogue. If it's mostly explanatory, give the speaker something to accomplish during the conversation.
- Promise more danger, and then take a step toward it.

If something is out of place, let a character in your story notice it: "That shouldn't be here. What's going on?" If your character doesn't acknowledge that something unusual is going on and readers notice it, they'll feel smarter than the character and might also think they found a "mistake."

If something is obvious, tell your readers: "Clearly no one would be at the office this early in the morning, but I called ahead just to make sure." If you don't point out that it's obvious that no one would be there, readers might be left thinking, *That's stupid. Why would he call the office this early in the morning?*

Sometimes you can just admit straight out that things don't quite make sense: "I couldn't quite tie all the threads together, but the killer had thought of everything so far. I figured he'd covered all his bases. And I really wasn't sure what else to do." If a comment like that comes late in the story, after you have the trust of your readers, that trust will allay their questions.

When a scene doesn't work, check these factors:

- **Honesty:** Is it honest about life?
- **Believability:** Does each character act in believable ways based on what she wants and who she is?
- **Escalation:** Is there an escalation of the struggle or too much repetition or exposition?
- **Causality:** Are things caused by the events that precede them?
- **Twists:** Is it too predictable, or, on the other end of the spectrum, too ridiculous?

Once I was reading a book about a federal agent who was trying to stop a terrorist from using the fireworks in New York City to infect millions of people with bubonic plague. A little twisted, but I liked it. So far so good.

But about a quarter of the way into the book, when a certain character was introduced, I thought, *Oh. I get it. He needs to forgive this other guy. The theme is forgiveness. Please don't let it go there.*

But as you've probably guessed, it did.

Needless to say, I was not blown away by that book.

We want to be surprised. We want to be pleased.

Never disappoint readers.

Never annoy them.

Or confuse them.

Or alienate them.

Remember, you're here to serve readers, and anything that gets in the way of your story undermines that goal.

Here's a list of some of the most common plot problems I see in novels, how to address them, and where to look in this book for a more in-depth explanation or analysis of each issue.

PROBLEM	TO FIX THE PROBLEM USE:	CHAPTER
TOO LITTLE TENSION	Promises and payoff: Make something go wrong, or promise that it will.	11
TOO MUCH REPETITION	Escalation: Identify and remove the early repetitious sections, and escalate the tension and action of the later ones.	4
TOO MUCH DESCRIPTION	Brevity: Find a way to say more by saying less.	18
UNCLEAR INTENTION	Desire: Remind the reader of the character's unmet desire, either for that scene or for the entire book. Or, sharpen the intention of the character in that scene.	1 and 22
THINGS DON'T FOLLOW LOGICALLY	Causality: Confirm that you are moving the story along from cause to effect, rather than effect to cause.	13
COINCIDENCE	Foreshadowing: (1) Show readers the object, skill, or character earlier, and (2) remove transitions that just happen to arrive at the right time to move a scene in a new direction.	14
LACKS UNITY/ COHESION	Polish: Make sure the mood and voice are consistent and the story pivots on complications and resolutions that escalate throughout the narrative.	18
NOTHING IS ALTERED	Scenes and setbacks: Summarize the scene rather than rendering it.	12
UNNECES-SARY SCENES	Fluidity: Delete the scene, or summarize it to fill in the transition its removal might cause to the narrative flow.	17

PROBLEM	TO FIX THE PROBLEM USE:	CHAPTER
TOO PREDICTABLE	Surprise: Make sure the story escalates in a direction readers don't expect but ends in a believable place to twist their expectations against them.	10
ENDING IS CONTRIVED	Inevitability: Work on foreshadowing to remove coincidences and sharpen causality to make sure everything is causally related. Verify that you're not being too authorially intrusive in the story.	13
MESSAGE/ AGENDA DRIVEN	Morality: Write from the center of a moral dilemma or a deep question about human nature rather than from an answer. Art's only desire is telling the truth about life. Let that be your guide. Also, make sure the story is tension-driven rather than trying to move things forward by relentless action or character descriptions.	19 and 20
STORY IS CHOPPY	Fluidity: Work on the flow, eliminate flashbacks, smooth out transitions, and keep things moving naturally from one event to the next.	17
ENDING IS ANTICLIMAC-TIC OR UNSAT-ISFYING	Twists: Focus on escalation and surprise. Keep all your promises. Then kill the story while it is still kicking.	10
PROSE WANDERS	Escalation: Rather than simply following believability and causality (everything makes sense), let the scenes also be shaped by the narrative force of escalation. Ask how you can make things worse.	4 and 8
PROSE IS BORING	Promises and payoff: Keep a promise, or put someone in peril.	11
INTERLUDES ARE TOO LONG	Scenes and setbacks: Make sure your interludes are only as long as they need to be for that story and that genre.	12

PROBLEM	TO FIX THE PROBLEM USE:	CHAPTER
CHAPTERS DON'T FLOW WELL	Fluidity: Check to see if you're moving from scene to interlude and the scenes are all causally and believably tied to the ones that precede and follow them.	17
NOTHING VITAL IS AT STAKE	Stakes: Raise them, and make them clear to your readers. Make bigger promises.	11
SEEMINGLY IMPORTANT CHARACTERS VANISH FROM THE STORY	Brevity: If they're not necessary, delete them. If they play the same role as other characters, combine them. If they are important, look for ways that their character arcs can be shaped by the progression of the story.	11 and 18
TOO MUCH INFORMATION ON MINOR CHARACTERS, PLACES, OR THINGS	Promises and payoff: Every word you write is a promise. Recast scenes so they bear only the narrative weight they need to in order to support the story.	11
STORY STALLS OUT	Escalation: Keep asking how you can make things worse. And apply the three questions detailed in Chapter 8 that shape stories and scenes.	4 and 8
READER CONFUSION	Tension: Clarify the protagonist's unmet desire. Also, make sure the story is moving forward from cause to effect.	1 and 13
READER APATHY	Empathy: (1) Confirm that the main character is someone readers care about, and (2) give the character a wound or deep human desire that we all share.	2
CAN'T PICTURE THE SETTING	Setting: Look at the scene through the eyes of the character. If they can see it, readers will, too.	2

PROBLEM	TO FIX THE PROBLEM USE:	CHAPTER
TOO MANY FLASHBACKS	Fluidity: If you choose to use a flash-back, just use one, tell that story, and then come back and get on with the main one you're telling. Only use a flashback if it propels the story forward more than if you didn't use it.	17
TOO MUCH DELIBERA-TION/SELF-REFLECTION	Characterization: Externalize emo-tion. Find a way to have your character express what he's feeling through his actions (slams a door), body language (tightens his fists), and posture (ram-rod straight or, conversely, wilted).	21 and 22
LONG, EXPLANATORY DIALOGUE	Fluidity: Work on the flow. Let charac-ters spar with words. Don't use dia-logue for exposition.	17
TOO MUCH TIME SPENT SETTING UP TRANSITIONS OF TIME AND PLACE	Scenes and setbacks: Make the char-acter's intention clear, and then get on with it. Let him go to sleep, attend the concert, or whatever.	12
TOO MUCH STORY AFTER THE RESOLU-TION	Story ingredients: Tension drives stories forward. When you have no more ten-sion, you'll lose readers' interest. If nec-essary, after the climax include a scene to wrap up any loose ends (that is, fulfill any unfulfilled promises), and then end with closure that makes it clear the story is done.	5 and 6
OVERWRITING	Brevity: Every word must matter.	18
THEME IS EVIDENT	Cohesiveness: Drop the idea of using a theme. Get rid of some of your blatant images and symbolism. Just tell the story.	20
EASILY IDENTI-FIABLE ACTS	Scenes and setbacks: Rethread the story so the transitions between the scenes are less visible.	1 and 12

PROBLEM	TO FIX THE PROBLEM USE:	CHAPTER
UNBELIEVABLE SCENES OR SEQUENCES	Believability: Evaluate each of the characters' choices and responses, and make sure they fit with that person's characterization. Use the tips in these chapters to remove coincidences and make the narrative believable.	13 and 14
SHOWING OFF YOUR RESEARCH	Distractions: Get on with the story. Anything that can lead a character to leave the world of the narrative should be changed or deleted.	25
OBVIOUS PLOT FLAW	Believability: Remove it, or, if you can't, let a character notice the problem and point it out. Typically, if you just admit that it's there, readers won't hold it against you.	14 and 24

In the final chapter, we'll wrap things up by detailing how to avoid the snares that trip up even the best-intentioned authors.

The solutions are often surprisingly simple and will take your writing to the next level.

CHAPTER 25

GIMMICKS

Common Traps Authors Fall into and What to Do About Them

If your novel isn't entertaining, it's not worth reading.

Fail at this, and nothing else will matter. Not grammar, not flow, not point of view or characterization or anything else. Fail at this and your novel won't sell, won't be recommended from one person to another, won't impact people or bring them closer to the truths of life.

If you're writing romance, you need to tug at the heartstrings. If suspense, your reader needs to be frightened. If action, you need to get readers' hearts pounding.

You must provide an emotionally satisfying experience for your readers.

Entertainment is inextricably woven into all the other aspects of fiction writing we've been covering.

If readers don't care about whether or not the protagonist succeeds in getting what he wants, they won't be entertained. If the story is too predictable or too abstruse, readers will either be too bored or too confused to be entertained. If the writing is too flowery or the story too dense or the descriptions too flat, readers will be annoyed or distracted or unimpressed—but not entertained.

In fiction, story matters more than anything else.

Yet all too often authors forget this, and in their zeal to impress readers or wow editors, they end up peppering their writing with distracting gimmicks that sabotage the readers' involvement with the story.

Ditch the gimmicks, and tell the story.

Here are four ways to remove some of the most common stumbling blocks that wedge themselves between stories and their readers.

1. Stop trying to be clever.

There's nothing less impressive than someone trying to be impressive. There's nothing less funny than someone trying to be funny. Forced eloquence doesn't impress anyone except for the person trying so hard to be eloquent.

So look for places in your story where you were trying to be funny, clever, or impressive, and change those sections or remove them.

Some authors resort to using a profusion of speaker attributions. Their characters chortle, grunt, sputter, rejoin, harrumph, exclaim, reiterate, gasp, howl, hiss, and bark. Whenever I read a book like that, I find myself skimming through the dialogue just to see what the next synonym for *said* will be. Readers get it. They know you own a thesaurus. Just tell the story.

Drop antiquated, obscure, or uncommon words unless they're necessary for character development or maintaining the narrator's voice. This isn't to say that you can't write intelligent, incisive, challenging stories, but any time the meaning of an unfamiliar word isn't immediately obvious within the context of the story, choose another word that won't trip up readers.

Over the years I've heard of authors who've written books without punctuation, or without using the word *said*, or without a semicolon, or they've written novels that contain an exact, predetermined number of words or only contain dialogue. But when those artificial constraints become more important to the author than the readers' experience with the story, they handcuff it. Scrap all those games with language, and focus on crafting a story that readers can't put down.

Also, avoid the temptation to impress your readers with your research, your vocabulary, your plot structure, or your knowledge of the flora and fauna of western North Carolina.

When readers pick up your book, they're not preparing for a spelling bee or a doctoral dissertation or a medical exam. Instead they're hoping for an entertaining, believable story that will transport them to another world and move them on a deep, emotional level.

Your goal shouldn't just be to meet, but to exceed, those expectations.

2. Avoid contrived literary devices.

The alliteration in "She cautiously closed the closet door and crept across the carpet" might have impressed your high school English teacher, but it does nothing to serve readers in today's hypercompetitive fiction market.

As soon as readers notice the alliteration, they'll be distracted. Whether they're counting up the number of times you used the letter *c* or rolling their eyes at your attempt to be literary, you've caused readers to momentarily disengage from your story.

You don't want that.

You don't even want readers to *admire* your writing. You want them to be so engaged in the story itself that they don't notice the way you use words to shape it. Anything that jars readers loose from the grip of the story needs to go, even if it seems to make the story appear more "literary."

Weed out figures of speech that don't serve the mood of the scene. During an airplane hijacking you wouldn't write, "The lofty clouds outside the window were castles in the sky." The words *lofty* and *castles* both carry a positive connotation and sabotage the suspense you're trying to create. If you were to use a figure of speech, you would choose one that accentuates the tense mood: "The jet plummeted through a dungeon of clouds."

Whenever you break the rules *or keep them*, it must be for the benefit of readers. If your writing style or techniques get in the way of the story or cause readers to question what's happening, analyze your writing, or page back through sections they've already read in order to understand the context, you've let your readers down.

You want your writing to be an invisible curtain between your readers and your story. Any time you draw attention to the narrative tools at your disposal, you insert yourself into the story and cause readers to notice the curtain.

In order to improve their writing, most authors need to cut back on the literary devices they use (whether that's assonance, onomatopoeia, hyperbole, overwrought similes, or whatever) rather than add more.

3. Just use normal names.

Don't use "Angela" to represent an angelic character. Don't use "Natasha" for the name of your Satan-worshipping character (spelled backward her name is "Ah, Satan!"). Readers are smart. They'll identify this stuff and then start looking for how you use every character to represent something. That exercise in story evaluation disconnects readers from the story itself.

Yes, you could choose the name "Marie Annette" for a character who's being used as a puppet. The name looks okay on the page, but say it aloud and you'll find that it sounds like "marionette." As soon as your readers notice this, what do you think they'll do?

Yes, of course. They'll start analyzing all the other names to see what they're supposed to "mean" as well. When that happens, the reader is studying the story instead of being wrapped up inside it.

Why do this to yourself?

Just use normal names.

4. Don't intrude on the story.

Whenever you include something in your story that distances, confuses, or distracts readers, you've undermined the effect that you are striving for.

Sometimes authors intrude on a story by:

- using it for therapy. Check that you're writing for the benefit of your readers, not just for yourself.
- trying to impose their political or religious views on readers or on a certain character.
- trying to impress readers by their style of writing, their research, or their expertise in a certain area.

Whenever something becomes more important to the author than the readers' engagement with the story, the integrity of the story world will suffer. We are here to serve our readers, not to get things off our chests, stand on our soapboxes, or show off.

IN CLOSING

On every page of your story, you'll have to break at least one "rule."

Acknowledging that frees us to focus on story rather than templates, formulas, and outlines.

When we offer up our stories to readers, it's like offering a piece of cake, and the greatest compliment is when someone asks for seconds.

As your story moves from promise to tension to surprise to resolution, it'll be shaped by the narrative forces that press against it: Context. Escalation. Believability. Causality. Continuity. Pace—and, of course, the many others we've covered in this book. As you keep the right questions in mind, and as you organically craft your tale, its true shape will reveal itself to you.

If you render a portrait of the protagonist's life in such a way that readers can picture his world and also care about what happens to him, they'll be drawn into the story.

If you present your protagonist with an emotionally stirring crisis or calling, readers will get hooked. If you show the stakes rising as she struggles to solve this crisis, you'll tug them in even more deeply.

If you end the story in a surprising and yet logical way that reveals a transformation of the main character's life, readers will be satisfied and entertained.

The ingredients come together, and the story tastes good.

Always be ready to break the rules for the sake of the story—which is another way of saying always be ready to do it for the sake of your readers.

Story trumps structure.

Story trumps everything that doesn't serve your readers.

So respect them, honor them, strive for excellence, write emotionally gripping fiction, and they'll thank you by clamoring to read more of your work.

INDEX